Other Books and Series by Jeff Bowen

Applications for Enrollment of Chickasaw Newborn Act of 1905
Volumes I thru VII

Cherokee Intermarried White 1906 Volume I, II, III, IV, V, VI & VII

Visit our website at **www.nativestudy.com** to learn more about these
and other books and series by Jeff Bowen

CHEROKEE INTERMARRIED WHITE 1906 VOLUME VIII

TRANSCRIBED BY

JEFF BOWEN

NATIVE STUDY
Gallipolis, Ohio
USA

Other Books and Series by Jeff Bowen

1901-1907 Native American Census Seneca, Eastern Shawnee, Miami, Modoc, Ottawa, Peoria, Quapaw, and Wyandotte Indians (Under Seneca School, Indian Territory)

1932 Census of The Standing Rock Sioux Reservation with Births And Deaths 1924-1932

Census of The Blackfeet, Montana, 1897- 1901 Expanded Edition

Eastern Cherokee by Blood, 1906-1910, Volumes I thru XIII

Choctaw of Mississippi Indian Census 1929-1932 with Births and Deaths 1924-1931   Volume I
Choctaw of Mississippi Indian Census 1933, 1934 & 1937, Supplemental Rolls to 1934 & 1935 with Births and Deaths 1932-1938, and Marriages 1936-1938 Volume II

Eastern Cherokee Census Cherokee, North Carolina 1930-1939
Census 1930-1931 with Births And Deaths 1924-1931 Taken By Agent L. W. Page Volume I
Eastern Cherokee Census Cherokee, North Carolina 1930-1939
Census 1932-1933 with Births And Deaths 1930-1932 Taken By Agent R. L. Spalsbury   Volume II
Eastern Cherokee Census Cherokee, North Carolina 1930-1939
Census 1934-1937 with Births and Deaths 1925-1938 and Marriages 1936 & 1938 Taken by Agents R. L. Spalsbury And Harold W. Foght Volume III

Seminole of Florida Indian Census, 1930-1940 with Birth and Death Records, 1930-1938

Texas Cherokees 1820-1839 A Document For Litigation 1921

Choctaw By Blood Enrollment Cards 1898-1914 Volumes I thru XVII

Starr Roll 1894   (Cherokee Payment Rolls) Districts: Canadian, Cooweescoowee, and Delaware Volume One
Starr Roll 1894 (Cherokee Payment Rolls) Districts: Flint, Going Snake, and Illinois   Volume Two
Starr Roll 1894 (Cherokee Payment Rolls) Districts: Saline, Sequoyah, and Tahlequah; Including Orphan Roll   Volume Three

Cherokee Intruder Cases Dockets of Hearings 1901-1909 Volumes I & II

Indian Wills, 1911-1921 Records of the Bureau of Indian Affairs Books One thru Seven;
Native American Wills & Probate Records 1911-1921

Other Books and Series by Jeff Bowen

Turtle Mountain Reservation Chippewa Indians 1932 Census with Births & Deaths, 1924-1932

Chickasaw By Blood Enrollment Cards 1898-1914 Volume I thru V

Cherokee Descendants East An Index to the Guion Miller Applications Volume I
Cherokee Descendants West An Index to the Guion Miller Applications Volume II (A-M)
Cherokee Descendants West An Index to the Guion Miller Applications Volume III (N-Z)

Applications for Enrollment of Seminole Newborn Freedmen, Act of 1905

Eastern Cherokee Census, Cherokee, North Carolina, 1915-1922, Taken by Agent James E. Henderson   *Volume I (1915-1916)*
Volume II (1917-1918)
Volume III (1919-1920)
Volume IV (1921-1922)

Complete Delaware Roll of 1898

Eastern Cherokee Census, Cherokee, North Carolina, 1923-1929, Taken by Agent James E. Henderson   *Volume I (1923-1924)*
Volume II (1925-1926)
Volume III (1927-1929)

Applications for Enrollment of Seminole Newborn Act of 1905 Volumes I & II

North Carolina Eastern Cherokee Indian Census 1898-1899, 1904, 1906, 1909-1912, 1914 Revised and Expanded Edition

1932 Hopi and Navajo Native American Census with Birth & Death Rolls (1925-1931) Volume 1 - Hopi
1932 Hopi and Navajo Native American Census with Birth & Death Rolls (1930-1932) Volume 2 - Navajo

Western Navajo Reservation Navajo, Hopi and Paiute 1933 Census with Birth & Death Rolls 1925-1933

Cherokee Citizenship Commission Dockets 1880-1884 and 1887-1889 Volumes I thru V

Originally published:
Baltimore, Maryland
2014

Reprinted by:

Native Study LLC
Gallipolis, OH
www.nativestudy.com
2020

Library of Congress Control Number: 2020917307

ISBN: 978-1-64968-077-8

Made in the United States of America.

This series is dedicated to
Jerry Bowen
the Brave and the Strong.

DEPARTMENT OF THE INTERIOR

Commissioner to the Five Civilized Tribes

Muskogee, Indian Territory, March 9, 1907.

NOTICE IS HEREBY GIVEN that the undersigned, the Commissioner to the Five Civilized Tribes, has been designated by the Secretary of the Interior, as the official to make and approve appraisals of the value of improvements upon land in the Cherokee Nation which were made prior to November 5, 1906, by white persons who intermarried with Cherokee citizens prior to December 16, 1895, and who have the right under the Act of Congress approved March 2, 1907 (Public 180), to sell improvements.

NOTICE IS FURTHER GIVEN that former claimants to citizenship by intermarriage who have made permanent and valuable improvements on lands of the Cherokee Nation and who claim the right to sell the same under and by virtue of said Act of Congress of March 2, 1907 (Public 180), must appear before the Commissioner to the Five Civilized Tribes prior to April 1, 1907, and designate the land upon which are located the improvements which they claim the right to sell by virtue of said Act; and if any such intermarried citizen shall fail to appear before the Commissioner to the Five Civilized Tribes prior to April 1, 1907, it will be considered that he makes no claim to the benefits conferred by said Act. Such appearance and designation of improvements must be made before the Commissioner at his office in Muskogee, Indian Territory, at any time between Monday, March 11th, 1907, and Saturday, March 30th, 1907, inclusive, or at any of the following named places between the dates named at which places the Commissioner will have a representative to receive said designations and hear testimony relative thereto:

Bartlesville, Ind. Ter., Monday March 18th, 1907, to Saturday March 23rd, 1907, inclusive.

Tulsa, Ind. Ter., Monday March 25th, 1907, to Saturday March 30th, 1907, inclusive.

Claremore, Ind. Ter., Monday March 18th, 1907, to Saturday March 23rd, 1907, inclusive.

Nowata, Ind. Ter., Monday March 25th, 1907, to Saturday March 30th, 1907, inclusive.

Vinita, Ind. Ter., Monday March 18th, 1907, to Saturday March 23rd, 1907, inclusive.

Pryor Creek, Ind. Ter., Monday March 25th, 1907, to Saturday March 30th, 1907, inclusive.

Tahlequah, Ind. Ter., Monday March 18, 1907, to Saturday March 23rd, 1907, inclusive.

Sallisaw, Ind. Ter., Monday March 25th, 1907, to Saturday March 30th, 1907, inclusive.

Designations must be made in person by the intermarried white claimant, or in case proper proof is made that he is physically unable to appear, by some adult member of his immediate family, or in case proper proof is made of the fact that the intermarried white claimant is physically unable to appear and has no adult member of his immediate family, by a person holding a properly executed power of attorney; provided, that in every case the designation must be made by a party familiar with the character, ownership, location and value of the improvements to be designated. At the time of said designation the testimony of any competent person will be taken by the Commissioner as to the location, character and value of said improvements.

No former intermarried white claimant will be permitted to designate improvements upon more land than he would have been entitled to take in allotment for him self had he been admitted to citizenship. If any intermarried white claimant has made a tentative selection of a full allotment he will not be allowed to designate improvements upon other land.

NOTICE IS FURTHER GIVEN that if any citizen of the Cherokee Nation entitled to select an allotment shall claim that the improvements on land tentatively selected by a former intermarried white claimant, or held by him, do not belong to said intermarried white claimant, or makes any adverse claim to said improvements, or to the right of the intermarried white claimant to sell said improvements under the Act approved March 2, 1907 (Public 180), said citizen must appear before the Commissioner to the Five Civilized Tribes either at Muskogee, Indian Territory, prior to April 1, 1907, or at one of the places above designated and within the dates above designated and make formal complaint before the Commissioner to the Five Civilized Tribes of his contention. At Muskogee, Indian Territory, between March 11th and March 30th, 1907, inclusive, and at the other places herein named during the hearings at said places as herein fixed, plats will be open for inspection showing the location of tentative allotments made by former claimants to citizenship by intermarriage and all other land on which such claimants claim improvements, so far as indicated by the records of this office.

All persons interested should take careful note of the limitation of time herein provided for, within which designations and complaints may be made, and that they must be made by appearance before the Commissioner.

TAMS BIXBY,
Commissioner.

This particular notice concerns the appraisals of improvements on properties held by Cherokee intermarried whites. You would have found notices like this throughout the Nation to bring in people to finalize the allotment question, of who belonged and who did not.

DEPARTMENT OF THE INTERIOR,

COMMISSIONER TO THE FIVE CIVILIZED TRIBES.

In the matter of the application for the enrollment of
ALBERTIN HAMPTON as a citizen by intermarriage of the Cherokee
Nation.

D E C I S I O N

THE RECORDS OF THIS OFFICE SHOW: That at Fairland, Indian
Territory, July 9, 1900, Albertin Hampton appeared before the Commission to the Five Civilized Tribes, and made application for the
enrollment of himself as a citizen by intermarriage, and for the
enrollment of his wife, Jane E. Hampton, et al. as citizens by
blood of the Cherokee Nation. The application for the enrollment of
the said Jane E. Hampton et al. as citizens by blood of the Cherokee
Nation has been heretofore disposed of, and their rights to enrollment will not be considered in this decision. Further proceedings
in the matter of said application were had at Muskogee, Indian
Territory, September 3, 1902, October 14, 1902, and January 2, 1907.

THE EVIDENCE IN THIS CASE SHOWS: That the applicant herein,
Albertin Hampton, a white man, was married, in accordance with
Cherokee law, January 20, 1874, to his wife, Jane E. Hampton, nee
Thomas, who was at the time of said marriage a recognized citizen
by blood of the Cherokee Nation, and whose name appears on the approved partial roll of citizens by blood of the Cherokee Nation,
opposite No. 195; that since said marriage the said Albertin Hampton
and Jane E. Hampton have resided together as husband and wife, and
have continuously lived in the Cherokee Nation. Said Albertin
Hampton is identified on the Cherokee authenticated tribal roll of
1880, and the Cherokee census roll of 1896, as "Bert Hampton", an
intermarried citizen of the Cherokee Nation.

IT IS, THEREFORE, ORDERED AND ADJUDGED: That in accordance with
the decision of the Supreme Court of the United States, dated November
5, 1906, in the case of Daniel Red Bird et al. vs. the United States,

under the provisions of Section twenty-one, of the Act of Congress approved June 28, 1898 (30 Stat., 495), Albertin Hampton is entitled to enrollment as a citizen by intermarriage of the Cherokee Nation, and his application for enrollment as such is accordingly granted.

                                          Commissioner.

Dated at Muskogee, Indian Territory,
this JAN 18 1907

The above is an accepted decision of the Commissioner to the Five Civilized Tribes. The Attorney for the Cherokee Nation had fifteen days after the date of Commissioner's decision in which to protest.

W.W.HASTINGS.
ATTORNEY

H. M. VANCE.
SECRETARY.

OFFICE OF

Attorney for the Cherokee Nation,

MUSKOGEE.I.T.   January 18, 1907.

The Commissioner to the Five Civilized Tribes,

Muskogee, Indian Territory.

Sir:

Receipt is acknowledged of the testimony and of your decision enrolling Albertin Hampton, as a citizen by intermarriage of the Cherokee Nation. Time for protesting said decision is waived and I consent that said person may be placed upon the schedule immediately.

Yours very truly,

J. W. Hastings

Attorney for Cherokee Nation.

The above is a notice of the Attorney waiving the time for protesting the Commissioner's decision (on the two previous pages) concerning Albertin Hampton's application and consenting to place the applicant upon schedule immediately.

INTRODUCTION

The *Cherokee Intermarried White*, National Archive film M-1301, Rolls 305-307, are found under the heading of Applications for Enrollment of the Commission to the Five Civilized Tribes. The genealogical value of this series concerning the relationships between many Cherokee tribesman and their marriages among another race is very important and virtually a treasure trove of information long sought after. While on the other hand what these cases are really about are the efforts of many to attain Cherokee land allotments. Referenced from the Supreme Court Decision, Cherokee Intermarriage Cases – 203 U.S. 76 (1906).

This collection of Intermarried claims involves two hundred and eighty-eight separate cases with a variety of scenarios from the divorced to the widowed to the deserving to the deceptive. During these times there were many that wanted what was rightfully only the Cherokees. You will see each case will be headed by the title from the first folder as an example: *Intermarried White I, Trans from Cher. 34*, the transfer number is the Dawes Commission number from the claimants spouse.

These cases are fascinating because of the generational bloodlines that can be verified by documentation rather than just word of mouth. From Kent Carter's book, *The Dawes Commission*, "The tribe also, continued to oppose the enrollment of whites who had married into the Cherokee tribe. That controversy dragged through the U.S. Court of Claims and then the Supreme Court, which finally ruled in favor of the tribe on November 05, 1906. The court upheld the Cherokee citizenship laws that denied rights to any white who had married into the tribe after November 1, 1877. It also upheld an 1839 law which stated that anyone who moved out of the nation lost their citizenship unless they were readmitted. The applications of 3,341 persons were rejected as a result of this ruling, and the allotment clerks were forced to undo a great deal of their work. With the issue finally settled by the courts, the commission was able to send the first schedule of Cherokees by intermarriage, containing fifty-five names, to the secretary of interior on June 10, 1907. Eventually only 286 people were enrolled as intermarried whites----far fewer than the number put on the rolls of the Choctaw and Chickasaw tribes, which had much more liberal laws on rights based on marriage." [1]

---

[1] The Dawes Commission and the Allotment of the Five Civilized Tribes, 1893-1914 by Kent Carter, pg. 121

In Cohen's Handbook of Federal Indian Law he states, "In the *Cherokee Intermarriage Cases,* the Supreme Court considered the claims of certain white persons, intermarried with Cherokee Indians, who wanted to participate in the common property of the Cherokee Nation. Such persons were permitted by tribal law to be tribal citizens with limited rights in tribal property. The tribe had also provided for the revocation of citizenship rights of a white person who intermarried with a Cherokee if the Cherokee spouse were abandoned or if a widower or widow married a non-Cherokee. The Court found that the Cherokee Nation had authority to qualify the rights of citizenship which it offered to its "naturalized citizens. Such tribal action defeated the claims of the plaintiffs:

The laws and usages of the Cherokees, their earliest history, the fundamental principles of their national policy, their constitution and statutes, all show that citizenship rested on blood or marriage; that the man who would assert citizenship must establish marriage; that when marriage ceased (with a special reservation in favor of widows or widowers) citizenship ceased; that when an intermarried white married a person having no rights of Cherokee citizenship by blood it was conclusive evidence that the tie which bound him to the Cherokee people was severed and the very basis of his citizenship obliterated."[2]

An important footnote that Cohen published within his pages for the above paragraph also needs to be studied. He noted, "Under Cherokee law white persons intermarrying with Cherokees before 1875 were tribal citizens for most purposes, including allotment of tribal land, but had no interest in tribal funds except those funds derived from tribal lands. A Cherokee law that became effective in 1875 provided that whites marrying Cherokees had no rights to tribal property but could obtain full citizenship by the payment of $500 to the tribe. In 1877 the tribe provided that no intermarried citizen could obtain any rights to tribal land or funds."[3]

During many years of study this author has found cases that should have been been accepted, especially with the particular documentation presented. All in all the outcome of the decision made should have rendered a different result. Also there have been many that numb the mind as to how they their cases were even considered. The years have given many the hopes that their ancestors were one of those that had a decent claim and an honest consideration. Like any time in history there are political struggles

---

[2] Felix S. Cohen's Handbook of FEDERAL INDIAN LAW 1982 ED. pgs 20-21.
[3] Felix S. Cohen's Handbook of FEDERAL INDIAN LAW 1982 ED. pg 21 footnote16.

and the human factor that points out man is not perfect. These pages were transcribed with the wish that another person somewhere along the line will find their relation from the past and give them the answers long hoped for.

Jeff Bowen
Gallipolis, Ohio
NativeStudy.com

Cher IW 221

◇◇◇◇◇

Cherokee
I.W. 221

Muskogee, Indian Territory, April 16, 1907.

Miles C. Jones,
    Dewey, Indian Territory.

Dear Sir:

Your marriage license and certificate filed in connection with your application for enrollment as a citizen by intermarriage of the Cherokee Nation is returned to you herewith, copies of the same being retained in the files of this office.

Respectfully,

Encl. W-13   Commissioner.
S.W.

◇◇◇◇◇

I.W. No. 221

Margaret S. Jones

Record and Decision

Not in 10829 - 4/15/07

Cher IW 222

◇◇◇◇◇

Cherokee Intermarried White 1906
Volume VIII

Department of the Interior,
Commission to the Five Civilized Tribes,
Vinita, I. T., October 3, 1900.

In the matter of the application of James Dencan[sic] for the enrollment of himself as a Cherokee citizen; being sworn and examined by Commissioner Breckinridge he testified as follows:

Q Give me your full name?   A James Duncan.

Q How old are you?   A I don't know, recollect exactly, I think I am going on 59.

Q What is your post-office?   A Afton.

Q What district do you live in?   A Delaware.

Q Who is it you want to put on the roll?   A Just myself.

Q Are you a Cherokee by blood?   A No sir.

Q You are a white man?   A Yes sir.

Q Where is your marriage license?   A (Produces papers)

Q When were you married, in 1868?   A Yes sir.

Q To whom were you married?   A Married to Tempy Ann Schrimpsher.

Q Is she living still?   A No sir.

Q When did she die?   A In 1880 I think.

Q Did you live with her from the time you married her until she died?   A No sir.

Q When did you separate from her?   A In 1871.

Q When did you marry again?   A In 1884.

Q Are you on the roll of 1880?   A I don't know; I don't think I am though, I wasn't here when the roll of 1880 was taken.

Q To whom did you marry that time?   A I married Sarah Miller.

Q Miller was her maiden name?   A Yes sir.

Q And before she married you she was a Copeland?   A Yes sir.

Q Is she living with you as your wife?   A Yes sir.

Q Is she living now?   A She was out here and enrolled the other day.

Q How old is she now?   A She is going on 60 I think. 50 or 60.

Q Have you got a certificate of your marriage to her?   A I have just got a little certified certificate. (Produces papers)

Q This is just a sort of certificate made out here afterwards?   A Yes sir, I never got no certificate from him at the time I got married?

A Did you get a divorce from your first wife?   A No sir.

Q Did you leave her or did she leave you?   A She left me and took another man and had a child by him.

Q And you were not married between the time she left you and the time you married your present wife, Sarah?   A Yes sir.

Q Have you lived with your wife Sarah ever since your marriage to her in 1884?
A Yes sir.

Q Where did you live from the time you left your first wife until your marriage to your last wife?   A I liven[sic] on the place I am living now while I was in the Nation here.

Cherokee Intermarried White 1906
Volume VIII

Q   Where did you live?   A I got into some trouble, them fellows robbing me of my houses[sic], and I was sent to the house of correction at Detroit, at the house of correction.

Q   The people robbed you and you were sent to prison?   A Yes sir.

Q   What became of the people that did the robbing?   A They was shot down up here on Caney.

Q   Where did you live between 1871 and 1884?   A Right at home where I am living now, in Delaware District, on Horse Creek 6 miles east of Afton.

Q   Do you mean to tell me that you were sent to prison because some one robbed you of your horses?   A Yes sir, there was 16 of us went to arrest them and because we went to arrest them without a warrent[sic] Judge Parler assigned it a violation of the law, it was sixty miles to Ft. Smith and there was sixteen of us went to arrest them and they fought.

Q   Then you were sent to prison for shooting a man?   A I was sent there for trying to arrest them.

Q   Is[sic] was for the assualt[sic], not for the horse stealing? A Yes sir assault.

Q   Were you in prison in 1880?   A Yes sir.

Q   In what year was it you got into trouble about the assault?   A 1874.

Q   How long did you stay in prison?   A I staid there five years and five months, and a half; there was three cases.

Q   Then when you got out you came right back here?   A Right home.

1880 roll for wife, page 242 #680 Sarah Copeland, Delaware Dist, native Cherokee, 39 years old.

1880 roll for applicant; page 569, #134 James Duncan Delaware Dist.

1896 roll for wife, page 461 #892 Sarah Duncan, Delaware District, native Cherokee.

Com'r: The applicant present license issued by the Clerk of Delaware District on the 6th day of February 1868, authorizing his marriage to Temap[sic] Schrimpsher a Cherokee citizen; and the certificate indorsed thereon shows that they were married on the 29th of the same month, 1868; this is filed herewith.

Examined by Cherokee Rep've Baugh:

Q   How long after your marriage to your first wife before you separated from her?

A   I married in 1868 and we separated in 1871.

Q   What was the cause of that separation?   A I went to Ft. Smith at the time of court and was gone about four weeks, and when I come back she had took another mand[sic] and had a child by him, and the child is on the roll.

Q   Had a child in four weeks?   A She lived with him and had a child by him.

Q   Was there any other cause for that separation besides that?   A No sir.

Q   Had you and she always lived tofether[sic] as man and wife up to that time?

A   Yes sir. We had never had not[sic] trouble. Before I got my license and married she went off and left me once, before; we married in 1865.

Q   Did you always treat her as man and wife?   A Yes sir, as near as I was able. I kept her plenty to eat.

Q   She neber[sic] lived with you after you can[sic] back from ft. Smith?   A No sir.

Q   Why didn't you procure a divorce from her after you came back?   A   After this first one left me she went and took up with another man and lived with him awhile and then she finally married a man named George Sutherlin.
Q   Why didn't you procure a divorce?   A   I wanted to give her a divorce once and the cleark[sic] told me it wasn't necessary.
Q   Why wasnyou[sic] going to give her a divorce, why didn't you sue her yourself?
A   I never married no more until after she died, and I married this wife.

The clerk told me I didn't need it; she had married a man named Sutherlin.
1880 roll page 181 #2806 Tempy Southerland, Cooweescoowee Dist.

Com'r Breckinridge: The applicant is shown to have married a Cherokee woman in 1868; he states that they separated in 1871, and he did not marry from that time until his present marriage, which was consummated in 1884; he is not on the roll of 1880, which he states is due to his being in prison at that time, arising from an attempt to arrest certain horse thieves; he never procured a divorce from the first wife, but states that he did not marry a second time until after her death; he is identified on the roll of 1896, and his present wife is identified on the rolls of 1880 and 1896; his first wife is identified under the name of the man who the applicant says married her after she left him on the roll 1880.

For the further consideration of the evidence in this case, this application will at present be placed upon a doubtful card the applicant being classed as a Cherokee by intermarriage.

M.D. Green, being first duly sworn states that as stenographer to the Commission to the Five Civilized Tribes he correctly recorded the testimony and proceedings in this case and that the foregoing is a true and complete transcript of his stenographic notes thereof.

M.D. Green.

Subscribed and sworn to before me this 4 day of October 1900.

C. R. Breckinridge.
Commissioner.

◇◇◇◇◇

(Copy of original document from case.)

◇◇◇◇◇◇

Cherokee Intermarried White 1906
Volume VIII

Supplemental Testimony to go with D Card #504.

DEPARTMENT OF THE INTERIOR,
COMMISSION TO THE FIVE CIVILIZED TRIBES,
VINITA, I.T., OCTOBER 3d, 1900.

Supplemental testinony[sic] in the matter of the application of James Duncan for enrollment as a citizen of the Cherokee Nation:

T.J. McGee, being sworn and examined by Commissioner C. R. Breckinridge, testified as follows:

Q Give your name?   A T. J. McGee.
Q How old are you?   A 56 years old.
Q What is your post office?   A Miami.
Q How long have you lived in the Cherokee Nation?   A 56 years.
Q You are hear[sic] to give woms[sic] additional testimony in a case?   A Yes, sir.
Q What is the name of the man whose case you want to give additional testimony in?
A James Duncan.
Q It is a question about his separating from his first wife is not it?   A Yes sir.
Q Who is to blame in that separation?   A She left him.
Q Did he give her any cause to leave him?   A He always provided for her; he was a man that always kept plenty around him.
Q What about his treatment of her?   A He always treated her all right.
Q What did she leave him for?   A He had a difficulty there at his house and killed his brother and then he was taken to Fort Smith and while he was there she took up with another man.
Q Did he do anything for her support when he left her?   A She was with another man. He came clear and came back.
Q Did he lead a correct life himself?   A The trouble there and trouble later on he got into was the only trouble I knew of him getting into. In 1877, he got into trouble with some folks coming there and took his houses[sic] away from him.
Q You think he always deported himself as a man ought?   A Always that way.
Q Did he treat his wife in a proper way?   A Yes sir.
Q You never heard of his mistreating her?   A Not while I was there.

---ooo OOO ooo---

J. O. Rosson, being first duly sworn, states that as stenographer to the Commission to the Five Civilized Tribes, he correctly recorded the testimony and proceedings in this case, and the foregoing is a true and complete transcript of his stenographic notes thereof.

J. O. Rosson.

Subscribed and sworn to before me this 8th day of September, 1900.

C. R. Breckinridge.
Commissioner.

◇◇◇◇◇

D. 504.

Department of the Interior,
Commissioner to the Five Civilized Tribes,
Muskogee, I. T., February 28, 1902.

In the matter of the application of James Duncan for the enrollment of himself as a citizen of the Cherokee Nation.

The applicant present in person and by attorney, W. P. Thompson, Vinita, I.T.

Cherokee Nation represented by W. W. Hastings.

The applicant was notified by registered letter February 12, 1902, that his application for enrollment as a citizen of the Cherokee Nation will be taken up for final consideration by the Commission at its offices in Muskogee, Indian Territory, on the 28th day of February, and the applicant this day appears in person, to wit the 28th day of February, 1902, and by his attorney, W. P. Thompson.

JAMES DUNCAN, being duly sworn testified as follows:

MR. THOMPSON; What is your name?   A James Duncan.
Q Your age?   A 60.
Q Postoffice?   A Afton.
Q You are the applicant in this case?   A Yes sir.
Q I notice the record in this case is reported as having you say in answer to this question: "Aand[sic] you were not married between the time she left you and the time you married your present wife, Sarah?" Your answer to avove[sic] question in the record is "Yes, sir". Is that correct or not?   A That is not correct.
Q You were never married from the time your wife Sarah left you until you married your present wife then?   A That is right.

LEWIS MOORE, being first duly sworn, testified as follows:

MR. THOMPSON: What is your name?   A Lewis Moore.
Q Postoffice?   A Needmore.
Q Age?   A 48.
Q Do you know the applicant, James Duncan?   A Ues[sic], sir.
Q Where was he?   A He was in Detroit I think in the penitentiary.
Q Was he confined at Detroit?   A Yes, sir.

Q Did you know his first wife?   A Yes, sir.

Q You know the time they separated?   A Well, not just exactly, I don't, no; recollect the time they separated.

Q Do you know the cause of the separation?   A Not exactly.

Q Well, do you know which one kept the home where they were living?   A Duncan.

Q And did they have any children?   A Yes, sir.

Q Who kept the children?   A Duncan till he was sent off.

Q Do you know about his first wife having an illegitimate child?   A Yes, sir.

Q How long was that after they separated?   A As well as I can recollect about a year I think.

Q Do you know whether she had taken up or was living with some one?   A Nothing only just what I heard.

Q Do you know whether his first wife was dead at the time he married his second? A No, sir, I couldn't be positive about that.

Q Well, had you heard anything of it?   A Yes, sir, I heard she was dead.

MR. HASTINGS: Well, now how did you hear it?   A Well just like you hear any other talk.

Q Well, how far did she live from you?   A Well, couldn't even tell you how[sic] where she lived when she died.

Q You don't know who you heard it from?   A No, sir, only just country talk.

Q Do you know what year you heard she died?   A No, sir, not exactly.

Q Do you know in five years of what year it was?   A Oh, yes, sir.

Q Well, now, tell it then?   A Well, it would be just a guess, it was between 1874, 1880 somewheres[sic] along there.

Q That is as near as you can come to it?   A Yes, sir.

Q How far did you live from them when they lived together as husband and wife, when Jim lived with his first wife?   A About four miles I guess.

Q You don't know anything about what caused the separation?   A Nothing only just talk.

Q Just talk?   A Yes sir.

Q You know nothing from this woman?   A No, sir.

Q It was not her talking?   A No, sir, it wasn't her talk.

Q Do you know the exact date of their separation?   A No, sir.

Q Do you know the exact date of the birth of this child after the separation?   A No, sir.

Q Do you know exactly how long it was afterwards?   A Somewheres near about a year, I know I had rented Duncan's place that next spring, and was living there.

Q How long was it after they separated before this man was cinvicted[sic] and sent off to the penitentiary?   A I couldn't tell you how long it it[sic] was after the separation, don't remember.

Q As much as twenty years?   A No, it wasn't that long.

Q Well fifteen?   A I couldn't say exactly how long.

Q Well, do you think it was as much as ten years?   A No, I don't think it was that long.

MR. THOMPSON: Well, about how long?   A Well, maybe two or three or four years.

Q Well is that your best judgment?   A Yes, sir.

Q You don't know much about the separation now way?   A No, sir, not about the separation.

MR. THOMPSON: Do you know whether you heard she was dead before 1884 or not? His first wife, you either know it or don't?   Q[sic] Well, I know that I heard she was dead.

Q Before 1880?   A Yes, sir.

Q Well, do you know that he was in the penitentiary in 1880 for that shooting of those horse thieves up there?   A Yes, sir.

Q Well you lived on his place when he was sent there?   A Yes, sir.

Q Well, you know about those facts don't you?   A Yes, sir.

T. J. McGee, being first duly sworn, testified as follows:

MR. THOMPSON: What is your name?   A T. J. McGee.

Q Age?   A 58.

Q Posteoffice[sic]?   A Daws, Indian Territory.

Q Do you know about the time of the marriage of James Duncan to Sarah Miller or Copeland?   A About 1884 is the best of my recollection.

Q Do you know whether his first wife, Tempy Ann Schrimpsher, was dead at the time that he married Sarah Miller or Copeland?   A Well, he was married by the deputy clerk, I was away, down at Tahlequah, Indian Territory and when I cam[sic] back home he said that he had married Jim Duncan, and he said they they[sic] states----

MR. HASTINGS: I don't think that would be----------

MR. THOMPSON: Well, had you heard of her death before that time?

A Yes, sir.

Q Do you know where Jim Duncan was in 1880?   A He was reported to be at the house of correction.

Q Well, do you know of the circumstance of the assault in regard to some horse thieves up there, for which he was sent?   A Well, I only heard of it.

MR. HASTINGS: Well now you lived on the east side of Grand River?

A Yes, sir.

Q And over on Cowskin Prairie Jim Duncan lived on the west side[sic] A Yes, sir.

Q Now how far did he live from you?   A We lived about fifteen miles miles[sic] apart, twelve or fifteen miles.

Q Is that all?   A Yes, sir.

Q Now how long before 1884 had you heard of this woman being dead?   A It would be hard matter to say.

Q Who did you ever hear say it?   A Why my deputy clerk that married them.

Q Well that was at the time?   A Yes, sir.

Q That was after the marriage. A Who did you hear it from?   A I heard it from Mr. Duncan.

Q From Mr. Duncan himself and that is since he has been here?   A No, sir.

Q Well, when did you hear it before?   A I couldn't say just exactly.

Q Had you heard it before from anybody else?   A Well, I couldn't say who else I might have heard it from.

Q You couldn't state that?   A No, sir.

COMMISSION: You submit the case, Mr. Thompson?

MR. THOMPSON: Yes, sir.

COMMISSION: The attorney for the applicant and the representative of the Cherokee Nation present submit the case. The same is ordered closed and reported to the Commission for a final decision based upon the evidence now of record. The attorney for the applicant requests and will be granted ten days in which to file a brief in this case, one copy with the Commission, and one copy with the representatives of the Cherokee Nation.

--: : --: :--: :--

Arthur G. Croninger, being duly sworn, states that as stenographer to the Commission to the Five Civilized Tribes he reported in full the proceedings and testinomy[sic] in the above case, and that the foregoing is a true and complete transcript of his stenographic notes thereof.

Arthur G. Croninger.

Subscribed and sworn to before me this 1st day of March, 1902.

T. B. Needles.
Commissioner.

◇◇◇◇◇

(Copy of original document from case.)

◇◇◇◇◇

Cherokee Intermarried White 1906
Volume VIII

DEPARTMENT OF THE INTERIOR.
Commission to the Five Civilized Tribes.
Muskogee, Indian Territory, October 9th, 1902.

In the matter of the application of James Duncan for the enrollment of himself as a citizen by intermarriage of the Cherokee Nation.

Supplemental to D-504.

Cherokee Nation appears by J. C. Starr.

JAMES DUNCAN, being duly sworn, testified as follows:--
Examination by the Commission.

Q. Your name is James Duncan?   A. Yes, sir.

Q. How old are you?   A. I will be 62 years old the sixth day of next April, is[sic] I live to see the day.

Q. What is your post office?   A. Afton.

Q. You are a white man?   A. Yes, sir.

Q. Claiming as an intermarried citizen, are you?   A. Yes, sir.

Q. What is the name of the wife through whom you claim citizenship?
A. Sarah Miller.

Q. Is she living?   A. She is living.

Q. Is she your first wife?   A. No, sir.

Q. How often were you married before you married Sarah?   A. Just once.

Q. Was your former wife dead when you married her?   A. Yes, sir.

Q. Was Sarah ever married before?   A. Yes, sir.

Q. How often?   A. Once.

Q. Was her first husband dead when she married you?   A. NO, sir; they parted.

Q. Were they divorced?   A. Yes, sir.

Q. Were[sic] were they divorced?   A. Delware[sic] district.

Q. When was that?   A. In '83.

Q. When did you marry her?   A. '84, sixth day of November.

Q. What is the name of her first husband?   A. Copeland.

Q. What is his first name?   A. Alex.

Q. Was he a white man or Cherokee?   A. He was a Cherokee.

Q. What was your first wife?   A. She was a Cherokee.

Q. Did you marry your first wife under a Cherokee license?   A. Yes, sir.

Q. Then you are claiming through your first wife, are you?   A. I have always been recognized as a citizen.

Q. You didn't marry your second wife under a Cherokee license?   A. No, sir.

Q. You were a citizen at that time?   A. Yes, sir.

Q. When did you marry your first wife?   A. '68.

11

Cherokee Intermarried White 1906
Volume VIII

Q. What was your first wife's name?   A. Tempy Ann Schrimpsher.

Q. How long did you live with her?   A. I lived with her until about '71 and she quit me.

Q. She quit you in '71?   A. Yes, sir.

Q. You lived with her continuously up to '71?   A. Yes, sir.

Q. You say she quit you in '71.   A. Yes, sir.

Q. What was the cause of the separation?   A. She took another man.

Q. Did she marry that other man?   A. No, sir; she left him and married another man by the name of Sutherland and quit Sutherland and married another man.

Q. You never lived with her after '71?   A. No, sir.

Q. When did she die?   A. Died in '81, I think. My daughter, she told me she died in '81. She was up there.

Q. Did you ever try to get your wife to come back with you?   A. Not after she took that man.

Q. Your present wife is living?   A. Yes, sir.

Q. Have you been living with her ever since you married her?   A. Yes, sir.

Q. Have you been residing in the Cherokee Nation ever since you married your first wife?   A. Yes, sir.

Q. Never lived outside of the Cherokee Nation since that time?   A. I never lived out.

Q. You have been out?   A. Yes, sir; I was out last fall about two weeks.

Q. But you have never been out to live?   A. I have never been out to live.

Examination by Mr. Starr.

Q. Was Tempy Ann Schrimpsher ever married before you married her?   A. No, sir.

Q. Was she your first wife?   A. Yes, sir.

Q. Where did you and she live during the time you lived together?   A. Right on the place we are living now.

Q. Where is that?   A. Six miles east of Afton.

Q. Who was living near you?   A. A. good many people lived around there. Bill Trott. Oce Trott.

Q. Bill Trott of Vinita?   A. Yes, sir.

Q. Can you name anybody that lived near you at that time?   A. There wasn't very many lived in that country then; '68 and to '71.

Q. Oce Trott and Bill Trott, did they live near you?   A. Lived about a mile from me.

Q. Who is the man you say your wife run away with?   A. Mansil.

Q. What was his first name?   A. Bob.

Q. Where did she go with him?   A. He took her and had her a while and run off.

Q. Where did he take her to?   A. Around the neighborhood.

Q. Where to.   A. I didn't follow up to see. I went off to Fort Smith and hired a woman to stay with her. She told me.

Q. How long did you stay there?   A. I was there about a month.

Q. When you came back your wife was gone?   A. She was there living with this fellow right there in my house. That woman told me. You will find her daughter on the eighty roll, Bell Mansil. Then she took another man by the name of Parks and they had some children.

Q. When you come back you found this woman living with another man?
A. Yes, sir.
Q. Did you see him?   A. Yes, sir. I saw him there.
Q. How long did he stay there after you got back?   A. He didn't stay at all. They left and went up to her uncles.
Q. What was her uncles[sic] name?   A. John Ward.
Q. How far did he live from there?   A. About three miles.
Q. Where is he?   A. He is dead.
Q. You never made any effort to get her to come back?   A. Never made any effort after she went with that other man.
Q. Why are you not on the eighty roll?   A. Simply because I got into trouble with them Barkers. They robbed me of four head of stock. They sent me to the house of correction at Detroit, Mich.
Q. When did you get into this trouble?   A. '78.
Q. When did your wife leave you?   A. '71.
Q. Did you have any trouble before you left for Fort Smith?   A. No, sir.
Q. What was the name of this man she run away with?
A. Bob Mansil.
Q. How long did he live with her?   A. Didn't stay only a month or so.
Q. Then where did she go?   A. Married this man Sutherland.
Q. What Sutherland?   A. George.
Q. Where did she go?   A. Up in Delaware, until they parted. She quit him and married a man by the name of George Parks.
Q. How long did she live with Sutherland?   A. I couldn't tell you exactly.
Q. After she quit living with Sutherland she married?   A. She married Sutherland first, then quit Sutherland and went to this man Parks.
Q. Where did she go then?   A. Went back to Sutherland.
Q. How long did she live with Sutherland?   A. I couldn't tell you. They live down here about 40 miles before from where I live.
Q. Where are you living now?   A. Living on my old place that I lived on ever since '68.
Q. Did you get a divorce from this first wife?   A. No, sir; I didn't. I never tried.

BY THE COMMISSION:
Q. I think I asked you if your present wife is a Cherokee by blood.
A. Yes, sir, she is a Cherokee. Born and raised here. Never was out of the nation.

IIIIIIIIIIIIIIIIIIIIIIIIIII

Jesse O. Carr, being first duly sworn, states that as stenographer to the Commission to the Five Civilized Tribes he reported the above entitled case and that the foregoing is a true and complete transcript of his stenographic notes thereof.

Jesse O. Carr

Subscribed and sworn to before me this 8th day of December, 1902.

BC Jones
Notary Public.

◇◇◇◇◇

Cherokee D 504

DEPARTMENT OF THE INTERIOR,

COMMISSION TO THE FIVE CIVILIZED TRIBES.

In the matter of the application of James Duncan for his enrollment as a citizen by intermarriage of the Cherokee Nation.

D E C I S I O N

The record herein shows that on October 3, 1900, James Duncan appeared before the Commission at Vinita, Indian Territory, and made application for his enrollment as a citizen by intermarriage of the Cherokee Nation. Further proceedings were had in the matter of said application at Muskogee, Indian Territory, on February 28, and October 9, 1902.

The evidence shows that James Duncan, a white man, was married under a Cherokee marriage license and in accordance with the laws of the Cherokee Nation on February 29, 1868, to Tempa Ann Schrimpser[sic], a citizen by blood of the Cherokee Nation, who is identified in the marriage license as "Temper Crimser". It appears that the applicant and his said wife lived together for about three years following their marriage and that she then left him, and there is no evidence that the said James Duncan abandoned his said wife. James Duncan is not identified on the authenticated tribal roll of 1880, having been in Prison during the preparation of such roll, and his identification on that roll as shown by the record is an error. An examination of the Cherokee tribal rolls in the possession of the Commission shows that the applicant is identified on the Cherokee Census roll of 1896 at page 569, #134.

Section twenty-one of the Act of Congress approved June 28, 1898 (30 Stats., 495), provides for the enrollment of Cherokee citizens "with such intermarried white persons as may be entitled to citizenship under Cherokee laws."

Section 666 of the compiled laws of the Cherokee Nation (1892), provides:

"Should any man or woman, a citizen of the United States, or of any foreign country, become a citizen of the Cherokee Nation by intermarriage, and be left a widow or widower by the decease of the Cherokee wife or husband, such surviving widow or widower shall continue to enjoy the rights of citizenship, unless he or she shall marry a white man or woman, or person, (as the case may be), having no rights of Cherokee citizenship by blood; in that case, all of his or her rights acquired under the provisions of this act shall cease."

It appears that James Duncan acquired the rights of Cherokee citizenship by virtue of his marriage to his first wife in 1868, and that subsequent to her death, which occurred in 1881, he married his present wife, Sarah, a citizen by blood of the Cherokee Nation.

The evidence further shows that the said James Duncan has resided in the Cherokee Nation since the date of his marriage to his first wife.

It is, therefore, the opinion of this Commission that James Duncan should be enrolled as a citizen by intermarriage of the Cherokee Nation, in accordance with the provisions of section twenty-one of the Act of Congress approved June 28, 1898 (30 Stats., 495), and it is so ordered.

COMMISSION TO THE FIVE CIVILIZED TRIBES.

Tams Bixby

Acting Chairman.

TB Needles

Commissioner.

C. R. Breckinridge

Commissioner.

Dated at Muskogee, Indian Territory,
this   JAN 30 1903

◇◇◇◇◇

DEPARTMENT OF THE INTERIOR,

COMMISSION TO THE FIVE CIVILIZED TRIBES,
Vinita, I.T., February 6th., 1903.

IN THE MATTER OF THE APPLICATION OF JAMES DUNCAN FOR ENROLLMENT AS A. CITIZEN BY INTER-MARRIAGE OF THE CHEROKEE NATION.

D--504

PROTEST OF THE CHEROKEE NATION.

Comes now the Cherokee Nation and respectfully protests against the decision of the Commission rendered in the above case on January 30th., 1903, and asks that the same, together with the record and a copy of the brief heretofore filed by the Cherokee Nation, be forwarded to the Honorable Secretary of the Interior for review.

Our objections to the enrollment of the applicant are fully stated in said brief, and we submit the same upon the argument contained therein.

Respectfully submitted,

W W Hastings
Attorney for the Cherokee Nation.

◇◇◇◇◇

At this point the reporting of the testimony was continued by Jesse O. Carr.

By the Commission:-

Q. This letter, Mrs. Grazier, that was written to your husband, notified him that further evidence would be necessary touching the question of his abandonment of his wife. Do you know what abandonment means?

A. I guess it means when he has left.

Q. That is what you think it means?

A. I think so.

Q. Because your husband hasn't left you alone all the time you think he hasn't abandoned you, as long as he give you some money?

A. If he provides for us all the time.

Q. If he lives with this other woman as much as you he hasn't left you?

A. No, he hasn't left.

Q. As long as he goes to see this other woman and then comes to see you and gives you money, that isn't abandonment?

A. No, sir. He provides for me all the time.

Q. When he brough[sic] this other woman to your house the first time did you ask him who that was?

A. No, sir.

Q. Who did he say it was?

A. He never said who she was.

Q. You knew that it was the owman[sic] your husband was living with?

A. No, I didn't know he was living with her. He didn't say she was. I knew who it was, though.

Q. Did you know then that you husband was living with her up in Kansas?

A. I didn't know what he was doing up there.

Q. You didn't know what he was doing up there?

A. Oh, yes, I knew he was practicing medicine.

Q. You found out since he was living with this woman?

A. I never inquired into it. I never tried to find out.

Q. Has he lived with this woman as much as you?

A. I don't know.

Q. He treats her as his wife, just as he treats you, and supports her?

A. I don't know nothing about what he does.

Q. He has children by her?

A. I don't know whether they are his children or whose they are.

Q. He admits they are his children?

A. I don't know.

Q. Doesn't he acknowledge the children?

A. I don't know what he says about that.

Q. Didn't he ever say anything to you about that?

A. No.

Q. You never said anything to him?

A. No.

Q. Do you know as a matter of fact that the children are his?

A. No, I don't know anything about that.

Q. What is your opinion about it?

A. I couldn't say. I don't know.

Q. How many children did you say this woman had?

A. She has got two.

Q. How old are they?

A. They are 5 years old, I think.

Q. The oldest one?

A. I think.

Q. How often has this woman come to your house with your husband?

A. I don't know.

Q. A great many times?

A. Yes, sir.

Q. Did he have the children along sometimes?

A. Yes, sir.

Q. Then he goes off with her again?

A. Yes, sir.

Q. Now, when they came to your house, this woman and her children, with your husband, how long did they stay there with you?

A. Why, I don't know. I never noticed now[sic] long they stayed.

Q. Did they stay over night?

A. I don't know. Longer than that I guess.

Q. More than one night?

A. Yes, sir.

Q. Stayed a week at a time?

A. I guess so.

Q. More than that?

A. I guess they do.

Q. Stayed several weeks, probably?

A. Yes, sir.

Q. And when you husband goes off she goes off with him?

A. Yes, sir.

Q. Then he would be gone may be 2 or 3 weeks?

A. Yes, I guess so.

Q. And then he came back with her?

A. No.

Q. He comes alone, does he?

A. Yes, sir; he most always comes alone.

Q. How long would he stay, 2 or 3 weeks?

A. As long as he want to.

Q. You say you and your husband have never talked about this matter? His relations with this woman?

A. No, sir.

Q. You never found it strange that he was living with another woman?

A. No. I am all right. He left my children with me. My children stays with me. They are all about grown.

Q. All you desire to testify to is that you husband never left you alone for any length of time and supports you?

A. Yes, that is all I thought I had to testify to and I knowed[sic] I could do that. I don't know who got up that kind of doings unless it is Randolph.

Homer Graxier[sic], being duly sworn, testified as follows:-

Examination by the Commission.

Q. State your name?

A. Homer Grazier.

Q. How old are you?

A. 19.

Q. What is your post office?

A. Narcissa.

Q. Are you the son of Moses L. Grazier?

A. Yes, sir.

Q. Martha Grazier is your mother?

A. Yes, sir.

Q. Have you ever testified in this case before?

A. No.

Q. Where were your father and mother living when you first remember? \

A. On Grand river, I guess.

Q. On a farm?

A. Yes, sir.

Q. You say you are 19 years old?

A. Yes, sir.

Q. Now, you can remember back to the time you were about 5 or 6?

A. I never kept track to see how long I can remember back.

Q. You remember back at the time you were 9 years old?

A. I guess I do.

Q. How much of the time have your father and mother lived together during the last 10 years?

A. I never kept track. They lived together all the time, so far as that is concerned, except when he would go off for a night or two.

Q. Have you been home all the time?

A. Yes, sir.

Q. Working on the farm?

A. Yes, sir.

Q. You say your father has been there except that he would be away?

A. Yes, sir. A. night or two or something like that.

Q. How long has he been away the longest time?

A. I never counted up to see.

Q. Would it be two days, two weeks or two months?

A. He has been away several times 2 or 3 days.

Q. Has he been away longer than that?

A. Yes, been away a week. I never kept track of it.

Q. You have an idea whether it was a week or month?

A. Yes, sir.

Q. What is your best judgment?

A. I didn't keep track of it.

Q. I am asking your judgment. You can say whether it was a week or a month?

A. I didn't say.

Q. I am asking you to say. Do you intend to answer that question?

A. No, sir.

Q. Why won't you?

A. I will.

Q. Answer it.

Q[sic]. He has been gone a week.

Q. I am asking if he has been away more than a week at one time?

A. I don't know whether he has or not.

Q. Would you say he had been gone a month at a time?

A. No, I wouldn't say that. I never did keep track of it.

Q. You answer is you don't know how long he has been gone?

A. No exactly. I didn't keep track.

Q. What do you mean by not exactly?

A. I mean not to the day or hour.

Q. I am asking whether he was gone a week, whether 2 weeks, or 3 weeks of a month.

A. Why, he has been gone 2 weeks, I guess.

Q. Where was he during the time he was gone?

A. I don't know anything about it. I didn't follow him.

Q. Did your mother know where he was?

A. I don't know that either.

Q. Did you[sic] father ever write home?

A. I suppose he did.

Q. Do you know whether he did or not?

A. I don't know.

Q. Did he ever write to you?

A. No. Yes, he did, too.

Q. He wrote you?

A. He wrote me once.

Q. Where was he then?

A. He was in Elk City.

Q. Elk city, Kansas?

A. Yes, sir.

Q. What was he doing there, do you know?

A. I don't know. I didn't ask him. He said he was practicing medicine. I suppose he was.

Q. How long ago was that, that he wrote you?

A. It has been a year.

Q. That is the first time he ever wrote you while he was gone; that is the only time?

A. That I remember of.

Q. How far do you live from the post office?

A. I live about 3 miles.

Q. You would go for the mail occasionally, would you?

A. Yes, sir

Q. Do you know whether your mother ever got any letter from your father?

A. I couldn't tell you anything about that.

Q. You couldn't say as to that?

A. No, sir; I don't know anything about that.

Q. You go for the mail?

A. Yes, I went after the mail.

Q. Don't you know whether your mother got any letters?

A. She got some. I don't know who from. I didn't come up here to answer all kinds of questions. I came up to answer whether he supported her or not.

Q. You will answer any question put to you. I am asking whether your mother got any letters from your father while he was gone.

A. I don't know anything about that.

Q. Can your mother read and write?

A. I suppose she can.

Q. Well, do you know?

A. She can read but she can't write very good, I don't think.

Q. Does she ever write letters?

A. No, sir.

Q. She can read a letter?

A. Yes, sir.

Q.   Did she ever read any letters to you that your father sent while he was gone?

A.   No, sir.

Q.   Now, you say in your best judgment the longest time your father was away from home was about two weeks?

A.   I never paid any attention to it.

Q.   He would be gone quite often, wouldn't he?

A.   Why, not so very often.

Q.   About how often in the course of a year would he be gone?

A.   About 3 or 4 times.

Q.   Did you ever see any woman at your mother's house who came there with your father?

A.   I saw a woman there; yes, sir.

Q.   What was her name?

A.   I don't know anything about it.

Q.   Did she have some children?

A.   I don't know anything about that.

Q.   Did you ever see any children there with the woman?

A.   There ain't no use of you asking me all them questions.

Q.   I am asking them, nevertheless.

A.   I ain't going to answer very many of them.

Q.   Did your father ever bring a woman down to his home with some children to visit there?

A.   I don't know anything about that. I couldn't swear he brought her there or anything of that kind. I ain't going to, more.

Q.   You saw some there, visiting there a week or more at a time?

A.   I never kept track of it.

Q.   She did visit there?

A.   How do you know. Did you see her there. You seem to know everything about it.

Q.   Now, Mr. Grazier, if you don't answer the questions properly I will report you to the United States court. I am asking you to state whether you saw any woman, during the past 5 or 6 years, come to your mother's house at the time your father returned and stay there a week or more at a time. Now answer that question yes or no.

A.   I guess so.

Q.   When that woman went away wouldn't your father go?

A.   I don't know anything about it.

Q.   Didn't they leave the house at the same time?

A.   I don't know that either.

Q.   You didn't know when this woman went away?

A.   No, sir.

Q.   You don't know if she ever went away?

A.   Yes, she isn't there now.

Q.   She isn't there now?

A.   No, sir.

Q.   Who is there besides your mother.[sic]

A.   No one only my wife.

Q. How long has this been, she was there?
A. I don't know.
Q. Has she been there within the past year?
A. Once, I think.
Q. How long did she stay there?
A. 2 or 3 days.
Q. She came there with your father when he came from Kansas?
A. I don't know anything about that. I wasn't there when he came.
Q. You don't know whether she came when your father came and went when he went away?
A. No sir.
Q. You don't know but what she might have come with him and gone back with him?
A. I don't know anything about it.
Q. Did you and your father have any talk about this woman?
A. Me and him never talked about it.
Q. Did you and your father ever talk about this case?
A. No, sir.
Q. At no time?
A. No, sir. Only he told me yesterday when he got the letter.
Q. That he had to come here?
A. Yes, sir.
Q. About how long did he talk to you about the case?
A. Never talked to me about it any.
Q. How did you happen to be here?
A. How did I happen to be here? I come in a buggy.
Q. Who asked you to come?
A. I come to file on my land.
Q. You happened to meet your father and mother here?
A. They came to[sic]. We live on the same place.
Q. Your father asked you to testify in his case?
A. He said he wanted me as a witness.
Q. Didn't he tell you what you would have to testify to?
A. I told you I don't know anything about it.
Q. Didn't your father tell you what you would have to testify to?
A. No, sir.
Q. What make you so reluctant to answer these questions?
A. Nothing, only I think it is all foolishness.
Q. Why do you?
A. Because the question is whether they are separated.
Q. How do you know.
A. Because I read the letter.
Q. I thought you said you didn't know anything about the case?
A. I don't know, only from the letter.
Q. What did the letter say?
A. That he had abandoned his Indian wife.

Q. Do you know what abandonment means?

A. I suppose I do.

Q. What does it mean?

A. It means to leave, I guess.

Q. Do you know whether your father has been living with this other woman?

A. I know nothing about it at all.

Q. Did your father and you talk about this case when you were out in the hall?

A. No, sir; nothing about the case at all.

Q. Nothing about what your testimony would be?

A. No, sir.

Q. The case wasn't mentioned at all?

A. No, sir. He was out there walking around, I was right there by the window.

Examination by Mr. Hastings.

Q. How far do you live from your mother's?

A. I live right close, about 10 steps from the other house.

Q. In the same yard?

A. Yes, sir.

Q. Isn't this other woman, that your father has been keeping, up there now?

A. Up there now?

Q. Wasn't she this morning, when you left?

A. I don't know anything about it.

Q. You know whether she was there or not?

A. I don't know anything about it.

Q. Was she there last night?

A. I don't know that, either. I stayed in my house and they stayed in theirs.

Q. How many rooms have they got in their house?

A. They have got two, I guess.

Q. You know, don't you?

A. Yes. Got two.

Q. Wasn't this other woman there yesterday?

A. I don't know. I wasn't there yesterday.

Q. What time did you come back yesterday?

A. I come along about dark.

Q. Were you over to their house last night?

A. No, sir.

Q. Did you see this woman at all yesterday?

A. No, sir.

Q. Where were you day before yesterday?

A. Day before yesterday. Let me see. I was in Miami day before yesterday, but yesterday I was looking after the place I was buying.

Q. Within the last few days have you seen this other woman?

A. No, sir; I haven't.

Q. You don't know whether she is up there?

A. No, sir.

Q. You didn't see her around up there. Have you seen her about that place within the last week?

A. I told you I hadn't been at home for the last week.

Q. Well, have you seen her?

A. No, I said.

At this point the witness refuses to testify and leaves the room.

Witness returns to witness stand and the examination is continued as follows:

BY THE COMMISSION:

If you will answer the questions put to you there will be no trouble. If you don't, there will.

A. I ain't afraid about the trouble at all.

Examination by Mr. Hastings.

Q. What I object to is you evade by saying something else. I am asking if you saw this woman, whom your father is reputed to be living with, and by whom he is said to have some children, about your mother's place? Have you seen her?

A. Yes, I have seen her,

Q. When was the last time?

A. It has been sometime along last winter.

Q. So far as you know, so far as your information is concerned, she hasn't been about there this last week?

A. Not that I noticed, no.

Q. How many times has this woman been at your mother's place?

A. I don't know.

Q. About how many time, according to your best judgment?

A. I suppose half a dozen time. I don't know exactly.

Q. With whom did she come?

A. I don't know.

Q. Were you ever there when she came?

A. No, sir; I never just happened to be there.

Q. You wouldn't see her there unless he was there?

A. No, sir.

Q. How many children has she?

A. She has one, if I am not mistaken.

Q. About how old is it?

A. I don't know, I am sure.

Q. How long has your father been at home this last time?

A. Now, I don't know.

Q. About how long?

A. I don't remember when he come home.

Q. Your best judgment?

Cherokee Intermarried White 1906
Volume VIII

A. I ain't been home myself, I reckon two weeks. I been down here at Afton. I been out there for the last two weeks. I don't know just when he came home. He was there when I left home, he was there when I came back.

Q. When did you leave home?

A. I come away along in February, I believe it was. Not February. Along about the middle of January.

Q. Now, Mr. Grazier, isn't it a fact that your father is reputed and generally believed to be living with this woman up in Kansas?

A. I don't know, sir.

Q. Do you know that it is the common report throughout the country that he has some children by her?

A. I don't know, sir. I never heard it. There was never any talk of that kind to me.

Q. Isn't it a fact that in the past two years a greater bulk of his time has been spent away from home?

A. No, sir.

Q. Isn't it a fact the he isn't up there only as he comes and goes, and that he stayed in Kansas?

A. No, sir. He stayed at home more than he was gone.

Q. He had no business. You say he was practicing medicine up in Kansas?

A. I suppose so. I have got his word for it.

Q. Has he a drug store up there?

A. I don't know.

Q. Did you ever hear him say?

A. Yes, sir. He did have one. I don't know whether he has it up there now.

Q. Did he say he did have one?

A. I don't know anything about it. I never asked.

Q. What is this woman's name?

A. I don't know.

Q. Did your ever hear it?

A. No, sir; never heard her name called in my life.

Q. Didn't you see her there at your house?

A. I have seen her there. I don't know her name, never asked it.

Q. She stayed there weeks at a time?

A. No, not weeks.

Q. How long did she stay there?

A. 6 or 7 days.

Q. She came with your father and both disappeared together?

A. I don't know.

Q. About the time[sic] time. When one left then both were gone.

A. Yes, sir. I don't know how they went. I wasn't there.

Q. Do you know a Mrs. Foley?

A. No, sir.

Q. Did you ever hear this woman called that?

A. Never heard her name at all.

Q. Do you think a woman would come up there, within 10 feet of your house, and stay there a week and you not hear her name?

A. The could come up in the same house and I wouldn't know it. I never make a practice of asking anybody's name.

Jesse O. Carr on oath states that as stenographer to the Commission to the Five Civilized Tribes he reported the above entitled case and that the foregoing is a true and complete transcript of his stenographic notes there.

Jesse O. Carr

Subscribed and sworn to before me this 6th day of November, 1903.

Samuel Foreman
Notary Public.

◇◇◇◇◇

C.F.B.   Cherokee D 505[sic]

DEPARTMENT OF THE INTERIOR
COMMISSIONER TO THE FIVE CIVILIZED TRIBES,
MUSKOGEE, IND. TER. JANUARY 5, 1907.

In the matter of the application for the enrollment of JAMES DUNCAN as a citizen by intermarriage of the Cherokee Nation.

APPEARANCES :   Applicant appears in person:
         Cherokee Nation represented by H. M. Vance,
         on behalf of W. W. Hastings, Attorney.

JAMES DUNCAN being first duly sworn by John E. Tidwell, a Notary Public, testified as follows:

On Behalf of Commissioner:

Q. What is your name?   A. James Duncan

Q. What is your age?   A. I am sixty-six years old; will be if I live to see the 5th day of next April.

Q. What is your Postoffice?   A. Afton.

Q. You are an applicant for enrollment as a citizen by intermarriage of the Cherokee Nation are you?   A. Yes sir.

Q. You have no Cherokee blood?   A. No sir.

Q. Your only claim to the right to enrollment as a citizen of the Cherokee Nation is by virtue of your marriage to a citizen by blood of that Nation is it?   A. Yes sir.

Q. What is the name of the citizen through whom you claim the right to enrollment?

A. Her name was Tempie Ann Schrimsher.

Q. When were you married to Tempie Ann Schrimsher?   A. I married her in 1868.

Q. Is she living or dead?   A. Dead.

Q. When did she die?   A. In 1881.

Q. Was she a recognized citizen of the Cherokee Nation at the time you married her?

A. Yes sir.

Q. Did you marry her in accordance with the laws of the Cherokee Nation?   A. I did.

Q. In what district did you secure your marriage license?   A. Delaware District.

Q. By whom were you married?   A. J. T. Trott.

Q. What was he?   A. He was a Minister of the Gospel.

Q. Were you ever married prior to your marriage to her?   A. No sir.

Q. Was she ever married prior to her marriage to you?   A. No sir.

Q. From the time of your marriage to your deceased wife, Tempie Ann Schrimsher, did you and she continuously live together as man and wife until her death?

A. No sir, she quit me and took another man.

Q. When did she leave you?   A. She left me in 1872.

Q. In 1872?   A. Yes sir.

Q. What reason had she, or did she give you, for leaving you?

A. Well, I had to attend Court at Fort Smith, stayed down there about a month, and when I came back she was living with another man by the name of Mansell.

Q. Did she tell you before you left that it was her intention to take up living with this man?

A. No sir.

Q. Had you any intimation of it?   A. No sir. I got a lady to stay with her while I was gone, and when I came home she told me about it, and that night he come in, and she acknowledged it.   She has one child by him, its name is Mansell, it is on the 1880 roll, and afterwards she left him and got a man by the name of George Southerland.

Q. Then your wife lived with two different men after she left you?   A. Yew she lived with them two and another one, she quit Southerland and took up with a man by the name of Meeks, and has a child by him named Andy, I think it is, Andy Meeks.

Q. Then how many men did she live with after she left you.

A. Three.

Q. Was she married to any of them?   A. Yes, she married George Southerland.

Q. Was she divorced from the one to whom she was married?

A. She just took up with them; and she was never divorced from me.   In '74 they had a payment at Vinita and she was living with Southerland and they tried to get on the '74 roll and they would not recognize him as a citizen because she was never divorced from me.   They put me on that roll all right and I drew Bread Money.   You have got my license in this office.

Q. Have you married since her death?   A. Yes sir.

Q. Is your second wife living?   A. Yes sir.

Q. What was her name? A. Sarah Miller. Before she ever married.

Q. When did you marry her? A. In 1885 or 1886.

Q. You did not marry your second wife until after your first wife's death? A. No sir, not until after she died.

Q. You did not marry any one from the time your first wife left you until after her death? A. No sir, never did. Both my wives was Cherokees by blood. I was administrator on my first wife's father's estate; he died during the war.

Q. Have you continuously lived in the Cherokee Nation since your marriage to your first wife? A. I have been recognized as a citizen by the Cherokee Nation ever since my marriage according to their laws.

Q. Have you lived continuously in the Cherokee Nation since your marriage?
A. I lived here all the time except in '77, some fellows robbed me and we went after them, and they put me in the House of Correction. We had no officers and they claimed I had no right to go after them without an officer.

Q. Where were you sent to the House of Correction? A. Detroit, Michigan.

Q. How long were you there? A. Five years, five months and a half.

Q. When were you sent? A. In '77.

Q. And you were there five years? A. Yes sir, I was there over five years.

Q. Your name does not appear upon the 1880 roll does it? A. No sir.

Q. You were confined in the house of Correction during the year 1880? A. Yes sir; and I had no people nor any body to put me on the roll. I am on every other roll that has been made while I was in the Nation.

Q. You say you filed the license and certificate showing your marriage to your first wife, Tempie Ann Schrimsher; at the time you made application for enrollment, did you? A. Yes sir.

Q. And it is now on file at this office? A. Yes sir, I reckon so; you took them from me there at Vinita, Indian Territory and never did return them.

The applicant, James Duncan is identified on the Cherokee Census Roll of 1896, Delaware District, No. 134.

The undersigned being first duly sworn states that as stenographer to the Commission to the Five Civilized Tribes she correctly recorded the testimony taken in this case on the first above mentioned date, and that the above and foregoing is a full, true and correct transcript of her stenographic notes thereof.

Lucy M Bowman

Subscribed and sworn to before me this 9th day of January, 1907.

Chas E Webster
Notary Public.

◇◇◇◇◇

CERTIFIED COPY.

(Honey Creek
(
(Del. Dist. C. N.
(
(February the 6th, 1868.

James Duncan,

        A citizen of the United States is hereby licensed to marry Tempie Crimser[sic], a citizen of the Cherokee Nation, the said James Duncan Having complied with the laws of the Cherokee Nation, the said James Duncan will be lawful married by some Minister of the gospel. The said James Duncan by oath truly allenates[sic] himself from the protection of all other governments, and from this day will abide by and support the laws of the Cherokee Nation.

Herein fail not - given from under my hand in the office this is the 6th day of February 1868.

        (Signed) T.J. McGhee, Clk. Dist Court

        In Delaware Dist.

        Cherokee Nation.

    This certifies that the undersigned, being duly sworn, states that as stenographer to the Commission to the Five Civilized Tribes she made the above and foregoing and that the same is a true, full and correct copy of the original instrument now on file in this office.

        Georgia Coberly
        Stenographer.

Subscribed and sworn to before me this 14th day of February, 1907.

        Walter W Chappell
        Notary Public.

◇◇◇◇◇

COMMISSIONERS:

HENRY L. DAWES,
TAMS BIXBY,
THOMAS B. NEEDLES,
C. R. BRECKINRIDGE.

ALLISON L. AYLESWORTH,
SECRETARY.

ADDRESS ONLY THE
COMMISSION TO THE FIVE CIVILIZED TRIBES.

DEPARTMENT OF THE INTERIOR,
COMMISSION TO THE FIVE CIVILIZED TRIBES.

Muskogee, Indian Territory,   **February 12,**   1902

Mr. James Duncan,
      Afton, Indian Territory.

Sir:-

You are hereby notified that the application of   **yourself**

for enrollment as ......citizen...... of the Cherokee Nation will be taken up for final consideration by the Commission to the Five Civilized Tribes, at its office in Muskogee, Indian Territory, on the   **28th**   day of   **February**   , 1902.

On said date, you may, if you desire, appear before the Commission, in person or by attorney, when an opportunity will be given you to introduce any additional testimony affecting your application.

You are further notified that the Representatives of the Cherokee Nation will also, at the same time, be afforded an opportunity to introduce testimony tending to disprove your right to enrollment, but said Representatives will be required to notify you of their intention to introduce such testimony before they will be permitted to do so.

Cherokee D-504
Register.

Yours truly,

xxxxxxxxxxxxxxx
Acting Chairman.
Commissioner in Charge.

◇◇◇◇◇

30

Cherokee D-504

COPY

Muskogee, Indian Territory, January 31, 1903.

W. W. Hastings,
   Attorney for the Cherokee Nation,
      Muskogee, Indian Territory.

Dear Sir:

There is herewith enclosed a copy of the decision of the Commission to the Five Civilized Tribes, dated January 30, 1903, granting the application of James Duncan for the enrollment of himself as a citizen by intermarriage of the Cherokee Nation.

You are hereby advised that you will be allowed fifteen days from date hereof, in which to file such protest as you may desire to make against the action of the Commission in this case, a copy of which protest you will be required to serve upon the applicant. If you fail to file protest within the time allowed, this decision will be considered final.

Respectfully,

Tams Bixby
Acting Chairman.

Enc. M-174

◇◇◇◇◇

Cherokee D-504

Vinita, Indian Territory, February 14, 1903.

Commission to the Five Civilized Tribes,
   Muskogee, Indian Territory.

Gentlemen:

Mr. W. P. Thompson of Vinita, Indian Territory who, the record in the case shows, represents as attorney James Duncan, an applicant for enrollment as a citizen of the Cherokee Nation, listed on doubtful card D-504, was in the office today and complained that although Mr. Duncan had received a copy of the decision of the Commission in his case and a notice to the effect that the decision had been protested by the Cherokee Nation, he, as attorney, did not receive a copy of the decision or a notice of the protest.

31

I request that a copy of the decision be furnished him at the earliest possible date.

Respectfully,

Clerk in Charge.

GRS

◇◇◇◇◇

Vinita, Indian Territory, February 17, 1903.

Commission to the Five Civilized Tribes,
    Muskogee, Indian Territory.

Gentlemen:

As directed in the Commission's letter of February 13, the original jackets and records in the following applications for enrollment as citizens of the Cherokee Nation are transmitted herewith:

> D-   20, Sarah B. Tiemeyer, et al.,
> D- 261, Theophilus Parker, et al.,
> D-1059, Surilda Scott,
> D- 504, James Duncan,
> D- 387, Hiram Blackfish,
> D- 270, Susan L. Brown, et al.

Respectfully,

Clerk in Charge.

Encl-6-3

GRS

◇◇◇◇◇

COPY

Cherokee D-504

Muskogee, Indian Territory, February 24, 1903.

The Honorable,
    The Secretary of the Interior.

Sir:

There is herewith transmitted the record of proceedings had in the matter of the application of James Duncan for the enrollment of himself as a citizen by intermarriage of the Cherokee Nation, including the Commission's decision, dated January 30, 1903, granting said application.

You are hereby advised that the Cherokee Nation protests against the action of the Commission in this case, a copy of which protest is enclosed.

Respectfully,

Tams Bixby

Chairman.

Enc. M-3130

Through the
    Commissioner of Indian Affairs.

◇◇◇◇◇

COPY

Cherokee D-504

Muskogee, Indian Territory, February 24, 1903.

W. W. Hastings,
    Attorney for Cherokee Nation,
        Vinita, Indian Territory.

Dear Sir:

You are hereby advised that the Commission has this day transmitted to the Secretary of the Interior, for review, the record of proceedings had in the matter of the application of James Duncan for the enrollment of himself as a citizen by intermarriage of the Cherokee Nation, including the Commission's decision, dated January 30, 1903, granting said application, and the protest of the Cherokee Nation against said decision, dated February 7, 1903.

The action of the Secretary will be made known to you as soon as the Commission is informed of same.

Respectfully,

Tams Bixby
Chairman.

◇◇◇◇◇

COPY

Cherokee D-504

Muskogee, Indian Territory, February 24, 1903.

W. P. Thompson,
     Attorney for James Duncan,
        Vinita, Indian Territory.

Dear Sir:

There is herewith enclosed a copy of the record of supplementary proceedings had in the matter of the application of James Duncan for the enrollment of himself as a citizen by intermarriage of the Cherokee Nation, together with a copy of the Commission's decision, dated January 30, 1903, granting said application. You have heretofore been furnished with a copy of the record of proceedings had in the original application.

You are hereby advised that the Cherokee Nation protests against the action of the Commission in this case, a copy of which protest has been furnished the applicant by the attorney for the Nation.

The decision, together with the record of proceedings had in this case, has this day been transmitted to the Secretary of the Interior for his review and decision. The action of the Secretary will be made known to you as soon as the Commission is informed of same.

Respectfully,

Tams Bixby
Chairman.

Enc. M-2130
Register

◇◇◇◇◇

COPY

Cherokee D-504

Muskogee, Indian Territory, February 24, 1903.

James Duncan,
Afton, Indian Territory.

Dear Sir:

There is herewith enclosed a copy of the decision of the Commission to the Five Civilized Tribes, dated January 30, 1903, granting your application for the enrollment of yourself as a citizen by intermarriage of the Cherokee Nation.

There has heretofore been furnished your attorney, W. P. Thompson, Vinita, Indian Territory, a copy of the record of proceedings had in the original application, and there has this day been forwarded to him a copy of the record of supplementary proceedings, together with a copy of the Commission's decision.

You are hereby advised that the Cherokee Nation protests against the action of the Commission in this case, a copy of which protest has been furnished you by the attorney of the Nation.

The decision, together with the record of proceedings had in this case, has this day been transmitted to the Secretary of the Interior for his review and decision. The action of the Secretary will be made known to you as soon as the Commission is informed of same.

Respectfully,

Tams Bixby
Chairman.

Enc. M-130

Register.

◇◇◇◇◇

Cherokee
D-504

Muskogee, Indian Territory, December 28, 1906.

James Duncan,
Afton, Indian Territory.

Dear Sir:

November 6, 1906, the United States Supreme Court held that white persons who intermarried with Cherokee citizens according to Cherokee law prior to November 1, 1875, are entitled to enrollment and allotments of land as citizens of the Cherokee Nation.

You are advised that to properly determine your right to enrollment as a citizen by intermarriage of the Cherokee Nation, it will be necessary for you to appear before the Commissioner for the purpose of giving testimony as to the date of your marriage and whether or not your wife, by reason of your marriage to whom you claim the right to enrollment as a citizen of the Cherokee Nation, was a recognized citizen of the Cherokee Nation at the time of your marriage to her, and whether or not you were married to her in accordance with Cherokee laws.

You are, therefore directed to appear before the Commissioner at Muskogee, Indian Territory, at 9 o'clock A. M., on Saturday, January 5, 1907, and give testimony as above indicated.

Respectfully,

JMH

Acting Commissioner.

◇◇◇◇◇

Cherokee
D-504

Muskogee, Indian Territory, December 28,1906.

W. P. Thompson,
Attorney for James Duncan,
Vinita, Indian Territory.

Dear Sir:

November 6, 1906, the United States Supreme Court held that white persons who intermarried with Cherokee citizens according to Cherokee law prior to November

1, 1875, are entitled to enrollment and allotments of land as citizens of the Cherokee Nation.

James Duncan has been advised that to properly determine his right to enrollment as a citizen by intermarriage of the Cherokee Nation, it will be necessary for him to appear before the Commissioner for the purpose of giving testimony as to the date of his marriage and whether or not his wife, by reason of his marriage to whom he claims the right to enrollment as a citizen of the Cherokee Nation, was a recognized citizen of the Cherokee Nation at the time of his marriage to her, and whether or not he was married to her in accordance with Cherokee laws.

James Duncan has this day been directed to appear before the Commissioner at Muskogee, Indian Territory, at 9 o'clock A. M., on Saturday, January 5, 1907, and give testimony as above indicated.

Respectfully,

J.M.H.   Acting Commissioner.

◇◇◇◇◇

Muskogee, Indian Territory, February 15, 1907

The Honorable,
   The Secretary of the Interior.

Sir:

February 24, 1903, the Commission to the Five Civilized Tribes transmitted the record of proceedings had in the matter of the application of James Duncan for enrollment as a citizen by intermarriage of the Cherokee Nation, together with the Commission's decision dated January 30, 1903 granting said application.

In view of the decision of the United States Supreme Court of November 5, 1906, in the cases of Daniel Red Bird et al. vs. the United States, the applicant was, on December 28, 1906, summoned before this office for the purpose of giving further testimony in his case, and his testimony taken January 5, 1907, is enclosed. This testimony is transmitted to be considered in connection with his case.

Respectfully,

Tthrough[sic] the Commissioner
   of Indian Affairs.

Encl. B-19   Commissioner
L M B

◇◇◇◇◇

Muskogee, I. T., January 25, 1907.

Commissioner to the Five Civilized Tribes,
Muskogee, Indian Territory.

Sir:

In considering the right of George Southerland, Cherokee 5216, to be enrolled as a citizen by intermarriage of the Cherokee Nation, I desire to call your attention to the testimony given by James Duncan, Cherokee D 505[sic], in the matter of his application to be enrolled as a citizen by intermarriage of the Cherokee Nation, on January 5, 1907, wherein he claims to have previously married Tempie Ann Schrimsher, she being the same woman through whom George Southerland claims his right to be enrolled as a citizen by intermarriage of the Cherokee Nation, and the said James Duncan testifies that she was never divorced from him prior to her marriage to Southerland.

Yours very truly,

(Signed) W. W. Hastings.
Attorney for the Cherokee Nation.

◇◇◇◇◇

-9Copy--[sic]

DEPARTMENT OF THE INTERIOR
OFFICE OF INDIAN AFFAIRS,
LAND   WASHINGTON
13780-1903.

February 2, 1907.

The Honorable,
The Secretary of the Interior.

Sir:

There is forwarded herewith report of the Commission to the Five Civilized Tribes, dated February 24, 1903, relative to the application of James Duncan for the enrollment of himself as a citizen by intermarriage of the Cherokee Nation, including the Commission's decision, dated January 30, 1903, granting the application. A copy of the protest of the Cherokee Nation against the action of the Commission in this case is enclosed.

The applicant herein claims the right to enrollment by reason of his marriage, in accordance with the laws of the Cherokee Nation, on February 29, 1868, to Tempa Ann Schrimpser[sic], a citizen by blood of the Cherokee Nation, who is identified on the marriage license, enclosed with the record, as "Temper Crimser".

The record shows that the applicant and his wife lived together for about three years following their marriage and that she then left him, and there is no evidence adduced to show that the applicant abandoned his wife.

The Commission finds that James Duncan is not identified on the authenticated tribal roll of 1880, having been in prison during the preparation of such roll, and his identification on that roll as shown by the record is an error, and that an examination of the Cherokee tribal rolls in the possession of the Commission shows that the applicant is identified on the Cherokee census roll of 1896, opposite No. 134.

Subsequent to the death of James Duncan's first wife, which occurred in 1881, he married his present wife, Sarah, a citizen by blood of the Cherokee Nation. It is also shown that the applicant has resided in the Cherokee Nation since the date of his marriage to his first wife.

Having married a citizen by blood of the Cherokee Nation prior to November 1, 1875, in accordance with Cherokee laws, the applicant under the ruling of the United States Court in the case of Daniel Red Bird, et al vs. The United States, is entitled to enrollment as a Cherokee citizen by intermarriage, and it is recommended that the decision of the Commission to that effect be affirmed.

Very respectfully,

C. F. Larrabee,

Acting Commissioner.

AJW-EH.

◇◇◇◇◇

D.C 8844-1907.   (COPY)

DEPARTMENT OF THE INTERIOR,   J.W.G.
DIRECT   WASHINGTON.   J.C.H.
I.T.D.2392-1907.

February 12, 1907.

L.R.S.

The Commissioner to the Five Civilized Tribes,
     Muskogee, Indian Territory.

Sir:

     February 24, 1903, the Commission to the Five Civilized Tribes transmitted the record in the matter of the application of James Duncan for enrolment[sic] as a citizen by intermarriage of the Cherokee Nation, together with its decision.

     Reporting February 2, 1907 (Land 13780-1903), the Indian Office recommends that the decision of the Commission be approved. Copy of its letter is inclosed.

     The Department concurs in said recommendation and the decision enrolling the applicant is hereby affirmed.

Respectfully,

Thos. Ryan

1 inclosure.   First Assistant Secretary.

3 inc. & carbon copy to Ind. O.

A FMc
2-13-07.

◇◇◇◇◇

Cherokee
10986.

Muskogee, Indian Territory, February 16, 1907.

James Duncan,
      Afton, Indian Territory.

Dear Sir:

You are hereby advised that the decision of the Commission to the Five Civilized Tribes, dated January 30, 1903, granting your application for enrollment as a citizen by intermarriage of the Cherokee Nation, was affirmed by the Secretary of the Interior, February 12, 1907.

Respectfully,

HJC   Commissioner.

◇◇◇◇◇

Cherokee
10986.

Muskogee, Indian Territory, February 16, 1907.

W. P. Thompson,
      Attorney for James Duncan,
            Vinita, Indian Territory.

Dear Sir:

You are hereby advised that the decision of the Commission to the Five Civilized Tribes, dated January 30, 1903, granting the application for the enrollment of James Duncan, as a citizen by intermarriage of the Cherokee Nation was affirmed by the Secretary of the Interior, February 12, 1907.

For your information there is enclosed herewith a copy of Departmental decision referred to.

Respectfully,

Encl. HJ-92.
    HJC   Commissioner.

◇◇◇◇◇

Cherokee
10986.

Muskogee, Indian Territory, February 16, 1907.

W. W. Hastings,
    Attorney for the Cherokee Nation,
        Muskogee, Indian Territory.

Dear Sir:

You are hereby advised that the decision of the Commission to the Five Civilized Tribes, dated January 30, 1903, granting the application for the enrollment of James Duncan as a citizen by intermarriage of the Cherokee Nation was affirmed by the Secretary of the Interior, February 12, 1907.

For you information a copy of the Departmental decision referred to is enclosed herewith.

Respectfully,

Encl. HJ-90.
    HJC   Commissioner.

◇◇◇◇◇

Cherokee
I.W. 222

Muskogee, Indian Territory, April 16, 1907.

James Duncan,
    Afton, Indian Territory.

Dear Sir:

Your marriage license and certificate filed in connection with your application for enrollment as a citizen by intermarriage of the Cherokee Nation is returned to you herewith, copies of the same being retained in the files of this office.

Respectfully,

Encl. W-24.   Commissioner.
S.W.

Cherokee Intermarried White 1906
Volume VIII

Cher IW 223

◇◇◇◇◇

Department of the Interior,
Commission to the Five Civilized Tribes,
Tahlequah, I. T. December, 3rd, 1900.

In the matter of the application of John H. Abbott for the enrollment of himself and children as Cherokee citizens. He being sworn before Commissioner Needles, testified as follows-

Q What is your name? A. John H. Abbott.
Q How old are you? [sic] 48.
Q What is your post office address? A. Tahlequah.
Q What district do you live in? A. Tahlequah
Q Are you a recognized citizen of the Cherokee Nation? A. By adoption.
Q For whom fo[sic] you apply? A. Myself and children.
Q Have you a certificate of marriage? A. No sir
Q Is your wife a Cherokee citizen by blood? A. Yes sir.
Q What was her maiden name? A. Helen Walker.
Q. When were you married to her? A. In 1874.
Q What are the names of your children? A. Carrie M.
 Q How old is she? A. 19
 Q Next child? A. Fannie E.
 Q How old_? A. 15.
Q What is the next child named? A. Butler L.
Q How old? [sic] 11.
Q What is the next one named? A. William G.
Q How old? [sic] 8.
Q Next child? A. Jane E.
Q How old? [sic] 6.
Q Are these children all alive and living with you at this time?
A. Yes sir.
Q Have you lived in the Cherokee Nation ever since you were married[sic]
A. Yes sir
Q Is your wife living? A. No sir.
Q Have you married since she died? A. No sir.
Q Did you live with her until she died? A. Yes sir.

1880 roll, page 347, No 16. John Abbott, Flint district.

1896	1275	6	John Abbott, Tahlequah dist.
1896	1131	31	Carrie Abbott, "
1896	1132	33	Annie Abbott, "
1896	1132	35	Butler Abbott "
1896	1132	36	William Abbott "
1896	1132	37	Jane Abbott, "

Cherokee Intermarried White 1906
Volume VIII

The name of John H. Abbott appears on the authenticated 1880 roll and the census roll of 1896 as John Abbott, a Cherokee citizen by intermarriage. The name of his wife Helen, now deceased, appears on the authenticated 1880 roll, and the name of their children, Carrie M., Fannie E., Butler T., William G., and Jane E. Abbott appear on the census roll of 1896. They are all fully identified and make satisfactory proof as to residence, consequently the said John H. Abbott will be duly listed for enrollment as a Cherokee citizen by intermarriage and his children as enumerated in the testimony will be listed for enrollment as Cherokee citizens by blood.

Chas. von Weise being sworn states that as stenographer to the Commission to the Five Civilized Tribes he reported in full all the proceedings in the above cause and that the foregoing is a full, true and correct transcript of his stenographic notes therein.

Chas. von Weise

Subscribed and sworn to before me this the 4th of December, 1900.

TB Needles
Commissioner.

◇◇◇◇◇

H.
Cher. 6028.

Department of the Interior.
Commission to the Five Civilized Tribes.
Tahlequah, I. T., October 6, 1902.

SUPPLEMENTAL TESTIMONY AND PROCEEDINGS in the matter of the application for the enrollment of JOHN H. ABBOTT as a citizen by intermarriage of the Cherokee Nation.

JOHN H. ABBOTT, being first duly sworn, and being examined, testified as follows:

BY COMMISSION: What is your name?   A John H. Abbott.
Q How old are you?   A Fifty-one.
Q What is your post office address?   A Tahlequah.
Q Are you a white man?   A Yes sir.
Q Have you heretofore made application to this Commission for enrollment as a citizen by intermarriage of?   A Yes sir.
Q What is the name of your wife?   A Ellen Abbott.
Q Is she living?   A No sir, she is dead.
Q Was she a Cherokee by blood?   A Yes sir.
Q When were you and she married?   A Married in 1874, September.
Q Did you and she live together continuously up to the time of her death?   A Yes sir.

44

Q When did she die?   A It has been about four years ago.

Q Do you claim your right to enrollment by reason of your marriage to her? A Yes sir.

Q Were you ever married before you married her?   A No sir.

Q Was she ever married before she married you?   A No sir.

Q Have you lived in the Cherokee Nation continuously since you made application for enrollment?   A Yes sir.

Q Did you make satisfactory proof to the Commission of your marriage to your wife according to Cherokee law?   A Yes sir, I think I did

Q Did you present your marriage license and certificate to the Commission?   A They asked me, and I told then, and they said it was all right.

> This testimony will be filed with and made a part of the record in the matter of the application for the enrollment of as a citizen by intermarriage of the Cherokee Nation, Cherokee straight card field No. 6028.

Wm. Hutchinson, being first duly sworn, states that as stenographer to the Commission to the Five Civilized Tribes he correctly recorded the testimony and proceedings in this case, and that the foregoing is a true and complete transcript of the stenographic notes thereof.

Wm Hutchinson

Subscribed and sworn to before me this 8th day of October, 1902.

John O Rosson
Notary Public.

◇◇◇◇◇

C. F. B.   Cherokee 6028.

DEPARTMENT OF THE INTERIOR,
COMMISSIONER TO THE FIVE CIVILIZED TRIBES.
Muskogee, Indian Territory, February 6, 1907.

In the matter of the application for the enrollment of John H. Abbott as a citizen by intermarriage of the Cherokee Nation.

Applicant appears in person.

APPEARANCES:

Cherokee Nation represented by
W. W. Hastings, Attorney.

John H. Abbott being first duly sworn by Mrs. Lyman K. Lane, Notary Public, testified as follows:

Cherokee Intermarried White 1906
Volume VIII

ON BEHALF OF COMMISSIONER.

Q	What is your name?	A	John H. Abbott.
Q	What is your age?	A	About 54.
Q	What is your post office address?	A	Foil, now.

Q   You are an applicant for enrollment as a citizen by intermarriage of?
A   Yes sir.

Q   You have no Cherokee blood?　　　　　A   Not a bit.

Q   Your only claim to the right to enrollment as a citizen of the Cherokee Nation is by virtue of your marriage to a citizen by blood of the Nation?
A   Yes sir.

Q   What is the name of the citizen through whom you claim?
A   Ellen Walker.

Q   Is she living?　　　　　A   No sir, she's dead.
Q   When did you marry her?　　　　　A   In 1874.

Q   Was she a recognized citizen by blood of the Cherokee Nation at the time you married her?
A   Yes sir.

Q   Living in the Cherokee country, was she?
A   Yes sir.

Q   Did you secure a license and marry her in accordance with the law of the Cherokee Nation?
A   Yes sir.

Q   In what district was the license issued?
A   Going Snake District.

Q   You secured your petition, did you?
A   Yes sir.

Q   And then got your license?　　　　　A   Yes sir.
Q   By whom were you married?　　　　　A   Michael Ghormley, preacher.

Q   You were married in Going Snake District, were you?
A   Yes sir.

Q   Were you ever married prior to your marriage to Ellen Walker?
A   No sir.

Q   Was she ever married before she married you?
A   No sir.

Q   When did she die?　　　　　A   '98 I believe.

Q   From the time of your marriage to her, did you and she continuously live together as husband and wife and reside in the Cherokee Nation until her death?
A   Yes sir.

Q   Have you married since her death?
A   No sir.

Q   Has your residence been continuous in the Cherokee Nation from the time of your marriage to her up until the present time?　　A   Yes sir.

Q   Have you any evidence of a documentary character showing your marriage to your deceased wife?
A   Not unless it is on the Going Snake records.

Q   You have no marriage license and certificate?
A   No sir; I lost them.

BY MR. HASTINGS.

Q   What is the exact date of your marriage?
A   It was September 4, 1874.
Q   You were married in Flint District?
A   I was married in Going Snake district at Uncle William Ghormley's.
Q   Have you ever married since the death of your wife?
A   No sir.
Q   You have lived continuously in the Cherokee Nation since your marriage to her?
A   Yes sir.
Q   And you lived with her continuously until her death?
A   Yes sir.
Q   And since that time you have lived continuously in the Nation and have never re-married?
A   No sir; I have never re-married, and have lived in the Nation.
Q   Did you have some children by this wife?
A   Yes sir.
Q   What was the oldest child's name?
A   Ethel.
Q   Is she living?   A   Yes sir.
Q   In what year was she born?
A   In '75; September, about the 5th I believe.
Q   What is the next child's name?   A   Eugene.
Q   How old is Eugene?
A   I don't remember just exactly how old he is; he was born about a year after she was.
Q   Is Eugene living?   A   Yes sir.
Q   You were enrolled in Flint District in '80?
A   Yes sir.

ON BEHALF OF COMMISSIONER.

The applicant, John H. Abbott, is identified on the Cherokee authenticated tribal roll of 1880, Flint District, No. 16. Immediately following his name on said roll appears the name of his deceased wife, E. T. Abbott, by virtue of his marriage to whom he claims the right to enrollment as a citizen by intermarriage of the Cherokee Nation, said E. T. Abbott being identified on said roll as a native Cherokee, age 24. Immediately following her name appears the name of E. L. Abbott, applicant's oldest child, who is identified as a native Cherokee, age 4 years, and immediately following the name of E. L. Abbott, appears the name of N. E. Abbott, native Cherokee, 2 years, and immediately following this name, appears the name of John W. Abbott, native Cherokee, 5 months old.

Q   Are all these children that I have mentioned, children of yourself and deceased wife Ellen Abbott?
A   Yes sir.

Q   Have you any witnesses here who have known you since your marriage?
A   Mr. Walker, my brother-in-law.
Q   Was he present at the marriage?
A   No; he wasn't present at the marriage.
Q   Was he acquainted with you prior to the time you married his sister?
A   Yes sir.

BY MR. HASTINGS.

Q   You swear positively, Mr. Abbott, that you did secure a marriage license prior to your marriage?
A   Yes sir.
Q   You got the regular number of signers?
A   I got 7 signers.
Q   What clerk issued the license?
A   Ben Goss, Going Snake District.
Q   You swear positively that that license was issued?
A   Yes sir.
Q   And you also swear positively that you were married to her in September, 1874, after the issuance of this license?
A   Yes sir; at William Ghormley's house.

Q   Are any of the people who signed your petition living at this time?
A   Charlie McClellan and James S. Stapler.
Q   They didn't see you married?
A   No, they just signd[sic] my petition. J. B. Jones, the Agent, drew my petition up for me.

William H. Walker being first duly sworn by Mrs. Lyman K. Lane, Notary Public, testified as follows:

ON BEHALF OF COMMISSIONER.

Q   What is your name?   A   William H. Walker.
Q   What is your age?   A   40.
Q   What is your post office address?
A   Tahlequah, Indian Territory.
Q   You are acquainted with John H. Abbott, are you?
A   Yes sir.
Q   Are you related to him?
A   By marriage; yes sir.
Q   What was his wife's name?   A   Ellen Walker.
Q   She was your sister was she?   A   Yes sir.
Q   Do you know when John H. Abbott was married to your sister, Ellen Walker?
A   I don't believe I could fix the date; I was quite small at that time.

Q   You can't swear positively as to the date?

A   No sir.

Q   Your sister was a recognized citizen by blood of the Cherokee Nation at the time of their marriage?

Q   And resided in the Cherokee country?

A   Yes sir.

Q   You knew John Abbott prior to his marriage to your sister, did you?

A   Yes sir.

Q   Is it your understanding and do you believe that John H. Abbott at the time he married Ellen Walker, secured a license from the Cherokee authorities and married your sister in accordance with the law of the Cherokee Nation?

A   Yes sir; I always so understood.

Q   Since that time, has he to your own personal knowledge exercised the rights of a citizen by intermarriage of the Cherokee Nation?

A   Yes sir; he has voted in the Cherokee elections, sat on juries and exercised all the rights of a citizen, - drew money.

Q   Was your sister, Ellen Walker, ever married prior to her marriage to James H. Abbott?

A   No sir.

Q   Was he to your knowledge ever married prior to his marriage to her?

A   No sir.

Q   They lived together continuously from the time of their marriage until her death?

A   Yes sir.

Q   And lived in the Cherokee Nation?

A   Yes sir.

Q   Since her death. John H. Abbott has continuously resided in the Cherokee Nation, has he?

A   Yes sir.

BY MR. HASTINGS.

Q   You have heard Mr. Abbott's testimony with relation to the date of his marriage to your sister, which he fixes as being sometime in September of 1874; have you any reason to believe that that is not the correct date?

A   No sir.

Q   While you state that you do not remember the date, it is your belief that that is the date, from family history?

A   Yes sir; I have heard it spoken of by my mother and others in the family; for that reason, I believe it is correct.

Q   You have no reason to doubt it?   A   No sir.

ON BEHALF OF COMMISSIONER.

Q   Do you remember when their oldest child was born?   Can you remember that?

A   Yes sir.

Q Do you have any idea as to how long it was after their marriage before that child was born?

A Well, no; not exactly; it seems to me like it was in the following year or possibly not until '76; I am not sure about that.

Q You know it was some time after their marriage?

A Yes sir.

Q What is this oldest child's present name?

A Ethel Corn.

Q What is her post office address?

A I don't know; they live up North somewhere.

An examination of the records of this case show that application was received by the Commission to the Five Civilized Tribes November 27, 1900, for the enrollment of the applicant's oldest child, whose name is now Ethel Corn, and that her age at that time was given as 25 years.

Ewing C. Ghormley being first duly sworn by Mrs. Lyman K. Lane, Notary Public, testified as follows:

ON BEHALF OF COMMISSIONER.

Q What is your name? A Ewing C. Ghormley.

Q What is your age? A 49 years.

Q What is your post office address?

A Adair.

Q Do you know a person in the Cherokee Nation by the name of John H. Abbott?

A Yes sir.

Q How long have you known him?

A I have known him a good while; I can't say.

Q Did you know him before he was married?

A Yes sir.

Q Do you remember when he was married?

A Yes sir.

Q Give the date of his marriage.

A I don't remember the date.

Q Do you remember the name of his wife before she was married?

A Yes sir; Ellen Walker.

Q Was she a recognized citizen by blood of the Cherokee Nation at the time he married her?

A Yes sir.

Q Was she his first wife? A I suppose so.

Q Was he her first husband? A Yes sir.

Q Is she living at this time? A No, she's dead.

Q When did she die?

A I don't know when she died.

Q   Do you know of your own personal knowledge that they resided together as husband and wife from the time of their marriage until the time of her death?

A   Well, of course, I wasn't living right close to them but I never heard of anything to the contrary.

Q   You say you were present at their marriage?

A   Yes sir.

Q   Is it your understanding that John H. Abbott secured a license and married his wife in accordance with the law of the Cherokee Nation?

A   That's my understanding.

Q   Did you see his license at the time of his marriage?

A   No sir.

Q   Did you know anything about his petition?

A   I don't know as I did.

Q   But you understand and believe that he secured a license and married his wife in accordance with the law of the Cherokee Nation?

A   That was my understanding.

Q   Do you know of your own personal knowledge that since that time he has been recognized as a citizen by intermarriage of the Cherokee Nation?

A   I reckon; I haven't been living near enough to him to know anything about it.

Q   You never heard his right as an intermarried citizen questioned?

A   No sir.

BY MR. HASTINGS.

Q   You are not prepared to state about the date of his marriage?

A   No sir; he was married at my father's house.

Q   And your father married them?

A   It was either my father or grandfather.

Q   Are they both ministers?

A   One was the Clerk and the other a minister. I think my father married them. I think he issued the license.

Q   You don't remember the date of it?

A   No sir.

ON BEHALF OF COMMISSIONER.

Q   Did you live near them just after their marriage?

A   Yes sir; something about like 8 or 9 miles.

Q   When was their first child born, do you remember?

A   I remember the circumstance.

Q   Do you know about how long it was after their marriage before their first child was born?

A   No, I don't.

Q   Was is a matter of a year or two years?

A   I don't remember.

Cherokee Intermarried White 1906
Volume VIII

The undersigned being first duly sworn states that as stenographer to the Commissioner to the Five Civilized Tribes, she recorded the testimony taken in this case and that the foregoing is a true and correct transcript of her stenographic notes thereof.

Myrtle Hill

Subscribed and sworn to before me this the 12th day of February, 1907.

Walter W. Chappell
Notary Public.

◇◇◇◇◇

E C M   Cherokee 6028.

DEPARTMENT OF THE INTERIOR,

COMMISSIONER TO THE FIVE CIVILIZED TRIBES.

In the matter of the application for the enrollment of JOHN H. ABBOTT as a citizen by intermarriage of the Cherokee Nation.

D E C I S I O N

THE RECORDS OF THIS OFFICE SHOW: That at Tahlequah, Indian Territory, December 3, 1900 application was received by the Commission to the Five Civilized Tribes for the enrollment of John H. Abbott as a citizen by intermarriage of the Cherokee Nation. Further proceedings in the matter of said application were had at Tahlequah, Indian Territory, October 6, 1902 and Muskogee, Indian Territory February 6, 1907.

THE EVIDENCE IN THIS CASE SHOWS: That the applicant herein, John H. Abbott, a white man, was married in accordance with Cherokee law in September, 1874 to his wife Ellen Abbott, nee Walker, since deceased, who was at the time of said marriage a recognized citizen by blood of the Cherokee Nation, who is identified on the Cherokee authenticated tribal roll of 1880, Flint District No. 17 as a native Cherokee. It is further shown that from the time of said marriage until the death of said Ellen Abbott, which occurred about the year 1898, the said John H. Abbott and Ellen Abbott resided together as husband and wife and continuously lived in the Cherokee Nation; that since the death of said Ellen Abbott the said John H. Abbott has not re-married and continuously lived in the Cherokee Nation up to and including September 1, 1902. Said

52

applicant is identified on the Cherokee authenticated tribal roll of 1880 and the Cherokee census roll of 1896 as an intermarried citizen of the Cherokee Nation.

IT IS, THEREFORE, ORDERED AND ADJUDGED: That in accordance with the decision of the Supreme Court of the United States, dated November 5, 1906, in the cases of Daniel Red Bird, et al. vs. the United States, Nos. 125, 126, 127, and 128, the said applicant, John H. Abbott is entitled under the provisions of Section Twenty-one of the Act of Congress approved June 28, 1898 (30 Stats., 495), to enrollment as a citizen by intermarriage of the Cherokee Nation and his application for enrollment as such is accordingly granted.

Tams Bixby
Commissioner.

Dated at Muskogee, Indian Territory,
this   FEB 23 1907

◇◇◇◇◇

Cherokee 6028

COPY

Muskogee, Indian Territory, February 23, 1907.

W. W. Hastings,
     Attorney for the Cherokee Nation,
          Muskogee, Indian Territory.

Dear Sir:

There is enclosed herewith a copy of the decision of the Commissioner to the Five Civilized Tribes, dated February 23, 1907, granting the application for the enrollment of John H. Abbott as a citizen by intermarriage of the Cherokee Nation.

Respectfully,

SIGNED Tams Bixby
Commissioner.

Encl. A-13
  RA

◇◇◇◇◇

Cherokee 6028

Muskogee, Indian Territory, February 23, 1907.

The Commissioner to the Five Civilized Tribes,
Muskogee, Indian Territory.

Sir:

Receipt is acknowledged of the testimony and of your decision enrolling John H. Abbott as a citizen by intermarriage of the Cherokee Nation. Time for protesting said decision is waived, and I consent that said person may be placed upon the schedule immediately.

Respectfully,

W. W. Hastings
Attorney for the Cherokee Nation.

◇◇◇◇◇

Cherokee 6028

COPY

Muskogee, Indian Territory, February 23, 1907.

John H. Abbott,
Tahlequah, Indian Territory.

Dear Sir:

There is enclosed herewith a copy of the decision of the Commissioner to the Five Civilized Tribes, dated February 23, 1907, granting the application for your enrollment as a citizen by intermarriage of the Cherokee Nation.

You will be advised when your name has been placed upon a schedule of citizens of the Cherokee Nation and approved by the Secretary of the Interior.

Respectfully,

SIGNED *Tams Bixby*
Commissioner.

Encl. A-12

Cher IW 224

◇◇◇◇◇

DEPARTMENT OF THE INTERIOR.
COMMISSION TO THE FIVE CIVILIZED TRIBES.
VINITA, I.T., OCTOBER 2nd, 1900.

IN THE MATTER OF THE APPLICATION OF Rachel J. McCullough, husband and child for enrollment as citizens of the Cherokee Nation, and she being sworn and examined by Commission, T. B. Needles, testified as follows:

Q What is your name? A Rachel J. McCullough.
Q What is your age? A Fifty four.
Q What is your Postoffice? A Afton.
Q What district do you live in? A Cooweescoowee.
Q Are you a recognized citizen of the Cherokee Nation? A Yes sir.
 Q By blood? A Yes sir.
Q What degree of blood do you claim? A One eighth.
Q For whom do you apply for enrollment? A My husband, M. H. McCullough and Charles, my youngest son.
Q Husband and child? A Yes sir.
Q Why is your husband not here? A He is visiting in Illinois.
Q What is your Husband's name? A Milton H. McCullough.
Q Is he a white man? A Yes sir.
Q Is he on the roll of 1880? A Yes sir.
Q What is the name of your child, Mrs. McCullough; the one you want to enroll?
A Charles H. McCullough.
Q How old is he? A He is seventeen.
Q Is he living now? A Yes sir.
Q You and your husband and child have always lived in the Cherokee Nation?
A Yes sir.

 (1880 Roll, Page 289, #1769, M. H. McCollough[sic], Delaware D'st)
 (1880 Roll, Page 289, #1770, Rachel J. McCollough, Delaware Dst)
 (1896 Roll, Page 498, #1892, Rachel J. McCullough, Delaware Dst)
 (1896 Roll, Page 581, #352, Milton H. McCullough, Delaware Dst)
 (1896 Roll, Page 498, #1896, Charles H. McCullough, Delaware District)

The name of Rachel J. McCullough and her husband, Milton H. McCullough appear upon the authenticated roll of 1880, as well as the census roll of 1896, his name appearing on the roll of 1880, as M. H. McCollough. The name of her son, Charles H. also appears upon the census roll of 1896. They all being duly identified according to the page and number of the rolls as indicated in the testimony, the said Rachel J. McCullough and her son, Charles H. McCullough will be duly listed for enrollment as Cherokee citizens by blood; and her husband, Milton H. McCullough as a Cherokee citizen by intermarriage.

The undersigned, being sworn, states that as stenographer to the Commission to the Five Civilized Tribes, he correctly recorded the testimony and proceedings in this case, and the foregoing is a true and complete transcript of his stenographic notes thereof.

R. R. Cravens

Subscribed and sworn to before
me this 5th day of October, 1900.   CR Breckinridge
                                                           COMMISSIONER.

◇◇◇◇◇

Cher
Supp'l to # 4007

Department of the Interior,
Commission to the Five Civilized Tribes,
Muskogee, I. T., October 31, 1902.

In the matter of the application of MILTON H. McCULLOUGH, for the enrollment of himself as a citizen by intermarriage, and his wife, RACHEL J. McCULLOUGH, and his son, CHARLES H. McCULLOUGH, as citizens by blood, of the Cherokee Nation.

WILLIAM P. McCULLOUGH, being duly sworn and examined by the Commission, testified as follows:

Q What is your name ?   A William P. McCullough.
Q How old are you ?   A Thirty two years old.
Q What is your post office address ?   A Fairland.
Q Are you acquainted with Milton H. McCullough who is an applicant for enrollment as an intermarried citizen of the Cherokee Nation ?   A Yes sir.
Q Is he a relative of yours ?   A Father.
Q What is his wife's name ?   A Rachel Jane.
Q Is she a citizen by blood of the Cherokee Nation ?   A Yes sir
Q Is she your mother ?   A Yes sir.
Q Have your father and mother lived together as husband and wife from 1880 up to the present time ?   A Yes sir.
Q They never have been separated since 1880 ?   A They never have only one time my father made a trip to Illinois in 1891, visiting there, and stayed probably two or three weeks; that's the only time.
Q I asked if they had ever been separated; I meant if they had ever fallen out and quit living together as man and wife ?   A No sir, they have lived together continuously.
Q Well, were they living together as man and wife on the first day of September, 1902 ?   A Yes sir.
Q They have lived in the Cherokee Nation since 1880 up to the present time ?

56

A Yes sir.

Q He has lived all his life in the Cherokee Nation ?   A Yes sir.

Q Your mother and father are both living ?   A Yes sir.

Q How old is your father ?   A I think he is sixty three years old now.

Q What is the condition of his health ?   A It is not good; he suffers from rheumatism, and can scarcely get around.

Q It would be hard for him to come here at this time ?   A Yes sir, I wouldn't say he couldn't come, but it would work a great hardship on him.

PHILLIP DONAHOO, being duly sworn and examined by the Commission, testified as follows:

Q What is your name ?   A Phillip Donahoo.

Q How old are you ?   A Thirty seven.

Q What is your business ?   A I am a physician.

Q Do you know Milton H. McCullough ?   A Yes sir.

Q Do you know his wife Rachel ?   A Yes sir.

Q How long have you known them doctor ?   A Since 1892.

Q What is Mr. McCullough's physical condition at this time ?   A Well, it is not very good, but for a man of his age it is fairly good.

Q Is he afflicted with rheumatism at all at this time ?   A I have treated him before I heard him complaining of that. I have been in the family frequently before I have ever treated him.

Q You haven't treated him then ?   A No sir, I never did just treat him, but I have been in the family frequently to see other members of the family.

Q Since 1892 have he and his wife lived together all the time ?   A Yes sir.

Q They have never separated ?   A No sir.

Q They were living together as husband and wife on the first day of September, 1902 ?   A Yes sir.

E. C. Bagwell, on oath states that, as stenographer to the Commission to the Five Civilized Tribes, he correctly recorded the testimony and proceedings had in the above entitled cause, and that the foregoing is an accurate transcript of his stenographic notes thereof.

E.C. Bagwell

Subscribed and sworn to before me this December 16, 1902.

BC Jones
Notary Public.

◇◇◇◇◇

DEPARTMENT OF THE INTERIOR,
COMMISSION TO THE FIVE CIVILIZED TRIBES.

In the matter of the death of **Milton H. McCullough**
a citizen of the **Cherokee** Nation, who formerly resided at or near
Afton , Ind. Ter., and died on the **21** day of
August , 1904

AFFIDAVIT OF RELATIVE.

UNITED STATES OF AMERICA, ⎱
  INDIAN TERRITORY, ⎰
  Northern District.

I, **Charles H. McCullough** , on oath state that I am **22**
years of age and a citizen by **blood** , of the **Cherokee** Nation;
that my postoffice address is **Afton** , Ind. Ter.; that I am
son of **Milton H. McCullough**
who was a citizen, by **adoption** , of the **Cherokee** Nation
and that said **Milton H. McCullough** died on the **21** day of
August , 1904

Chas H McCullough

Witnesses To Mark:

{ _____
  _____

Subscribed and sworn to before me this **21** *day of* **Nov** , 190 4

Samuel Foreman
Notary Public.

AFFIDAVIT OF ACQUAINTANCE.

UNITED STATES OF AMERICA, ⎱
  INDIAN TERRITORY, ⎰
  _____ District.

I, _____ , on oath state that I am ____
years of age, and a citizen by _____ of the _____Nation;
that my postoffice address is _____ , Ind. Ter.;
that I was personally acquainted with _____
who was a citizen, by _____ , of the _____Nation;
and that said _____ died on the _____day of
_____ , 1____

58

Witnesses To Mark:

{ _____

  _____

Subscribed and sworn to before me this _____ *day of* _____, *190*__

_____

Notary Public.

◇◇◇◇◇

C.F.B.   Cherokee 4007.

DEPARTMENT OF THE INTERIOR,
COMMISSIONER TO THE FIVE CIVILIZED TRIBES.
MUSKOGEE, I. T., FEBRUARY 9, 1907.

In the matter of the application for the enrollment of MILTON H. McCULLOUGH as a citizen by intermarriage.

CHARLES H. McCULLOUGH, being first duly sworn by Mrs. Lyman K. Lane, Notary
      Public, testified as follows:

ON BEHALF OF THE COMMISSIONER:

Q   What is your name?   A Charles H. McCullough.
Q   What is your age?   A 24.
Q   What is your post office address?   A Fairland, I. T.
Q   You appear here today, do you, on behalf of your father, Milton H. McCullough,
      who is an applicant for enrollment as a citizen by intermarriage of the Cherokee
      Nation?   A Yes sir.
Q   Is he living or dead?   A Dead.
Q   When did he die?   A August 21, 1904.
Q   What is the name of your mother?   A Rachel J. McCullough.
Q   Is she living or dead?   A Living.
Q   Has she ever appeared before this office to give testimony relative to the right to
      enrollment of your father as a citizen by intermarriage of the Cherokee Nation?
      A No sir.
Q   What is the condition of her health? Could she appear here if necessary?
      A I don't know whether she could nor not; her health is bad; she has heart
      trouble.
Q   Your father claims the right to enrollment by virtue of his marriage to your mother,
      Rachel J. McCullough, does he?   A Yes sir.
Q   Have you any evidence of a documentary character showing the marriage of your
      father and mother?   A Yes sir.

Cherokee Intermarried White 1906
Volume VIII

The applicant presents an original marriage license showing that on October 1, 1868, license was issued by John L. Springston, Clerk District Court, Saline District, Cherokee Nation, authorizing the marriage of M. H. McCullough, a citizen of the United States, and Miss Rachel J. Adair, a citizen of the Cherokee Nation. On the back of said license appears a certificate signed by David Rowe showing that on October 6, 1868, he performed the marriage ceremony in accordance with the terms of said license.

Q   From the time you can first remember did your father and mother live together as husband and wife until his death?   A Yes sir.

Q   And lived continuously in the Cherokee Nation, did they?   A Yes sir.

Q   Did you ever hear of your father and mother being out of the Cherokee Nation since their marriage?   A No sir.

Q   They have always, since their marriage, to the best of your knowledge, considered the Cherokee Nation their home?   A They have.

Q   Have you been appointed to look after your father's estate?   A Yes sir.

Q   You present here an instrument showing that you have been appointed as administrator of your father's estate. Do you desire that this be filed with the papers in this case?   A I have one of those, already signed, here.

Q   To the best of your knowledge, was your father ever married prior to his marriage to you[sic] mother?   A No sir.

Q   You never heard that eh[sic] was?   A No sir.

Q   Did you ever hear that your mother was married prior to her marriage to your father? A No sir.

W. W. HASTINGS, ATTORNEY FOR CHEROKEE NATION:

Q   How old are you?   A 24.

Q   You say that you never heard that your father was married prior to his marriage to your mother?   A No sir.

Q   You never heard it in any sort of way?   A No sir.

Q   I mean by that that you never knew of it personally, and that you never heard of it? A No sir.

The applicant, Milton H. McCullough, is identified on the Cherokee authenticated tribal roll of 1880, Delaware District, No. 1789. His wife, Rachel J. McCullough, by virtue of his marriage to whom he claims the right to enrollment as a citizen by intermarriage of the Cherokee Nation, is identified on the said roll, in said District, at No. 1770, and her name is on the approved partial roll of citizens by blood of the Cherokee Nation, opposite No. 9687.

"It will be necessary for you, Mr. McCullough, before the application for the enrollment of your father, Milton H. McCullough, as an intermarried citizen of the Cherokee Nation will be complete, to introduce the testimony of witnesses who have knowledge as to whether or not either your father or your mother was ever married prior to the time of their marriage."

Cherokee Intermarried White 1906
Volume VIII

(Witness excused).

The undersigned, being first duly sworn, states that, as stenographer to the Commissioner to the Five Civilized Tribes, she correctly reported the above and foregoing testimony, and that the same is a full, true and complete transcript of her stenographic notes thereof.

Sarah Waters

Subscribed and sworn to before me this 12th day of February, 1907.

J. L. Gary
Notary Public.

◇◇◇◇◇

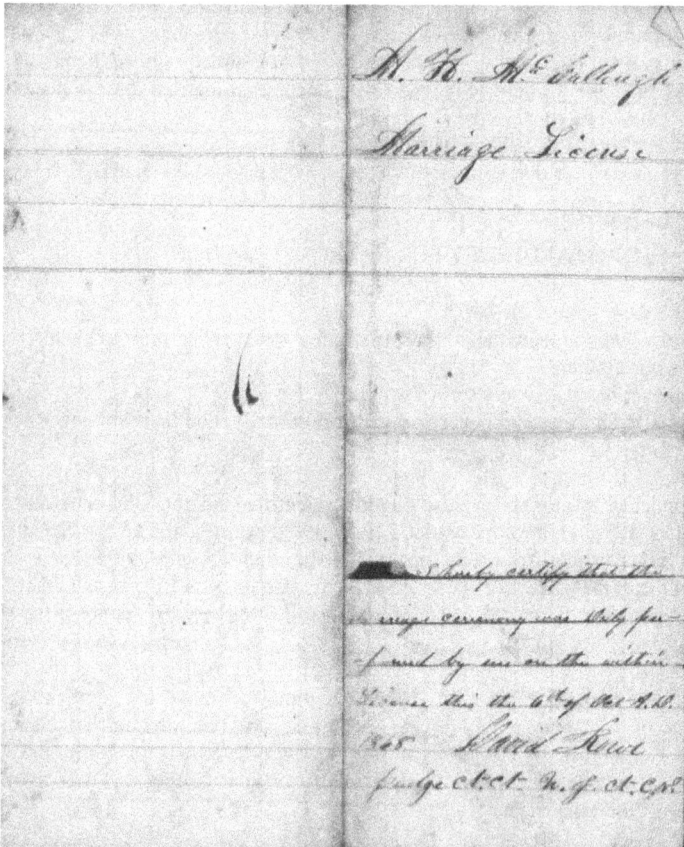

Saline District
Cherokee Nation

Be it known to all whom it may concern that marriage license are hereby granted to M. H. McCullough a *white man* citizen of the United States to marry Miss Rachel P. Adair a citizen of the aforesaid Dist and Nation Said M. H. McCullough having complied with the laws and customs of the Cherokee people and Nation and any of the judges of the several Courts of this Nation or any Regular ordained Minister of the gospel having the Care of souls are hereby authorized to perform the marriage ceremony required and return the same with a certificate of service as the law directs

Given from under my hand and seal in office this the 16th of October 1868

John L. Springston Clk
Dist Ct Saline Dist Cher. N.t.

(Copy of original document from case.)

◇◇◇◇◇

C.F.B.   Cherokee 4007.

DEPARTMENT OF THE INTERIOR,
COMMISSIONER TO THE FIVE CIVILIZED TRIBES.
Muskogee, I. T., February 23, 1907.

In the matter of the application for the enrollment of Milton H. McCullough as a citizen by intermarriage of the Cherokee nation[sic].

Cherokee Nation represented by H. M. Vance.

J. F. Thompson, being first duly sworn by Walter W. Chappell, a Notary Public for the Western District of Indian Territory, testified as follows:

By the Commissioner:

Q State your name and postoffice address?   A J. F. Thompson, Tahlequah, Indian Territory.

Q How old are you?   A Sisty-sis[sic] years.

Q Were you at one time acquainted with Milton H. McCullough, who was the husband of Rachael J. McCullough?   A Yes sir.

Q He is not living at this time?   A No sir.

Q When did he die?   A I think 2 or 3 years ago.

Q He was a white man, was he?   A Yes sir.

Q What was his wife's name?   A Rachael J. McCullough.

Q She was a Cherokee by blood?   A Yes sir, sister to my wife.

Q Is she living at this time?   A Yes sir.

Q How long have you known these persons, Milton H. McCullough and Rachael J. McCullough?   A I have known Rachael J. McCullough since 1856, and I have known Milton H. McCullough since 1868.

Q When were they married?   A They were married I think September, 1868.

Q Did you know both parties prior to their marriage?   A No, I didn't know Milton H. McCullough intimately. I saw him; he was in the family of my mother-in-law; I was a tenant.

Q You were not personally acquainted with him?   A No sir.

Q Was Rachael J. Adair ever married prior to her marriage to Milton H. McCullough?   A No sir.

Q Was he, to your knowledge, ever married prior to his marriage to her?   A Not that I know of.

Q Did you ever hear that he was?   A I heard such a rumor but I never knw[sic] as to the truth of it.

Q But you never got any information as to whether or not it was true?   A No sir.

Q You know that they continuously lived together as husband and wife from the time of their marriage until the death of Milton H. McCullough?   A Yes sir.

Q Did you understand from what you heard that Milton H. McCullough was married prior to his marriage to Rachael J. Adair and that his former wife was dead at the time he married Rachael Adair?   A I have no means of knowing.

Q You can give no information then, in regard to a former marriage or reputed former marriage?   A No sir.

By Mr. Vance:

Q Do you know where he was said to have been married prior to his other marriage? A No, but I rather think it was Illinois, however.

Q You don't know the exact date?   A No sir.

Q Or place?   A No sir.

Q Do you know the name of the person to whom he is said to have been married? A No sir.

Q Do you know anybody in this country who would know the facts in the case? A No, I don't.

Frances R. Lane upon oath states that as stenographer to the Commissioner to the Five Civilized Tribes she reported the testimony in the above entitled cause and that the foregoing is an accurate transcript of her stenographic notes thereof.

Frances R Lane

Subscribed and sworn to before me this February 23, 1907.

Walter W Chappell
Notary Public.

◇◇◇◇◇

C.F.B.   Cherokee 4007

DEPARTMENT OF THE INTERIOR,

COMMISSIONER TO THE FIVE CIVILIZED TRIBES.

In the matter of the application for the enrollment of Milton H. McCullough as a citizen by intermarriage of the Cherokee Nation.

D E C I S I O N

THE RECORDS OF THIS OFFICE SHOW: That at Vinita, Indian Territory, October 2, 1900, application was received by the Commission to the Five Civilized Tribes for the enrollment of Milton H. McCullough as a citizen by intermarriage of the Cherokee Nation. Further proceedings in the matter of said application were had at Muskogee, Indian Territory, October 31, 1902, and February 9 1907.

THE EVIDENCE IN THIS CASE SHOWS: That the applicant herein, Milton H. McCullough, is a white man, and claims the right to enrollment as a citizen of the

Cherokee Nation by virtue of his marriage, in accordance with Cherokee law October 6, 1868, to one Rachel J. Adair; that the said Rachel J. Adair was, at the time is said marriage, a recognized citizen by blood of the Cherokee Nation, is identified on the Cherokee authenticated tribal roll of 1880, Delaware District No. 1770, as a native Cherokee, and whose name is included in the approved partial roll of citizens by blood of the Cherokee Nation opposite No. 9687. It is further shown that since said marriage said parties have lived together as husband and wife, and have continuously resided in the Cherokee Nation. Said applicant is duly identified on the Cherokee authenticated tribal roll of 1880 as an intermarried citizen of the Cherokee Nation.

IT IS, THEREFORE, ORDERED AND ADJUDGED: That in accordance with the decision of the Supreme Court of the United States, dated November 5, 1906, in the cases of Daniel Red Bird, et al., vs. the United States, Nos. 125, 126, 127, and 128, the said applicant, Milton H. McCullough is entitled, under the provisions of Section twenty-one of the Act of Congress approved June 28, 1898 (30 Stats. 495), to enrollment as a citizen by intermarriage of the Cherokee Nation, and his application for enrollment as such is accordingly granted.

Tams Bixby
Commissioner.

Dated at Muskogee, Indian Territory,
this   FEB 23 1907

◇◇◇◇◇

Cherokee 4007   COPY

Muskogee, Indian Territory, February 23, 1907.

W. W. Hastings,
        Attorney for the Cherokee Nation,
                Muskogee, Indian Territory.

Dear Sir:

        There is enclosed herewith a copy of the decision of the Commissioner to the Five Civilized Tribes, dated February 23, 1907, granting the application for the enrollment of Milton H. McCullough as a citizen by intermarriage of the Cherokee Nation.

Respectfully,

SIGNED *Tams Bixby*
Commissioner.

Enc I--29
RPI

◇◇◇◇◇

Cherokee 4007

Muskogee, Indian Territory, February 23, 1907.

The Commissioner to the Five Civilized Tribes,
Muskogee, Indian Territory.

Sir:

Receipt is acknowledged of the testimony and of your decision enrolling Milton H. McCullough as a citizen by intermarriage of the Cherokee Nation. Time for protesting said decision is waived, and I consent that said person may be placed upon the schedule immediately.

Respectfully,
W. W. Hastings
Attorney for the Cherokee Nation.

◇◇◇◇◇

Cherokee 4007 COPY

Muskogee, Indian Territory, February 23, 1907.

Milton H. McCullough,
Afton, Indian Territory.

Dear Sir:

There is enclosed herewith a copy of the decision of the Commissioner to the Five Civilized Tribes, dated February 23, 1907, granting the application for your enrollment as a citizen by intermarriage of the Cherokee Nation.

You will be advised when your name has been placed upon a schedule of citizens of the Cherokee Nation and approved by the Secretary of the Interior.

Respectfully,

SIGNED *Tams Bixby*
Enc I-30   Commissioner.

RPI

Cher IW 225

◇◇◇◇◇

Cherokee Intermarried White 1906
Volume VIII

DEPARTMENT OF THE INTERIOR,
COMMISSION TO THE FIVE CIVILIZED TRIBES,
VINITA, I.T., SEPTEMBER 20, 1900.

In the matter of the application of Emeline L. Jones for the enrollment of herslef[sic] as a citicen[sic] of the Cherokee Nation; said Jones being sworn by Commissioner T. B. Needles, testified as follows

Q What is your name? A Emeline L. Jones.
Q How old are you? A 77.
Q What is your post office address? A Vinita.
Q What district do you live in? A Cooweescoowee.
Q Are you a recognized citizen of the Cherokee Nation? A Ye, sir.
Q By blood? A No, sir.
Q By inter-marriage? A My husband was adopted. John B. Jones is my husband, I am a widow. I was adopted after I come here.
Q You say your husband was John B. Jones? A Yes, sir.
Q Is he living? A No, sir, been dead 24 years.
Q Does your name appear upon any roll 1880[sic]? A Yes, sir, I drew a payment.
Q Whom do you apply for? A Myself and five step-children.
Q They are living with you? A No, sir, they are not living now with me.
Q Their mothers and fathers living are they? A No, sir; their mothers are dead.
   1880 enrollment; pager 773, #1155, Emeline L. Jones, Tahlequah.

Q Were you enrolled in 1896? A They pretended to enroll me.
Q How long have you been living in the Cherokee Nation? A I have been living here ever since 1868.
Q Lived here continuously since 1868? A I went to Denver with my husband before he died. I went to New York and made a visit one[sic].

W. W. Hastings, Representative of the Cherokee Nation:

Q Were you living in the Cherokee Nation in the year of 1880?
A Yes, sir, I was here that year.
Q Have you lived continuously since that time every year? A Yes, sir.
Q What has been your post office? A Sometimes at Tahlequah and some times at other places.
Q Where have you been for the past ten years, what has been your post office? A I have been here for the last nine years?[sic] My post office before I come here has been Minopa[sic].
Q You live here now? A Yes, sir.
Q You live here continuously? A Yes, sir.

Com'r Needles:--The name of Emeline L. Jones appears upon the authenticated roll of 1880, and she makes satisfactory proof as to her residence, and is duly identified upon

Cherokee Intermarried White 1906
Volume VIII

said roll and having been fully identified, she will be duly listed for enrollment by this Commission as a Cherokee citizen by inter-marriage.

---oooOOOooo---

J. O. Rosson, being first duly sworn, states that as stenographer to the Commission to the Five Civilized Tribes, he correctly recorded the testimony and proceedings in this case, and the foregoing is a true and complete transcript of his stenographic notes thereof.

JO Rosson

Subscribed and sworn to before me this 22d day of September, 1900.

TB Needles
Commissioner.

◇◇◇◇◇

Statement of Applicant Taken Under Oath.

CHEROKEE BY BLOOD AND ADOPTION.

Date **SEP 20 1900** 1900.

Name .... **Vinita I.T.** ....

District........................ Year .... Page .... No. ....

Citizen by blood .... Mother's citizenship ....

Intermarried citizen ....

Married under what law.................................... Date of marriage.........................

License ....**77**.................................... Certificate................

Wife's name................ **Emiline**[sic] **L Jones**...........................

District................**TAHLEQUAH**.................... Year....**1880**....Page....**773**....No.........**1155**........

Citizen by blood................ Mother's citizenship.................

Intermarried citizen........ **Yes**..............................

Married under what law.................................... Date of marriage.........................

License .... Certificate................

Names of Children:

	Dist.	Year	Page	No.	Age
	Dist.	Year	Page	No.	Age
	Dist.	Year	Page	No.	Age
	Dist.	Year	Page	No.	Age
	Dist.	Year	Page	No.	Age

#3125

◇◇◇◇◇

DEPARTMENT OF THE INTERIOR.
Commission to the Five Civilized Tribes.
Muskogee, Indian Territory, October 24th, 1902.

In the matter of the application of Emiline[sic] L. Jones for the enrollment of herself as a citizen by intermarriage of the Cherokee Nation.

Supplemental to #3125.

J. J. Spencer, being duly sworn, testified as follows:
Examination by the Commission.
Q.   What is your name?   A. J. J. Spencer.
Q.   How old are you?   A. I am 62 years old, sir.
Q.   What is your post office address?   A. Vinita.
Q.   Are you acquainted with the applicant in this case, Emiline L. Jones? A. Yes, sir.
Q.   How old is he, about?   A. Well, sir; I couldn't tell you. She must be way up in the eighties.
Q.   Is she physically unable to come and testify in her own case?   A. Yes, sir.
Q.   Is she a white woman?   A. Yes, sir.
Q.   How long have you known her?   A. I have known her for 5 years.
Q.   Have you known her continuously for five years?   A. Yes, sir.
Q.   Where has she been living during that time?   A. Living right in Vinita.
Q.   Is she a single woman, or a widow?   A. She is a widow.
Q.   She has been a widow ever since you have known her?   A. Yes, sir.
Q.   Was she a widow on the first of September, 1902?   A. Yes, sir.
Q.   Has she been living in the town of Vinita for the past 5 years?   A. Yes, sir.

-:-

Jesse O. Carr, being first duly sworn, states that as stenographer to the Commission to the Five Civilized Tribes he reported the above entitled case and that the foregoing is a true and complete transcript of his stenographic notes thereof.

Jesse O. Carr

Subscribed and sworn to before me this 29th day of January, 1903.

Samuel Foreman
Notary Public.

Copy

◇◇◇◇◇

69

C. F. B.   Cherokee 3125.

DEPARTMENT OF THE INTERIOR,
COMMISSION TO THE FIVE CIVILIZED TRIBES.
Muskogee, Indian Territory, January 11, 1907.

In the Matter of the Application for the Enrollment of Emiline L. Jones as a citizen by intermarriage of the Cherokee Nation.

APPEARANCES:

James S. Davenport for Applicant.

Cherokee Nation represented by
W. W. Hastings, Attorney.

James S. Davenport being first duly sworn by B. P. Rasmus, Notary Public, testified as follows:

ON BEHALF OF COMMISSIONER.

Q   What is your name?   A   James S. Davenport.
Q   What is your age?   A   42.
Q   What is your post office address?
A   Vinita.
Q   Do you know a person in the Cherokee Nation by the name of Emiline L. Jones?
A   Yes sir.
Q   She is an applicant for enrollment before this office as a citizen of the Cherokee Nation?
A   Yes sir.
Q   Do you know whether or not she has received any notice from the commissioner[sic] of late, to come here and give testimony in her case?
A   Yes sir, I do; she had me read the notice at one time and I was here the day that she should have appeared; I advised Mr. Rosson of the Commission that her physical condition was such that she couldn't come.
Q   It will not be possible then for her to appear to give testimony in her case?
A   No sir; I think not. She is an invalid and can only get around a little on crutches; it would be necessary for her to be hauled to the depot in some kind of a conveyance and helped on the train, and hauled from the depot up here. She has lived for the last 10 years within 150 feet of my home and I know her condition.

Miles C. Jones being first duly sworn by B. P. Rasmus, Notary Public, testified as follows:
Q   What is your name?   A   Miles C. Jones.
Q   What is your age?   A   62 years old.
Q   What is your post office address?
A   Dewey, Indian Territory.

Cherokee Intermarried White 1906
Volume VIII

Q   You appear here to-day for the purpose of giving testimony relative to the right to enrollment of Emiline L. Jones as a citizen by intermarriage of the Cherokee Nation?

A   Yes sir.

Q   How long have you known Emiline L. Jones?

A   Since 1868.

Q   Is she related to you in any way?

A   She is my brother's widow.

Q   She is a white woman?   A   Yes sir.

Q   You say she married your brother?

A   Yes sir.

Q   When did she marry him?

A   To the best of my recollection, it was in October, '68.

Q   Is your brother a white man?   A   Yes sir.

Q   He neither claims nor possesses any Cherokee blood?

A   No sir.

Q   They were married in the Cherokee Nation?

A   No sir; in Lawrence, Kansas.

Q   Was your brother a recognized citizen of the Cherokee Nation at the time of their marriage?

A   Yes sir.

Q   How did he acquire citizenship in the Cherokee Nation?

A   By special act of Council.

Q   When was he admitted to citizenship in the Cherokee Nation by the special act of council?

A   If I remember correctly, it was on the 7th of November, 1965[sic].

The resolution of thanks to the Baptist Missionary Society of Boston, and an Act granting citizenship to Evan Jones and John B. Jones, made a part of the record in the case of John J. Harrison, M M 19, will be made a part of the record herein.

      "Copy

Resolution of thanks to the Babtist[sic] Missionary Society of Boston; And, An Act granting citizenship to Evan Jones and John B. Jones.

Resolved by the National Council:

That our sincere thanks are hereby tendered to the Babtist[sic] Missionary Society of Boston.

It is now more than forty years since Missionaries of that Society came into the Cherokee Nation; When the Cherokees were poor and covered with darkness, light with regard to the other world was brought to us by Evan Jones, and at a later date by his son John B. Jones. And we do bear witness that they have done their work well, and that they have striven to discharge the duties incumbent upon them in doing good to the people, and performing faithfully their duties to God. And we bear witness that their work was highly prospered up to the time when they were driven out of our country by the United States Agents in 1861.

And now after the close of the war, we are informed that the Missionary Society have determined to resume their work in the Cherokee Nation. For their determination we do hereby return to them our thanks.

And we hereby declare; that it is our desire that they will more strongly than ever push forward their work of enlightening our land.

And we do further declare that we hold in high esteem Evan Jones, and his son J. B. Jones.

Now, therefore; Be it enacted by the National Council; That Evan Jones and John B. Jones be, and they are hereby admitted to citizenship in this Nation together with their families; and all the rights allowable to white men under the Constitution is hereby granted to them.

Our object in so doing is that our people may be instructed by them in good morale and general intelligence.

Smith Christie

Tahlequah C. N.   Pres. N. Committee.

Nov. 7th, 1865.   W. D. Reese, Clerk N. C.

Approved: Lewis Downing, Acting Chairman P. Chief.

A True Copy, W. D. Reese, Clk. N. Comt.

C. F. B.   Cherokee 3125.

Fort Gibson, C. N.

February 11th, 1868.

I heredo certify that this paper is a true copy of the official one, now in the possession of Evan Jones.

J. E. Munson

1st Lieut. 6th U. S. Infantry

Judge Advocate.

Exhibit A."

Q Have you any evidence with you of a documentary character showing the marriage of Emiline L. Jones to John B. Jones?

A Yes sir.

The applicant presents an original marriage certificate which is too voluminous to be made a part of the record in this case but reads as follows:

"This is to certify that John B. Jones of Tahlequah in the Cherokee Nation, and Emiline L. Smith of Redman in the State of New York, were by me joined together in holy matrimony on the 16th day of October, in the year of Our Lord 1868."

Signed Evan Jones, Minister of the Gospel, in presence of M. S. Beach and O. W. MvAllaster[sic].

Q Is John B. Jones living at this time?

A No sir; he is dead.

Q   When did he die?
A   I don't know just exactly but I think it was in the early part of 1876. It wa before the middle of the year; I know that by the fact that his family returned from Colorado where they had gone the year previous on account of his ill health. He became quite feeble and they went there in '75. They returned in perhaps the last of May or the first of June, 1876.
Q   From the date of their marriage did John B. and Emiline L. Jones live continuously together as husband and wife until the death of John B. Jones?
A   Yes sir.
Q   And they lived continuously in the Cherokee Nation except the year they spent in Colorado?
A   Yes sir.
Q   They didn't go to Colorado at that time for the purpose of making it their home.
A   No sir; they went on account of his health.
Q   Was Emiline L. Jones, John B. Jones' first wife?
A   His second wife.
Q   Was his former wife living or dead at the time he married Emilie L. Jones?
A   Dead.
Q   Was he Emiline L. Jones' first husband?
A   Yes sir.
Q   Since the death of John B. Jones, has Emiline L. Jones lived continuously in the Cherokee Nation?
A   She has; I don't think she has ever been out.
Q   She is living at this time?
A   Yes sir; in the Cherokee Nation.

The applicant, Emiline L. Jones, is identified on the Cherokee authenticated tribal roll of 1880, Tahlequah District, No. 1155.

Q   Emiline L. Jones has not married since the death of her husband, John B. Jones?
A   No sir.

The undersigned being first duly sworn states that as stenographer to the Commission to the Five Civilized Tribes, she recorded the testimony taken in this case and that the foregoing is a full, true and correct transcript of her stenographic notes thereof.

Myrtle Hill

Subscribed and sworn to before me this the 14th day of January, 1907.

John E. Tidwell
Notary Public.

E.C.M.   Cherokee 3125.

DEPARTMENT OF THE INTERIOR,

COMMISSIONER TO THE FIVE CIVILIZED TRIBES.

In the matter of the application for the enrollment of Emeline L. Jones as a citizen by intermarriage of the Cherokee Nation.

D E C I S I O N

THE RECORDS OF THIS OFFICE SHOW: That at Vinita, Indian Territory, September 20, 1900, application was received by the Commission to the Five Civilized Tribes for the enrollment of Emeline L. Jones as a citizen by intermarriage of the Cherokee Nation. Further proceedings in the matter of said application were had at Muskogee, Indian Territory, October 24, 1902, and January 11, 1907.

THE EVIDENCE IN THIS CASE SHOWS: That the applicant herein, Emeline L. Jones, is a white woman, and neither claims nor possesses any right to enrollment as a citizen of the Cherokee Nation, other than such right as she may have acquired by virtue of her marriage, in October 1868, to one John B. Jones; that the said John B. Jones was not a Cherokee by blood, and acquired citizenship in the Cherokee Nation by virtue of his admission, November 7, 1865, by an Act of the Cherokee National Council admitting, among others, John B. Jones, to citizenship in the Cherokee Nation, and adjudging the applicants[sic] entitled to all the rights allowable to white men under the constitution of the Cherokee Nation. In view of the foregoing, it is considered that the applicant herein, Emeline L. Jones, did not marry a citizen by blood of the Cherokee Nation prior to November 1, 1875.

IT IS, THEREFORE, ORDERED AND ADJUDGED: That in accordance with the decision of the Supreme Court of the United States, dated November 5, 1906, in the cases of Daniel Red Bird, et al., vs. the United States, Nos. 125, 126, 127, and 128, the said applicant, Emeline L. Jones, is not entitled, under the provisions of Section twenty-one of the Act of Congress approved June 28, 1898 (30 Stats., 495), to enrollment as a citizen by intermarriage of the Cherokee Nation, and her application for enrollment as such is accordingly denied.

Tams Bixby
Commissioner.

Dated at Muskogee, Indian Territory,
this   FEB 6 1907

Copy

◇◇◇◇◇

COPY

Cherokee-3125.

Muskogee, Indian Territory, June 14, 1905.

W. S. Upham,
      Coffeyville, Kansas.

Dear Sir:

      The Commission is in receipt of your letter of June 5, 1905, asking to be advised as to the status of the application for the enrollment of Emiline L. Jones as a citizen of the Cherokee Nation.

      In reply you are advised that the Commission has not yet rendered a decision in this case, and will not until the question of the rights of applicants to enrollment as citizens by intermarriage of the Cherokee Nation has been finally determined by the Courts.

                            Respectfully,

                              SIGNED *Tams Bixby*
                                     Chairman.

◇◇◇◇◇◇

Cherokee
3125.

Muskogee, Indian Territory, December 24, 1906.

Emeline L. Jones,
      Vinita, Indian Territory.

Dear Madam:

      November 6, 1906, the United States Supreme Court held that white persons who intermarried with Cherokee citizens according to Cherokee law prior to November 1, 1875, are entitled to enrollment and allotments of land as citizens of the Cherokee Nation.

      You are advised that to properly determine your right to enrollment as a citizen by intermarriage of the Cherokee Nation, it will be necessary for you to appear before the Commissioner for the purpose of giving testimony as to the date of your marriage and whether or not your husband, by reason of your marriage to whom you claim the right to enrollment as a citizen by intermarriage of the Cherokee Nation, was a recognized Cherokee citizen at the time of your marriage to him.

You are therefore directed to appear before the Commissioner at Muskogee, Indian Territory, at 9 o'clock A. M., on Friday, January 4, 1907, and give testimony as above indicated.

Respectfully,

H.J.C.   Acting Commissioner.

<><><><><>

Cherokee 3125

Muskogee, Indian Territory, February 6, 1907.

Emiline L. Jones,
        Vinita, Indian Territory.

Dear Madam:

There is enclosed herewith a copy of the decision of the Commissioner to the Five Civilized Tribes, dated February 6, 1907, rejecting the application for your enrollment as a citizen by intermarriage of the Cherokee Nation.

The decision, together with the record of proceedings had in the case, has this day been transmitted to the Secretary of the Interior for his review and decision. The action of the Secretary will be made known to you as soon as this office is informed of the same.

Respectfully,

Encl. H-24   Commissioner.
    JMH

Register.

<><><><><>

Cherokee 3125

Muskogee, Indian Territory, February 6, 1907.

Starr & Patton,
Attorneys for Emiline L. Jones,
Vinita, Indian Territory.

Dear Sirs:

There is enclosed herewith a copy of the decision of the Commissioner to the Five Civilized Tribes, dated February 6, 1907, rejecting the application for the enrollment of Emiline L. Jones as a citizen by intermarriage of the Cherokee Nation.

The decision, together with the record of proceedings had in the case, has this day been transmitted to the Secretary of the Interior for his review and decision. The action of the Secretary will be made known to you as soon as this office is informed of the same.

Respectfully,

Encl. H-26   Commissioner.
JMH

◇◇◇◇◇

Cherokee 3125

Muskogee, Indian Territory, February 6, 1907.

W. W. Hastings,
Attorney for the Cherokee Nation,
Muskogee, Indian Territory.

Dear Sir:

There is enclosed herewith a copy of the decision of the Commissioner to the Five Civilized Tribes, dated February 6, 1907, rejecting the application for the enrollment of Emiline L. Jones as a citizen by intermarriage of the Cherokee Nation.

The decision, together with the record of proceedings had in the case, has this day been transmitted to the Secretary of the Interior for his review and decision. The action of the Secretary will be made known to you as soon as this office is informed of the same.

Respectfully,

Encl. H-25   Commissioner.
JMH

◇◇◇◇◇

Cherokee Intermarried White 1906
Volume VIII

Muskogee, Indian Territory, February 6, 1907.

The Honorable,
    The Secretary of the Interior.

Sir:

There is transmitted herewith the record of proceedings had in the matter of the application for the enrollment of Emiline L. Jones as a citizen by intermarriage of the Cherokee Nation, together with the decision of the Commissioner, dated February 6, 1907, denying said application.

Respectfully,

Encl. H-27   Commissioner.
    JMH

Through the Commissioner
of Indian Affairs.

◇◇◇◇◇

Refer in reply to the following:
    Land 13138-1907.

DEPARTMENT OF THE INTERIOR,
OFFICE OF INDIAN AFFAIRS,
WASHINGTON.

February 23, 1907.

The Honorable,
    The Secretary of the Interior.

Sir:

I have the honor to transmit herewith a communication from the Commissioner to the Five Civilized Tribes, dated February 6, 1907, enclosing the record in the matter of the application for the enrollment of Emeline L. Jones as a citizen by intermarriage of the Cherokee Nation, together with his decision of the same date adverse to the applicant.

The record shows that application was duly made to the Commission to the Five Civilized Tribes on September 20, 1900, for the enrollment of Emeline L. Jones as a citizen of the Cherokee Nation. Testimony was taken in the matter on October 24, 1902, and January 11, 1907. It appears that the applicant is a white woman and neither claims nor possesses any right to enrollment as a citizen of the Cherokee Nation except such as she may have acquired by reason fo[sic] her marriage in October, 1868, to one John B. Jones who was also a white, but acquired his citizenship in the Cherokee Nation on November 7, 1865, by an act of the Cherokee National Council, which declared that John B. Jones, among others, was entitled to all the rights allowable to white men under the constitution of the Cherokee Nation. The same act that admitted the persons mentioned in it reads, "together with their families" but the applicant was not at that time a member of the family of John B. Jones. Her name appears on the authenticated roll of 1880 opposite number 1155.

In view of the fact that the applicant did not marry a citizen by blood of the Cherokee Nation prior to November 1, 1875, the Office is of the opinion that the decision of the Commissioner denying the application is correct and in accordance with the decision of the United States Supreme Court in the case of Daniel Red Bird, et. al vs. the United States, and it is recommended that it be affirmed.

Very respectfully,

C. F. Larrabee,

Acting Commissioner.

EWE

◇◇◇◇◇

JFJr

O.K.

DEPARTMENT OF THE INTERIOR,
Washington-

I. T. D. 4858-1907.
D.C. 12339-1907.   February 28, 1907.

L.R.S.
Direct.

Commissioner to the Five Civilized Tribes,
    Muskogee, Indian Territory.

Sir:

On February 23, 1907 (Land 13138), the Indian Office transmitted your report, dated February 6, 1907, in the matter of the application for the enrollment of Emeline L. Jones as a citizen by intermarriage of the Cherokee Nation, together with your decision of the same date, denying said application. The Indian Office concurs in your decision.

Cherokee Intermarried White 1906
Volume VIII

It appears that the applicant is a white woman, and neither claims nor possesses, any right to enrollment as a citizen of the Cherokee Nation, except such as she may have acquired by reason of her marriage in October, 1868, to one John B. Jones, who was also a white, but acquired his citizenship in the Cherokee Nation on November 7, 1865, by an Act of the Cherokee National Council, which declared that he, among others, was entitled to all the rights allowable to white men under the Constitution of the Cherokee Nation.

Your attention is called to the opinion of the Assistant Attorney General for this Department, dated and approved February 9, 1907, in the case of Miles C. Jones et al., wherein it was held that a white man adopted by act of the legislative council was in all respects of the status of a Cherokee citizen by blood, and that the decision of the Supreme Court of the United States in Red Bird v. the United States, has no reference to persons of this class.

In view of this opinion, your decision dated February 6, 1907, is hereby reversed, and you are directed to enroll said Emeline L. Jones as a citizen by intermarriage of the Cherokee Nations[sic].

The papers in the case, together with a carbon copy hereof, have been returned to the Indian Office.

Copy of Indian Office letter, above referred to, is enclosed.

Respectfully,

(Signed) Jesse E Wilson
Assistant Secretary.

1 inc. and 2 inc.
for Ind. Of.

AFMc
3-1-07

◇◇◇◇◇

80

Cherokee Intermarried White 1906
Volume VIII

Cherokee 3125   COPY

Muskogee, Indian Territory, March 8, 1907.

Emiline L. Jones,
      Vinita, Indian Territory.

Dear Madam:

      You are hereby advised that the application for your enrollment as a citizen by intermarriage of the Cherokee Nation, was granted by the Secretary of the Interior February 28, 1907.

Respectfully,

SIGNED *Jams Bixby*
Commissioner.

◇◇◇◇◇

Cherokee 3125   COPY

Muskogee, Indian Territory, March 8, 1907.

Starr & Patton,
      Attorneys for Emiline L. Jones,
            Vinita, Indian Territory.

Gentlemen:

      You are hereby advised that the application for the enrollment of Emiline L. Jones, as a citizen by intermarriage of the Cherokee Nation, was granted by the Secretary of the Interior February 28, 1907.

Respectfully,

SIGNED *Jams Bixby*
RPI   Commissioner

◇◇◇◇◇

81

Cherokee 3125

COPY

Muskogee, Indian Territory, March 8, 1907.

W. W. Hastings,
     Attorney for the Cherokee Nation,
         Muskogee, Indian Territory.

Dear Sir:

     You are hereby advised that the application for the enrollment of Emiline L. Jones as a citizen by intermarriage of the Cherokee Nation, was granted by the Secretary of the Interior February 28, 1907.

     For your information, there is enclosed herewith a copy of Departmental letter referred to.

             Respectfully,

             SIGNED *Tams Bixby*

Enc I-14   Commissioner.

RPI

Cher IW 226

◇◇◇◇◇

I.W. No. 226

Leonidas Dobson

Record and Decision
Not in 5997   4/25/07

◇◇◇◇◇

Cherokee Intermarried White 1906
Volume VIII

COPY

This certifies that Revd Leonidas Dobson formerly of Montgomery Square Philada and citizen of the U. S. has complied with the requirement of our laws "Regulating Intermarriage with white men", passed by the National Council and approved Oct 15th 1870, and has been recorded as a citizen in the Clerks[sic] Office for Tahlequah Dist Cherokee Nation.

W. M. Turner Clk
Dist Ct. for Tahlequah
District Cherokee Nation.

This the 27th day of October 1870.

I, the undersigned, a Stenographer to the Commissioner to the Five Civilized Tribes, do hereby certify that the above is a true and correct copy of the original instrument now on file in this office.

Lola M. Champlin

Subscribed and sworn to before me this the 13th day of May 1907.

Frances R Lane
Notary Public.

◇◇◇◇◇

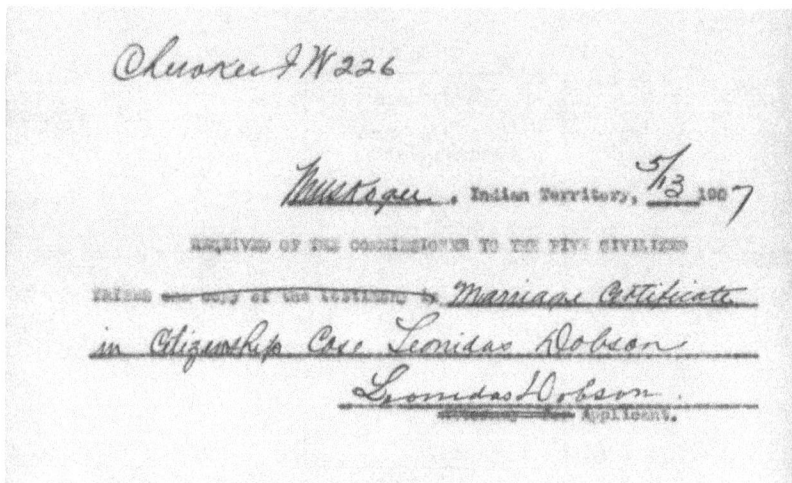

(Copy of original document from case.)

Cher IW 227

◇◇◇◇◇

```
I.W. No. 227

Rebecca Miller


Record and Decision
Not in 7135  4/25/07
```

Cher IW 228

◇◇◇◇◇

(No information given.)

Cher IW 229

◇◇◇◇◇

DEPARTMENT OF THE INTERIOR,
COMMISSION TO THE FIVE CIVILIZED TRIBES,
VINITA, I.T., SEP., 29, 1900.

In the matter of the application of Nancy Reed for enrollment of herself, husband and five children, as citizens of the Cherokee Nation, said Reed being sworn by Commissioner Breckinridge, testified as follows:

Q   What is your name?   A   Nancy Reed.
Q   How old are you?   A   38.
Q   What is your postoffice address?   A   Zena.
Q   In what district do you live?   A   Delaware.
Q   Whom do you want to have put on the rolls?   A   Myself, husband and five children.
Q   Do you apply for yourself as a Cherokee by blood?   A   Yes.
Q   Is your husband a Cherokee by blood or white man?   A   White man.
Q   Are you a native of the Cherokee Nation?   A   Yes.

Q   Lived here all your life?   A Yes.

Q   What was your father's name?   A Jess Woods.

Q   Dead or alive?   A Dead.

Q   How long since he died?   A About 15 years.

Q   Give me your mother's name?   A Mandy.

Q   Is she dead or alive?   A Alive.

Q   Cherokee or white woman?   A Cherokee.

Q   Was your father a Cherokee?   A No sir, white man.

Q   Have you your marriage license and certificate?   A Yes.

   The applicant presents a marriage certificate showing that on September 12, 1890, Nancy Miller was married to Joseph Reed by Rev. R. T. Parks. That was your marriage to your husband?   A Yes.

   It is filed herewith.

Q   This is not your first marriage?   A No sir.

Q   How many times have you been married before?   A Twice.

Q   When did you marry Miller?   A About 23 years ago I guess.

Q   What was your husband Miller's full name?   A Martin Miller.

Q   Is he a Cherokee or white man?   A Cherokee.

Q   When did you marry him?   A About 23 years ago.

Q   Is he dead or alive?   A Alive.

Q   How long did you live with him as his wife?   A About 4 years.

Q   Then did you get a divorce from him?   A Yes.

Q   Is this a copy of the decree of divorce?   A Yes.

   Applicant files official copy of the decree of divorce between herself and her former husband, Martin Miller, dated September 3, '90. It is filed herewith.

Q   Now you were married before that-- that was your second marriage to Miller?

A   Yes.

Q   What was your first marriage?   A William Woodard.

Q   When did you marry him?   A About 25 years ago.

Q   How long did you and he live together as husband and wife?   A 2 years.

Q   Did he die?   A Yes.

Q   And he was dead when you married Miller?   A Yes.

Q   Well, then in the year '80 you are on the roll as a Miller?   A Yes.

Q   Your present husband's name is Joseph Reed?   A Yes.

Q   What is [sic] age?   A 49.

Q   And he claims his citizenship by adoption through his marriage in '94 with Julia Chouteau. How do you present this marriage license and certificate that I hold in my hand as the paper on which your husband claims citizenship by adoption?   Is this to establish your husband's claim?   A I don't know, he didn't tell me to give it to you.

   Upon further examination it appears that the date of the marriage license is 1874.

Q   What was the name of his Chouteau wife?   A Julia.

   The applicant presents what is now disclosed to be a marriage license issued by the Clerk of Delaware district March 4, 1874, to Joseph Reed authorizing his marriage to Joey or July Chouteau, and the certificate shows that they were united in marriage in March by the Judge of the District on the 5th of the same month and year?[sic] It is filed herewith.

Q   How long did your husband live with July Chouteau?   A I cannot tell you.

Q   Is she dead?   A Yes.

Q   You do not know when she died?   A He said she had been dead about 20 years.

Q   Do you know whether they were separated before her death?   A No sir, they were not separated.

Q   Now you and your husband were married in '90 as shown here- 10 years ago?
A   Yes.

Q   And your husband said that July Chouteau was dead 20 years ago?   A Yes.

Q   You do not know the name of her father or mother?   A No sir.

Q   Now after July Chouteau died did your husband marry again?   A No sir, not until he married me.

Q   Give me the names of these children?   A Looney Reed, 17 years old.
         On '96 roll, page 523, number 2595, as Luna.

Q   Next?   A Lula Reed, 17 years old. (Twins.)
         On '96 roll, page 523, number 2596.

Q   Next?   A Etty Reed, age 14.
         On '96 roll, page 523, number 2597, as Etta.

Q   Next?   A John Reed, 12 years old.
         On '96 roll, page 523, number 2598.

Q   Next?   A Pearl Reed, 10 years old.
         On '96 roll, page 523, number 2599.

Q   These children are all alive now?   A Yes.

Q   These are all the children of your present husband?   A Yes.
         Applicant on the '80 roll, page 283, number 1636, as Nancy M. Miller.
         On '96 roll, page 523, number 2594, as Nancy Reed.

Q   Where is your husband at this time?   A He is at home.

Q   Has your husband lived in the Cherokee Nation ever since '80?   A Yes.

The applicant applies for the enrollment of herself, husband and five children. She is identified on the rolls of '80 and '96 as a Native Cherokee, and states that she has lived in the Cherokee Nation all her life. Her change of name is established by the marriage certificate filed herewith, and she will be listed now for enrollment as a Cherokee by blood. Her five children are identified with her on the roll of '96 as native Cherokees. They are living at this time. They are all minors and will be listed now for enrollment as Cherokees by blood.

In regard to the enrollment of her husband: He is identified on the authenticated rolls of '80 and census rolls of '96, and she states that he has lived in the Cherokee Nation ever since '80. Now his enrollment in '80 as an adopted citizen is shown to have arisen from his marriage previous to that time to a former Cherokee wife. She is said to have died in '84, and the applicant is shown to have been married to her present husband in '90. Now she states that her husband was not married between the death of his former wife in '84 and his marriage to herself in '90, but she has applied for children 17 and 14 and 12 years of age, which she states are her children by this husband which shows that they lived together in some capacity before the marriage that is shown in the record. This discredits his whole conduct and throws doubts upon his status during the period intervening between the deadt[sic] of his first wife and his declared marriage to his present wife. Therefore, the application for his enrollment will be placed upon a doubtful card for further consideration.

The applicant now reveals since the foregoing was declared that her two children, Luna, and Lula Reed, are married; therefore their names will be stricken from the present enrollment and they will be required to make application for themselves.

The undersigned, being first duly sworn, states that as stenographer to the Commission to the Five Civilized Tribes, he correctly recorded the testimony and proceedings in this case, and the foregoing is a true and correct transcript of his stenographic notes thereof.

B McDonald

Subscribed and sworn to before me this 1st day of October, 1900.

C R Breckinridge
Commissioner.

◇◇◇◇◇

(Copy of original document from case.)

◇◇◇◇◇

D 468

Department of the Interior,
Commission to the Five Civilized Tribes.
Muskogee, I. T., February 27, 1902.

In the matter of the application of Joseph Reed, for the enrollment of himself as a citizen of the Cherokee Nation:

The applicant was notified by registered letter on February 11, 1902, that his application for the enrollment of himself as a citizen of the Cherokee Nation would be taken up by the Commission for final consideration on the 27th day of February, 1902, and that he could on said date appear before the Commission in person or by attorney, and an opportunity would be given him to introduce any further testimony affecting his application.

Receipt has been acknowledged of the Commission's letter.

Applicant having this day, to-wit: the 27th day of February, 1902, been called three times, and failing to respond either in person or by attorney, it is ordered that this case be closed, and reported to the Commission for final decision based upon the evidence now of record.

C R Breckinridge
Commissioner.

◇◇◇◇◇

Cher
Supp'l to D 468

Department of the Interior,
Commission to the Five Civilized Tribes,
Vinita, I. T., February 11, 1903.

In the matter of the application of JOSEPH REED, for the enrollment of himself as a citizen by intermarriage of the Cherokee Nation.

JOSEPH REED, being first duly sworn, and examined, testified as follows:

Examined by the Commission:

Q   What is your name ?   Joseph W. Reed.
Q   How old are you ?   A Fifty.
Q   What is your post office ?   A Zena.
Q   Are you a white man ?   A Yes sir, supposed to be.
Q   Are you claiming the right to be enrolled as a citizen by intermarriage ?
A   Yes sir.
Q   What is your wife's name ?   A Nancy Reed.

88

Q   Is she the wife through whom you are claiming your citizenship ?
A   Yes sir.
Q   Was she your wife in 1880 ?   A No sir, I have been married twice, my first wife was Julia Chouteau.
Q   Then she is the one through whom you are claiming ?   A Yes sir.
Q   How long did you live with her ?   A Why seven or eight years; I lived with her until she died.
Q   She was your wife in 1880 ?   A Yes sir.
Q   You lived with her from 1880 until she died ?   A Yes sir.
Q   You have married since she died ?   A Yes sir.
Q   Your present wife is name Nancy ?   A Yes sir.
Q   She is your second wife ?   A Yes sir.
Q   Have you lived with her ever since you married her ?   A Yes sir.
Q   Was she ever married before ?   A Yes sir.
Q   Had she any living husband when you married her ?   A Yes sir.
Q   Is she a Cherokee by blood ?   A Yes sir.
Q   You say she had a living husband when you married her ?   A Yes sir.
Q   Weren't they divorced ?   A They were, yes sir.
Q   Were they divorced when you married her ?   A Yes sir.
Q   She didn't have a living husband then ?   A Why he was living of course.
Q   Have you been residing in the Cherokee Nation ever since 1880 ?   A Yes sir.
Q   Never lived anywhere else ?   A No sir.

Examined by Mr. Hastings:

Q   Had Julia Chouteau ever been married when you married her ?   A No sir.
Q   Were you ever married before you married her ?   A No sir.
Q   Did you file a Cherokee license and all ?   A Yes sir.
Q   You lived with Julia Chouteau until she died ?   A Yes sir.

E. C. Bagwell, on oath states that, as stenographer to the Commission to the Five Civilized Tribes, he correctly recorded the testimony and proceedings had in the above entitled cause, and that the foregoing is an accurate transcript of his stenographic notes thereof.

E.C. Bagwell

Subscribed and sworn to before me this March 3, 1903.

Samuel Foreman
Notary Public.

◇◇◇◇◇

C. F. B.   Cherokee D 468.

DEPARTMENT OF THE INTERIOR,
COMMISSIONER TO THE FIVE CIVILIZED TRIBES.
Muskogee, Indian Territory, February 6, 1907.

In the matter of the application for the enrollment of Joseph Reid[sic] as a citizen by intermarriage of the Cherokee Nation.

APPEARANCES:
                    Applicant appears in person.

                    Cherokee Nation represented by
                    W. W. Hastings, Attorney.

Joseph Reid being first duly sworn by Mrs. Lyman K. Lane, Notary Public, testified as follows:

ON BEHALF OF COMMISSIONER.

Q   What is your name?   A   Joseph Reid.
Q   What is your age?   A   54.
Q   What is your post office address?
A   Zena.
Q   You are an applicant for enrollment as a citizen by intermarriage of the Cherokee Nation?
A   Yes sir.
Q   You have no Cherokee blood?   A   No sir.
Q   Your only claim to the right to enrollment as a citizen of the Cherokee Nation is by virtue of your marriage to a citizen by blood of the Nation?
A   Yes sir.
Q   What is the name of the citizen by virtue of your marriage to whom you claim the right to enrollment as a citizen by intermarriage of the Cherokee Nation?
A   Her name was Julia Choutou[sic].
Q   Is she living?   A   No sir; she's dead.
Q   When did you marry her?   A   In '74.
Q   Was she a recognized citizen by blood of the Cherokee Nation at the time you married her?
A   Yes, I suppose so.
Q   Living in the Cherokee country?   A   Yes sir.
Q   Was she a Shawnee?
A   No, she was a Cherokee.
Q   She wasn't admitted to citizenship after you were married,- she was recognized as a citizen prior to your marriage?
A   Yes sir; she was recognized as a Cherokee citizen before I married her.
Q   Was she your first wife?   A   Yes sir.
Q   Were you her first husband?   A   Yes sir.

Cherokee Intermarried White 1906
Volume VIII

Q   When did she die?   A   I think she died in '79.

Q   When did you say you married her?   A   In '74.

Q   From the time of your marriage to her, did you and she continuously live together as husband and wife until her death?

A   Yes sir.

Q   What was the name of her father?

A   Her father was a Choutou,- Paul I think.

Q   What was her mother's name?

A   I don't know as I can tell you her given name; her mother was dead when I married her; I think though it was Sarah Chambers.

Q   When did her father die?   A   I can't tell you.

Q   Did he die prior to your marriage to her?

A   He died I think when she was small.

Q   Did she have any brothers and sisters?

A   She had one half sister.

Q   What was the name of her half sister in 1880?

A   Ann Kell I think was her half sister's name.

Q   Did your deceased wife and her half sister, Ann Kell, derive their Cherokee blood from the same person?

A   From the same mother; yes sir; I suppose so.

Q   Where was your deceased wife born, do you know?

A   No sir; I never heard her say.

Q   Didn't she ever tell you where she was born?

A   I suppose she did but I have forgotten it; as well as I remember I think she was born in the territory; I never heard her speak of being anywhere else.

Q   Have you any evidence of a documentary character showing your marriage to her? I mean any license or certificate?

A   Yes sir.

BY MR. HASTINGS.

Q   Was your wife a Cherokee by blood?   Julia Choutou?

A   Yes, she was recognized as a citizen by blood.

Q   You know Choutou is a Shawnee name and I am asking you if you are positive--

A   All I know about it is that there are some Choutous up there that claim to be Shawnee but she never did; she is not related to them.

Q   Do you know he mother's maiden name?

A   I think she was a Chambers.

Q   Who was her father,- Paul Chambers?

A   Yes sir.

Q   Where did he live?

A   I don't know; when he died he lived on Cabin Creek over here in the territory.

Q   You think he died before your wife did?

A   Yes sir.

Q   Did your wife have any full brother or sister?

A   No sir; none that I ever heard of.

Q Do you know whether your wife claimed here[sic] Cherokee blood through her father or mother or both?
A Through her mother.
Q And not through her father?
A I think she said her father claimed to be part Osage but she claimed her Cherokee blood by her mother.
Q She had a half sister by the same mother?
A Yes sir.
Q And what was her name?   A Ann Kell.
Q Is she living?   A No sir; she's dead too.
Q When did she die?   A I can't tell you.
Q Before or after your wife died?
A After my wife died.
Q About how long?
A I don't have no idea how long.
Q Was Ann Kell an old woman; about what age was she when you wife died, say in '79?
A Somewhere along in 20 I reckon.
Q Was she unmarried?
A No, she was married when she died. She married Nat Skinner.
Q Do you know who Ann Kell's father was?
A I seen him; his name was Lewis Kell.
Q And he was a Cherokee?
A Supposed to be; I don't know whether he was a Cherokee or not.
Q This half sister of your wife's, whose name was Ann Kell, married Nat Skinner?
A Yes sir; that's the way I understand it.
Q Did you live with your first wife until she died?
A Yes sir.
Q You and she were living together at that time?
A Yes sir.
Q And your last wife is a Cherokee?   A Yes sir.

ON BEHALF OF COMMISSIONER.

Q Whom did you marry after the death of your first wife?
A I married Nancy Miller.
Q She was a Cherokee by blood?
A Always recognized as a Cherokee by blood.
Q Is she living?   A Yes sir.
Q Is she on the final roll as a citizen by blood of the Cherokee Nation?
A Yes sir.
Q And has filed on her land?   A Yes sir.
Q Were you ever married other than to these two women?
A No sir.

Cherokee Intermarried White 1906
Volume VIII

Q Since your marriage to your second wife, you and she have continuously lived together as husband and wife?

A Yes sir.

Q And in the Cherokee Nation?   A   Yes sir.

Q Your residence then has been continuously in the Cherokee Nation since your marriage to your first wife in 1874?

A Yes sir; never have lived nowhere else only right here in the Cherokee Nation.

The applicant presents a certified copy of the records of Delaware District, showing that on March 4, 1874, license was granted by J. E. Harlin, Clerk Delaware District, Cherokee Nation, authorizing the marriage of Joseph Reid, a citizen of the United states, and Josie Choutou, a citizen of the Cherokee Nation; and that said license was returned executed March 6, 1874. This instrument will be filed with and made a part of the record in this case.

The applicant, Joseph Reid, is identified on the Cherokee authenticated tribal roll of 1880, Delaware District, No. 2145.

Mr. Reid, before the application for your enrollment as a citizen by intermarriage of the Cherokee Nation will be complete, it will be necessary for you to introduce the testimony og[sic] witnesses who were acquainted with your first wife and knew her family, and by whom you can establish that she was a citizen by blood of the Cherokee Nation at the time you married her, if she was such citizen.

Sarah Mayfield being first duly sworn by Mrs. Lyman K. Lane, Notary Public, testified as follows:

BY MR. HASTINGS.

Q What is your name?   A   Sarah Mayfield.

Q What is your age?   A   70.

Q What is your post office address?   A   Oolagah.

Q Did you know Nat Skinner's first wife, who was Nan Skinner after he married her?

A Yes sir.

Q Did you know Nan Skinner's mother's name?

A Yes; her name was Sarah Chambers.

Q That was her maiden name?   A   Yes sir.

Q You say you used to go to school with her before the war?

A Yes sir; I went to school with her.

Q She was a well recognized Cherokee citizen?

A Yes sir; she was.

Q Did you know her after the war?   A   No sir.

Q Did you know her children?   A   I knew Nat's wife.

Q Did you know that she had any other children?

A No sir; I didn't.

Q Did you ever know that she was married to a Choutou?

A I didn't know it but I heard she was.

Q You never knew him while she was married to him?

A No sir.

Q Do you know whether or not she had any children while she was married to him?

A No sir; I don't; I just knowed[sic] her and went to school with her and then knowed[sic] her daughter, Nat Skinner's wife.

Q You didn't know any other children she had?

A No sir; I didn't.

The undersigned being first duly sworn states that as stenographer to the Commission to the Five Civilized Tribes, she recorded the testimony taken in this case and that the foregoing is a true and correct transcript of her stenographic notes thereof.

Myrtle Hill

Subscribed and sworn to before me this the 11th day of February, 1907.

J L Gary
Notary Public.

◇◇◇◇◇

(The Marriage License and Certificate below typed as given.)

1	This is to certify that Joseph Reid
2	a citizen of the U States was Licens to
3	Marry Josie Choutou a Citizen of the
4	Cherokee Nation On March 4th 1874
5	And the Licens Return Executed And
6	hereby Recorded March 6th 1874 In
7	Conformity with the Act Entitled
8	And Act to provide for the Licensing
9	of citizens of U States to Entermarry
11	With Citizen of the Cherokee Nation
12	Approved Oct. 15th 1855
13	J. E. Harlin Clerk
14	Del Dist C N

Clerk Office Delaware District Cherokee Nation this is to Certify by me the above 14 lines is a true Coppy Trancribed from the Record Book of Marriage Now on file in the Clerk office Delaware District Cherokee Nation   On this the 9th Day of January 1891

T J McGhee
Clerk Delaware District
Cherokee Nation.

(SEAL)

Cherokee Intermarried White 1906
Volume VIII

The undersigned being first duly sworn states that as stenographer to the Commission to the Five Civilized Tribes, she made the above copy and that same is a true and correct copy of a certified copy of the original marriage records, which certified copy is now on file in this office.

Myrtle Hill

Subscribed and sworn to before me this the 13th day of February, 1907.

Walter W Chappell
Notary Public.

◇◇◇◇◇

Cherokee D. 468.

DEPARTMENT OF THE INTERIOR,

COMMISSION TO THE FIVE CIVILIZED TRIBES.

In the matter of the application for the enrollment of Joseph W. Reed as a citizen by intermarriage of the Cherokee Nation.

D E C I S I O N.

The record in this case shows that on September 29, 1900, Nancy Reed appeared before the Commission at Vinita, and made application for the enrollment, among others, of her husband, Joseph W. Reed, as a citizen by intermarriage of the Cherokee Nation. The other parties to the application are differently classified and are not embraced in this decision. Further proceedings in the matter of said application were had at Vinita, on February 11, 1903.

The evidence in this case shows that Joseph W. Reed, a white man, was lawfully married under authority of a Cherokee marriage license on March 5, 1874, to Julia Chouteau, named in the marriage license, "Joey Choutou," a citizen of the Cherokee Nation, who died prior to the marriage of Joseph W. Reed to his wife Nancy. The said Joseph W. Reed is identified on the Cherokee authenticated tribal roll of 1880 and also on the Cherokee census roll of 1896.

Section twenty-one of the Act of Congress approved June 28, 1898 (30 Stats., 495), provides for the enrollment of Cherokee citizens "with such intermarried white persons as may be entitled to citizenship under Cherokee laws."

"Should any man or woman, a citizen of the United States or of any foreign country, become a citizen of the Cherokee Nation by intermarriage, and be left a

95

widow or widower by the decease of the Cherokee wife or husband, such surviving widow or widower shall continue to enjoy the rights of citizenship, unless he or she shall marry a white man or woman, or person, (as the case may be), having no rights of Cherokee citizenship by blood; in that case, all of his or her rights acquired under the provisions of this act shall cease."

The evidence in this case shows that Joseph W. Reed secured rights of Cherokee citizenship through intermarriage with his first wife, Julia Chouteau, and that subsequent to her death he was lawfully married to his present wife Nancy, a Cherokee citizen by blood.

The evidence further shows that Joseph W. Reed has lived in the Cherokee Nation continuously since 1880, and has lived with his present wife, Nancy, in the Cherokee Nation since his marriage to her up to and including September 1, 1902.

It is, therefore, the opinion of this Commission that Joseph W. Reed shall be enrolled as a citizen by intermarriage of the Cherokee Nation, in accordance with the provisions of section twenty-one of the Act of Congress approved June 28, 1898 (30 Stats., 495), and it is so ordered.

COMMISSION TO THE FIVE CIVILIZED TRIBES.

_____

Chairman.

_____

Commissioner.

_____

Commissioner.

_____

Commissioner.

Dated at Muskogee, I. T.,

this _____

◇◇◇◇◇

COMMISSIONERS:
HENRY L. DAWES,
TAMS BIXBY,
THOMAS B. NEEDLES,
C. R. BRECKINRIDGE.

DEPARTMENT OF THE INTERIOR,
COMMISSION TO THE FIVE CIVILIZED TRIBES.

ALLISON L. AYLESWORTH,
SECRETARY.

ADDRESS ONLY THE
COMMISSION TO THE FIVE CIVILIZED TRIBES.

Muskogee, Indian Territory, **February 11,** 1902

Mrs. Nancy Reed,
Zena, Indian Territory,

Madam:-

You are hereby notified that the application of **Joseph Reed**

for enrollment as ....citizen..... of the Cherokee Nation will be taken up for final consideration by the Commission to the Five Civilized Tribes, at its office in Muskogee, Indian Territory, on the **27th** day of **February** , 1902.

On said date, you may, if you desire, appear before the Commission, in person or by attorney, when an opportunity will be given you to introduce any additional testimony affecting your application.

You are further notified that the Representatives of the Cherokee Nation will also, at the same time, be afforded an opportunity to introduce testimony tending to disprove your right to enrollment, but said Representatives will be required to notify you of their intention to introduce such testimony before they will be permitted to do so.

You are required to supply the Commission with marriage certificate of Joseph Reed to yourself; also license.

Yours truly,

Cherokee D-468
Register.

Acting Chairman.

◇◇◇◇◇

Cherokee D-1468[sic].

Vinita, Indian Territory, January 26, 1903.

Joseph Reed,
Zena, Indian Territory.

Dear Sir:-

You are hereby notified that before your application for enrollment as a citizen by intermarriage of the Cherokee Nation will be complete, it will be necessary that you introduce before the Commission, testimony showing your status as a citizen by intermarriage of the Cherokee Nation on September 1, 1902.

This testimony should be introduced before the Cherokee Land Office of this Commission at Vinita, on or before February 17, 1903.

You are requested to present this letter when you appear for the purpose of introducing this testimony.

Respectfully,

Acting Chairman.

RP

◇◇◇◇◇

Cherokee D-468.

Vinita, Indian Territory, March 10th, 1903.

Commission to the Five Civilized Tribes,
Muskogee, Indian Territory.

Gentlemen:

I have the honor to transmit herewith for decision, the record in the matter of the application of Joseph Reed, Cherokee D-468, the same being now deemed complete.

Respectfully,

Clerk in Charge.

Enc. C-67.
JOC.

◇◇◇◇◇

Cherokee No.
D. 468

Muskogee, Indian Territory, January 10, 1907.

Joseph Reed,
    Zena, Indian Territory.

Dear sir[sic]:

There is inclosed a copy of the decision of the Commissioner to the Five Civilized Tribes, dated January 10, 1907, rejecting, among others, the application for your enrollment as a citizen by intermarriage of the Cherokee Nation. The Commissioner's decision has this day been forwarded to the Secretary of the Interior for review. You will be advised of the Secretary's action as soon as this office is informed of same.

Respectfully,

Incl. Decn. __D__   Commissioner.

◇◇◇◇◇

REFER IN REPLY TO THE FOLLOWING:
Cherokee
D 468

DEPARTMENT OF THE INTERIOR,
COMMISSIONER TO THE FIVE CIVILIZED TRIBES.

Muskogee, Indian Territory, January 29, 1907.

Joseph Reed,
    Care of T. S. Remson, N.P.
        Grove, Indian Territory.

Dear Sir:

Receipt is acknowledged of an affidavit executed by you on January 23, 1907, relative to your right to enrollment as a citizen by intermarriage of the Cherokee Nation.

In reply you are advised that on January 10, 1907, the Commissioner to the Five Civilized Tribes rendered his decision denying, among others, your application for enrollment as such is accordingly granted. a citizen by intermarriage of the Cherokee Nation, and on the same date said decision was forwarded to the Secretary of the Interior for review.

For your information there is quoted to you the following provision of the Act of Congress approved April 26, (24 Stat., 137):

".....and no motion to reopen or reconsider
and citizenship case, in any of said tribes, shall be
entertained unless filed with the Commissioner to
the Five Civilized Tribes within sixty days after the
date of the order or decision sought to be reconsidered,
except as to decisions made prior to the passage of this
Act, in which cases such motion shall be made within
sixty days after the passage of this Act: . . . . ."

Respectfully,

Tams Bixby

L M B   Commissioner

◇◇◇◇◇

Muskogee, Indian Territory, February 18, 1907.

The Honorable,
    Secretary of the Interior.

Sir:

January 10, 1907 the Commissioner to the Five Civilized Tribes rendered his decision denying, among others, the application for the enrollment of Joseph Reed as a citizen by intermarriage.

Said decision was on January 25, 1907 (I.T.D.1396-1907), affirmed by the Department.

Further proceedings had in this case at Muskogee, February 6, 1907 show that the decision of the Commissioner in the case is erroneous.

The records show that Joseph Reed, a white man, who married in accordance with Cherokee law March 4, 1874 to Josie Reed, nee Choutou, since deceased, who was at the time of said marriage a recognized citizen by blood of the Cherokee Nation. It is further shown that from the time of said marriage until the death of said Josie Reed, which occurred in 1879, the said Joseph Reed and Josie Reed resided together as husband and wife and continuously lived in the Cherokee Nation. It is also shown that on September 12, 1890 Joseph Reed was married to Nancy Reed, formerly Miller, who was at the time of said marriage a recognized citizen by blood of the Cherokee Nation, who is identified on the Cherokee authenticated tribal roll of 1880, Delaware District, No. 1636 as a native Cherokee, and whose name appears upon the approved partial roll of citizens by blood of the Cherokee Nation opposite No. 9060. It is further shown that from the time of said marriage the said Joseph Reed and Nancy Reed resided together as husband and wife and continuously lived in the Cherokee Nation up to and including September 1, 1902. Said applicant is identified on the Cherokee authenticated tribal roll of 1880 and the Cherokee census roll of 1896 as an intermarried citizen of the Cherokee Nation.

In view of the decision of the Supreme Court, dated November 5, 1906, in the cases of Daniel Red Bird, et al. vs. the United States, Nos. 125, 126, 127 and 128, it is respectfully recommended that the Department rescind its said decision of January 26, 1907, so far as it relates to this applicant, and that the application for the enrollment of Joseph Reed as a citizen by intermarriage of the Cherokee Nation be granted. The record of proceedings had in the case is inclosed.

Commissioner.

Through the Commissioner
    of Indian Affairs.

(Initials illegible)

◇◇◇◇◇

W.W.HASTINGS. ATTORNEY.	OFFICE OF	H.M. VANCE. SECRETARY.

Attorney for the Cherokee Nation,

MUSKOGEE, I. T.   February 21, 1907.

The Commissioner to the Five Civilized Tribes,
    Muskogee, Indian Territory.

Sir:

I have examined the record in the matter of the application for the enrollment of Joseph Reed as a citizen by intermarriage of the Cherokee Nation. I do not desire to protest against the enrollment of this applicant as a citizen by intermarriage of the Cherokee Nation and I consent to his enrollment.

Respectfully,
W. W. Hastings
Attorney for the Cherokee Nation.

◇◇◇◇◇

Muskogee, Indian Territory, February 22, 1907.

Arthur F. McGarr,
    Room 116 Department of the Interior,
        Washington, D.C.

Dear Sir:

There are enclosed herewith copies of three letters addressed to the Department under dates of February 18 and 21, 1907, recommending that the Department rescind its decision of January 26, 1907, adverse to Joseph Reed, and reverse the Commissioner's decision of January 10, 1907, adverse to Mary J. Thompson and Louvena Alberty, applicants for enrollment as citizens by intermarriage of the Cherokee Nation, and that they be enrolled.

In the event the Department concurs in the Commissioner's recommendation in these cases, date from which schedules containing their names can be prepared is as follows:

Reed, Joseph,	51	M	
Alberty, Louvena	50	F	5891
Thompson, Mary J.	64	F	5492.

Respectfully,

Encl. B-37

Commissioner

L M B

◇◇◇◇◇

Cherokee
Deed 416

Muskogee, Indian Territory, February 23, 1907.

Joseph Reed,
Zena, Indian Territory.

Dear Sir:-

There is returned herewith marriage license issued by the clerk of Delaware District, Cherokee Nation, authorizing the marriage of yourself and Julia Choteau, copies of same have been retained in the files of this office.

Respectfully,

HSS
23-1

Commissioner.

◇◇◇◇◇

(COPY)

DEPARTMENT OF THE INTERIOR,
OFFICE OF INDIAN AFFAIRS,

Washington.   February 27, 1907.

Land
18969-1907.

The Honorable,
The Secretary of the Interior.

Sir:

There is forwarded herewith report of Commissioner Bixby dated February 18, 1907, relative to the application for the enrollment of Joseph Reed as a citizen by intermarriage of the Cherokee Nation.

On January 26, 1907 (I T D 1395-1907), the Department affirmed the decision of the Commissioner of January 10, 1907, denying, among others, the application of Joseph Reed.

It is shown by the record, however, that the applicant is entitled to enrollment as a citizen by intermarriage of the Cherokee Nation under the decision of the Supreme Court in the case of Daniel Red Bird, et al. vs. The United States, and it is recommended that the Department rescind its decision of January 26, 1907, so far as it relates to this applicant, and that he be enrolled as a citizen by intermarriage of the Cherokee Nation.

Very respectfully,
C. F. Larrabee,
Acting Chairman Commissioner.

AJW-EH.

◇◇◇◇◇

(COPY)   S P E C I A L   JP.

DEPARTMENT OF THE INTERIOR,
Washington,   FHE
March 1, 1907.

I T D 8988-1907   LRS

DIRECT.

Commissioner to the Five Civilized Tribes,
Muskogee, Indian Territory.

Sir:

In accordance with your recommendation of February 18, 1907, you are authorized to enrol[sic] Joseph Reed as a citizen by intermarriage of the Cherokee Nation, and the decision of the Department of January 26, 1907, adverse to him, is rescinded.

It is shown that he was married in accordance with the Cherokee law, to his first Cherokee wife, a citizen by blood, in 1874.

A copy of Indian Office letter of February 27, 1907 (land 18969-07), submitting your report and recommending that the party be enroled[sic], is inclosed.

A copy hereof and the papers in the case have been sent to the Indian Office.

Respectfully,

Jesse E. Wilson
1 Inc. & 3 for Ind. Of.   Assistant Secretary.
A F Mc
  3-2-07

Cherokee Intermarried White 1906
Volume VIII

◇◇◇◇◇

Cherokee D468   COPY

Muskogee, Indian Territory, March 8, 1907.

Joseph Reed,
        Zena, Indian Territory.

Dear Sir:

        You are hereby advised that the application for your enrollment as a citizen by intermarriage of the Cherokee Nation, was granted by the Secretary of the Interior March 1, 1907.

                                        Respectfully,

                                        SIGNED *Jams Bixby*
Enc I-1   Commissioner.

RPI

◇◇◇◇◇

Cherokee D
    468

                                        COPY

Muskogee, Indian Territory, March 8, 1907.

W. W. Hastings,
        Attorney for the Cherokee Nation,
                Muskogee, Indian Territory.

Dear Sir:

        You are hereby advised that the application for the enrollment of Joseph Reed as a citizen by intermarriage of the Cherokee Nation, was granted by the Secretary of the Interior March 1, 1907.

        For your information, there is enclosed herewith copy of Departmental letter referred to.

                                        Respectfully,

                                        SIGNED *Jams Bixby*
Enc I-2   Commissioner.
RPI

◇◇◇◇◇

Cherokee
10999

Muskogee, Indian Territory, March 30, 1907.

Davis, Mason & Bland,
    Afton, Indian Territory.

Gentlemen:

In reply to your letter of March 26, 1907, in which you request to be advised the status of the Cherokee intermarried case of Joseph Reed, you are advised that on March 1, 1907, the application for the enrollment of Joseph Reed as a citizen by intermarriage of the Cherokee Nation was granted by the Secretary of the Interior. Mr Reed will be advised of his final enrollment number when the schedule containing his name is returned to this office approved by the Secretary of the Interior.

Respectfully,

L M B

Acting Commissioner.

<><><><><>

468

Ready for review

Marriage Certificate to
present wife Nancy required
and are in Case 3735
also license to prst wife

<><><><><>

Cherokee Intermarried White 1906
Volume VIII

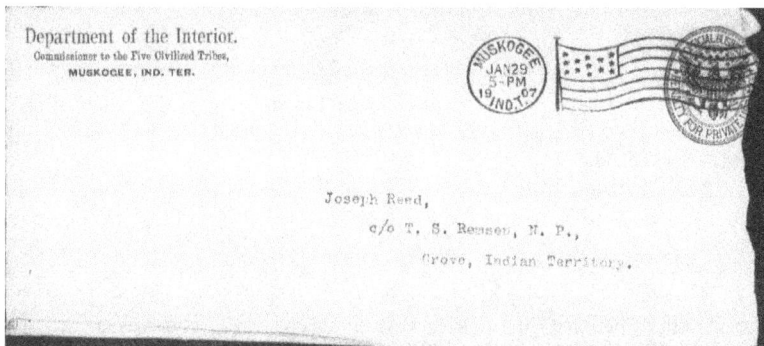

(Copy of original document from case.)

◇◇◇◇◇

(Copy of original document from case.)

◇◇◇◇◇

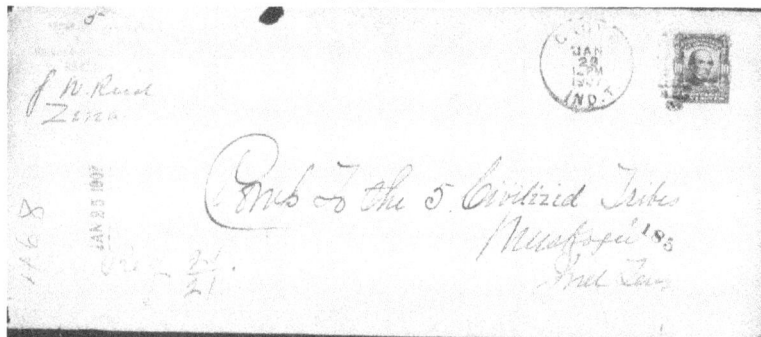

(Copy of original document from case.)

Cher IW 230

◇◇◇◇◇

> I.W. No. 230
>
> James W. McSpadden
>
> Record and Decision
> Not in No 5724   4/26/07

Cher IW 231

◇◇◇◇◇

> I.W. No. 231
>
> Calvin P. Guthrie
>
> Record & Decision not
> in No. 747 - 4/16/07

Cher IW 232

◇◇◇◇◇

```
                                I.W. No. 232

            Napoleon B. Luckey


            Record & Decision  not
            in No. 2796
```

Cher IW 233

◇◇◇◇◇

COPY

DEPARTMENT OF THE INTERIOR
COMMISSION TO THE FIVE CIVILIZED TRIBES,
MUSKOGEE, I.T., FEBRUARY 21st, 1901.

In the matter of the application of John W. Gleeson for enrollment as a citizen of the Cherokee Nation; and said Gleeson being sworn and examined by Commissioner Needles, testified as follows:

Q What is your name?   A John W. Gleeson.
Q How old are you?   A I will be 82 years old the 13th day of next August.
Q What is your post office?   A Muskogee here.
Q What district?   A Canadian District.
Q Are you a recognized citizen of the Cherokee Nation?   A Yes, sir
Q By blood or intermarriage?   A By marriage.
Q Who do you wnt[sic] to enroll A John W. Gleeson.
Q Anybody else?   A No, sir.
Q When were you married?   A There is my license. (Hands papers to Commissioner.)

Cherokee Intermarried White 1906
Volume VIII

Tribal Rolls of the Cherokee Nation examined and applicants[sic] name found thereon as follows:

1880 Authenticated roll; page 20, #562, Jno. W. Gleeson, Canadian district.

1896 Census Roll; page 87, #97, John W. Gleeson, Canadian district.

Com'r:-- Applicant presents satisfactory proof of his marriage to one Clarry Crittendon, a Cherokee citizen by blood, on the 21st day of January, 1873.

Q Is your wife living?   A No, sir.

Q When did she die?   A About 12 years ago.

Q Have you always lived in the Cherokee Nation since you were married?   A Yes, sir.

Q Are you living in the Cherokee Nation now?   A Yes, sir.

Q Did you live with your wife continuously from the time you married her until her death?   A I come down here to make a place; I lived in Going Snake district and then I come down here to make a place and then she come down here and went back and she died before I got ready to have her come down her.

Q You say she died 12 years ago?   A Yes, sir.

Q You married her in 1873?   A Yes sir.

Q Did you live with her from the time you were married until she died?   A No, sir.

Q Were you ever separated?   A Yes, sir: I tell you why, because she had a negro baby after I married her, and the Cherokees told me, the Cherokees and all told me I had a right to quit her because she did not do right.

Q When did you quit her?   A I can't tell you just exactly.

Q Well about what time?   A I could not tell you.

Q Were you ever divorced from her?   A No, sir, never was divorced in the world.

Q How long did you live with her after you married her?   A I could not tell you exactly.

Q About how many years?   A We lived together a good while.

Q She never had but the one child?   A No, sir.

Q Is it living?   A No, sir.

Q About how old was the child when it died?   A About eight years old.

Q You say she had a negro baby?   A Yes, sir.

Q Did you live with her until that time?   A No, sir.

Q How long did you live with her before that?   A I can't tell you that.

Q You can estimate about that, Mr. Gleeson; did you live with her two years?   A Yes, sir.

Q Three years?   A Yes, sir, more than that.

Q Five years?   A I don't know whether I lived that long.

Q Between three and four years?   A Yes, sir.

Q Then how long after that did she have this colored baby?   A Just a little while. She married again, her own coursin[sic], after she had that negro baby.   She left me altogether.

Q Had you left her before?   A I come down here to make her a place and left her on the place up yonder?[sic]

Q Up where?   A In Goingsnake district.

110

Cherokee Intermarried White 1906
Volume VIII

Q You left her in Going Snake district and come down to Canadian district?
A Yes, sir.
Q How far was that?   A Perhaps 20 miles.
Q Never lived with her afterwards?   A I have been back there to see her but never made my home up there.
Q Well now, how long was it after you left her until she had this colored baby?
A It must have been more than a year or two.
Q When you left her you did not know that she was going to have the colored baby did you?   A No, sir.
Q Then what made you leave her?   A I did not leave her; I come down to make a place here in Canadian district and before she come down she had the negro baby; her and the negro come down here and she had the negro baby and she had a husband with her.
Q And you left her about a year before that?   A She never knowed[sic] a stranger; she had a bastard before I married her; she told me that it was a legal marriage; everybody could use her.
Q Didn't you know that when you married her?   A No, sir; I come down here from Missouri and rented a place and first my father and I rented a place and when I was making a crop there they persuaded me to marry her; and they told me that she was a widow.
Q Was she a full blood?   A She was not more than a quarter indian[sic].
Q Now, you left your wife before 1880 did you?   (No response.)
Q You say you were married in 1873?   A Yes, I was down here before 1880; she had that youngen[sic] before 1880.
Q You have never married since?   A Never married since.
Q Hal[sic] all the experience you wanted in that line, did you?   A I lived up to the Cherokee laws.
Q Have you always been recognized as a Cherokee citizen by intermarriage? A Yes, sir.
Q Have you voted?   A I have; sir.
Q Right along?   A Yes, sir.
Q Do you own any property?   A Oh! I have a good farm and never have been interrupted.

Com'r Needles:-- The name of John W. Gleeson appears upon the 1880 authenticated roll as well as the census roll of 1896 as an intermarried citizen. He makes satisfactory proof of his marriage to his wife, Clarry Crittendon, a Cherokee citizen by blood, in the year 1873. The testimony develops the fact that he separated from his wife after living with her some three or four years but that separation occurred before 1880. Since 1880 he has never been remarried; consequently said John W. Gleeson will be duly listed for enrollment as a Cherokee citizen by intermarriage.
---oooOOO---[sic]
J. O. Rosson, being first duly sworn, states that as stenographer to the Commission to the Five Civilized Tribes, he correctly recorded the testimony and proceedings in this case, and that the foregoing is a true and complete transcript of his stenographic notes thereof.

J.O. Rosson

Cherokee Intermarried White 1906
Volume VIII

Subscribed and sworn to before me this 23d day of February, 1901.

T.B. Needles
Commissioner

◇◇◇◇◇

Can.

CHEROKEE BY BLOOD AND ADOPTION.

82

Date **FEB 21 1901** 1900.

Name **John W. Gleeson** **Muskogee I.T.**

District **Can** Year **1880** Page **20** No. **562**

Citizen by blood **No** Mother's citizenship

Intermarried citizen **Yes**

Married under what law Date of marriage

License Certificate

Wife's name

District Year Page No.

Citizen by blood Mother's citizenship

Intermarried citizen

Married under what law Date of marriage

License Certificate

Names of Children:

	Dist.	Year	Page	No.	Age
	Dist.	Year	Page	No.	Age
	Dist.	Year	Page	No.	Age
	Dist.	Year	Page	No.	Age
	Dist.	Year	Page	No.	Age

No. 1 on 1880 roll as Jno. W. Gleeson

◇◇◇◇◇

(The Marriage Certificate and License below were originally handwritten on the microfilm.)

This is to certify that I solemized[sic] the ceremony of matrimony between John W. Gleason[sic] and Clarry Crittenden this the 21 January A.D. 1873

T.B. Whitmire
Judge dist court
G. S. D. C.N.

112

Cherokee Intermarried White 1906
Volume VIII

Cher. Nation }
Going S. Dist }

Be it known that authority is hereby granted to any of the Judges of any of the County of this Nation & to all Ministers of this gospel haveing[sic] the Care of Souls are hereby authorized & empowered to solemnize the rights of matrimony according to the ceremonies usually observed in such cases between John W. Gleason an unmarried citizen of the U. States to Miss Clara Crittenden a Cherokee citizen The said John W. Gleason have complied with the law in such cases.

Given from under my hand in office this day & date the 6th of January A.D. 1873

J. W. Starr
Clk. Dist Ct
G. S. Dist
Cher. Nat.

◇◇◇◇◇

DEPARTMENT OF THE INTERIOR.
COMMISSION TO THE FIVE CIVILIZED TRIBES.

In the matter of the death of **John W. Gleason**
a citizen of the **Cherokee** Nation, who formerly resided at or near **Muskogee**, Ind. Ter., and died on the **30th** day of **November** , **1903**

AFFIDAVIT OF RELATIVE.

UNITED STATES OF AMERICA, Indian Territory, }
Western DISTRICT. }

I, _____ , on oath state that I am _____ years of age and a citizen by _____ , of the _____ Nation; that my postoffice address is _____ , Ind. Ter.; that I am _____ of _____ who was a citizen, by _____ , of the _____ Nation and that said _____ died on the _____ day of _____ , 1_____

Witnesses To Mark:
{ _____
_____

Subscribed and sworn to before me this _____ day of _____ , 190__

_____ Notary Public.

113

AFFIDAVIT OF ACQUAINTANCE.

UNITED STATES OF AMERICA, Indian Territory,
Western   DISTRICT.

I,   **John G. Lieber**   , on oath state that I am   **34**
years of age, and a citizen by   **nativity**   of the **United States**   ~~Nation~~;
that my postoffice address is   **Muskogee**   , Ind. Ter.;
that I was personally acquainted with   **John W. Gleason**
who was a citizen, by   **adoption**   , of the   **Cherokee**   Nation;
and that said   **John W. Gleason**   died on the   **30th**   day of
November   , 1903

John G. Lieber

Witnesses To Mark:

Subscribed and sworn to before me this   **5th**   day of   **January**   , 1907

Edward Merrick
Notary Public.

◇◇◇◇◇

COPY

Cherokee 7340.

C.F.B.

DEPARTMENT OF THE INTERIOR,
COMMISSIONER TO THE FIVE CIVILIZED TRIBES.
MUSKOGEE, I. T., JANUARY 17, 1907.

In the matter of the application for the enrollment of JOHN W. GLEESON as a
citizen by intermarriage of the Cherokee Nation.

APPEARANCES: W. W. Hastings, Attorney for Cherokee Nation;
John G. Lieber, Executor of estate of the ap-
plicant, John W. Gleeson.

MARGARET CRITTENDON, being first duly sworn by Chas. E. Webster,
Notary Public, testified as follows:

BY MR. HASTINGS:

Q What is your name?   A Margaret Crittendon.
Q How old are you?   A 66, will be in the spring.

Cherokee Intermarried White 1906
Volume VIII

Q What is your post office address?   A Wagoner.

Q Are you a citizen of the Cherokee Nation?   A Well, I reckon so.

Q You claim citizenship by intermarriage?   A Yes sir.

Q What was your husband's name?   A Mose Crittendon.

Q Did you know the applicant during his lifetime, John W. Gleeson?
A Yes sir, I knowed[sic] him.

Q Did you know his wife, through whom he claims citizenship by intermarriage in the Cherokee Nation?   A Yes sir.

Q What was her name?   A Her name was Clary Crittendon before she married Gleeson.

Q Was she related to you or to your husband?   A She was my step-daughter.

Q Was living with you and your husband at the time of her marriage to John W. Gleeson, was she?   A Yes sir.

Q Where were you living at the time of this marriage?   A On the prairie, about 12 milses[sic] this side of Siloam.

Q In Going Snake District?   A In Going Snake District.

Q Do you remember the circumstances of their marriage, were they married at your house?   A No sir, they went to the Clerk's and got married.

Q Where did they live, then, after they married?   A In about a mile of us.

Q On a place of their own?   A Yes sir.

Q Did they build a house?   A It was a place my man give them.

Q That was her father?   A Yes sir.

Q How long did they continue to live there?   A Well, something about 2 or 3 year[sic]; I dont[sic] recollect just exactly the time.

Q Well, did they separate?   A Yes sir.

Q What became of John W. Gleeson?   A Why, he went off down in Canadian.

Q Came off down here in Canadian from up there?   A Yes sir.

Q What became of her, Mrs. Gleeson?   A She stayed up there on the prairie awhile, then she went to Arkansas Bottoms, and died.

Q You mean she lived there?   A No sir.

Q Immediately after the time he left her, what became of her?   A He left her at my house.

Q Well, did he ever come back up there?   A Yes sir, he come back.

Q How long had he been gone?   A I dont[sic] recollect just the time; maybe 5 or 6 weeks.

Q Had he made a trip down here in Canadian District?   A Yes sir.

Q What did he come back for, do you know?   A Well, he had taken her cattle, and he came to get a bill of sale.

Q Dhow do you know that?   A Because he said so.

Q Did she have some cattle that he removed off?   A Yes sir.

Q Is she living now?   A No sir, she is dead.

Q Has been dead some time?   A Yes sir, a good while; I dont[sic] know just how long.

Q Do you remember how may[sic] cattle of hers he removed from there down here?
A 8 or 10 head; something like that.

Q Do you know whether or not she know that there was a separation when he first moved those cattle?   A No sir, she didn't think of such a thing.

Q What was said, if you know, when he first moved the cattle?   A He was going down there to get a place, and was going to come back and get her, and move down there.

Q And he went in advance, with the cattle?   A Yes sir.

Q You say in about 6 weeks he returned?   A Yes sir, maybe not that long.

Q Now, where did he leave from when he went with the cattle?   Did he leave her at your place?   A He left her where they was living.

Q And said he was coming back?   A Yes sir.

Q And he did come back in about 6 weeks?   A Yes sir.

Q What did he say to her then?   A He told her he was not going to live with her any more.

Q She was at your house when he came back?   A Yes sir.

Q How long did he remain?   A He stayed a few days.

Q Did he live with her any more?   A No sir, he never did.

Q Where did she make her home immediately thereafter?   A She went and stayed with her grandmother.

Q Did her grandmother live there in the neighborhood? A Yes sir; in about 10 miles of me.

Q How long did she stay at your house after Gleeson left before she wnt[sic] to her grandmother's?   A A week or two, something like that; I dont[sic] know just how long.

Q After that time did she and Gleeson ever live together?   A No sir, he never did come back any more.

Q Do you remember where he went?   A He come back in Canadian.

Q About how far was that from where they had formerly lived?   A It was in Going Snake.

Q How far was it from the Arkansas line; what was the post office?   A Wagoner.

Q Not while he was in Going Snake District?   A Yes sir. O[sic], no sir, it was Cincinnati. It has been so long I forgot.

Q Your present post office is Wagoner?   A Yes sir.

Q Then you were about 8 or 10 miles from the line of Arkansas? A Yes sir.

Q And he came off down here in Canadian, did he? A Yes sir.

Q Do you know about how far that was from his former home in Going Snake District? A I dont[sic] know just how far.

Q Was it 50 or 60 miles? A About that, something like that.

Q What became of those cattle?   A Why, her father come back here, and took the cattle and sold them, and carried the mony[sic] to her.

Q That was your husband?   A Yes sir.

Q His name was, what?   A Mose Crittendon.

Q He is also dead, is he? A Yes sir.

Q Do you know what was the attitude of Mrs. Gleeson toward Mr. Gleeson; as to whether she was kind toward him, or whether they were falling out or not?   A She was always kind to him.

Q Did you know of any reason that he had for going off and leaving her?   A No sir, I did not.

Q About how long did they live together after the birth of that child?   A Not a great while; it was just a small baby.

Q Was they any dispute about the parentage of that child?   A No sir

Q Never any dispute?   A No sir.

Q Did he ever dispute being the father of it?   A No sir.

Q Was any question raised about it at any time?   A No sir.

Q Then it was not because of the fatherhood of this child that they separated? A No sir.

Q Do you know what reason he had, if any, for leaving her?   A No sir, I dont[sic].

Q Did he give any reason?   A No sir, he never did.

Q All you know is that he got up and left her. A Yes sir, she thought he was coming back, but when he come he told her he wouldn't live with her any more.

Q Did they have any other property beside those cattle?   A Well, he had son horses.

Q Did he take those?   A Yes sir, carried all the stock with him.

Q Do you remember whether they had any hogs, or any other stock? A Cattle and horses was all they had.

Q He took the cattle and horses with him?   A Yes sir. The cattle was hers.

Q What about their household effects?   A He taken a little in the wagon, and the balance he left.

Q And you say the the[sic] place upon which they lived was given to her by her father? A Yes sir.

Q She retained that, did she? A Yes sir.

BY MR. LIEBER:

Q Now, Mrs. Crittendon, you say that Gleeson left there to come down to Canadian to start a place? A Yes sir.

Q That was agreeable to his wife, wat[sic] it?   A Yes, I suppose so.

Q You never heard anything to the contrary?   A No sir.

Q How long did you say he was gone from home when he went to Canadian?   A I dont[sic] know just how long; about 6 weeks as well as I can recollect.

Q What time of the year was it that he went to Canadian?   A In the summer time, but I dont[sic] know just when.

Q And you are positive that he was not away from home but 6 week[sic]? A That is the best of my knowledge; I dont[sic] recollect just how long; maybe not quite so long, maybe a little longer.

Q You are not positive about the length of time that he was gone?   A No sir.

Q Now, this child that his wife had was born while he was down here in Canadian? A No sir, he was at home when it was born?[sic]

Q Was it before he went to Canadian to establish the place that the child was born? A Yes sir.

Q What was the name of the child? A I believe that they called it William.

Q William what?   A William Gleeson.

Q Is the child living?   A No sir, it is dead.

Q How long did it live, Mrs. Crittendon?   A I don't know just how long it did live; maybe one year old, or two years; she went to Arkansas Bottoms, near Fort Smith.

Q Did you ever see her after she left home?   A No sir.

Q Did the child die before she left?   A It died after she went to the Bottoms.

Q About how old was the child when she left?   [sic] I dont[sic] recollect; it must have been about a year old, maybe.

Q You never saw this woman after she left you[sic] place that time?

A No sir, not after she went to Arkansas Bottoms.

Q Did you ever see old man Gleeson after he left you[sic] place there that time, when you say he said he wouldn't live with her any more?   A No sir, never saw him any more.

Q You do not know how long his wife lived after she left you[sic] place?   A No sir, I dont[sic] know how long it was.

Q You do not know of your own personal knowledge how long the child lived.

A The child died first.

Q You simply heard that?   A I sent my brother to get the child when I heard it was dead; that is how I know the child died first.

Q Where was she living when you sent your brother to her?   A Arkansas Bottoms, not far from Fort Smith.

Q What was his name?   A Isaac Howell.

Q Is he living?   A No sir, he is dead.

Q Can you swear, of your own personal knowledge, Mrs. Crittendon, that Gleeson's wife never lived with him after he returned to the Canadian District the second time?

A No sir, she never did.

Q How do you know that she didn't?   A Because she lived close to me, and he lived down here.

Q You say she left your place for the Arkansas Bottoms?   A No, she went to her grandmother's, and stayed awhile, then she married again, and went to the Bottoms.

Q Who did she marry the second time?   A I dont[sic] know what the fellow's name was

Q How long after Gleeson left her the second time was it when she married again?

A Some 2 or 3 weeks.

Q What was the name of the second man that she married?   A I dont[sic] know; I did know, but I have forgot.

Q Did he marry her while whe[sic] was at her grandmother's?   A Yes sir.

Q After she left her grandmother's you never saw her any more?   A No sir, I never did.

Q Then, as a matter of fact, Mrs. Crittendon, you do not know of your own personal knowledge that she didn't live with old man Gleeson after he came back her[sic] to the Canadian District?   A I never did know of it; she lived within 10 miles of me until she married and went to the Bottoms.

Q You never saw her in the Bottoms yourself?   A No sir, I never did

Q Did she ever have a child by this second husband?   A If she did, I never heard it.

Q How far was her grandmother's place from where you lived?

A About 10 miles.

Q Did you see her frequently while she lived at her grandmothers[sic]?

A No sir, I was not up there ofter[sic]; when I was there I saw her.

Q And you say you do not know the name of her second husband?

A I did know it, but I have forgot it; I dont[sic] recollect his name

Q He was related to her, was he, Mrs. Crittendon?   A I dont[sic] know whether he was or not.

Q How many children did she have before she left that neighborhood[sic]

A She had 2. If she had any more I dont[sic] recollect anything about it.

Q She had one child before she married Gleeson, didn't she?

A Yes sir, had one before she married Gleeson.

Q Had she ever been married before she married Mr. Gleeson?

A No sir, she hadn't.

Q Now, you say that when Gleeson came back there he told her that he was not going to live with her any more?   A Yes sir.

Q Did you hear the conversation that they had then?   A Yes sir.

Q Just tell the Commissioner the conversation they had at that time, as near as you can give it. A Well, that would be hard to do. He just told her he was not going to live with her any more; he was not going to take her and live with her any more.

Q Now, they had had[sic] some take about it before he told her that, hadn't they?

A Well, if they had, I didn't know anything about it.

Q Were you present while they were having their little dispute?   A They didn't have no dispute that I know of, but when he come back he told her he was not going to take her, and he was going back.

Q Was she living at your house, then, when he came back? A Yes sir

Q How long was he there?   A He didn't stay but 2 or 3 days.

Q How long had he been back when he told her that he was not going to live with her any more?   A He came in the morning, and told her that evening.

Q And then after that he stayed a few days, did he? A Yes sir, a day or two.

Q You say she had that second child at that time?   A Yes sir.

Q Where did Gleeson sleep, then?   A He selpt[sic] in a bed to himself.

Q In the same room with his wife?   A Well, we just had two rooms, and I dont[sic] recollect just where he slept, but he slept to himself, and she slept to herself.

Q Had they slept that same way before he left?   A Well, I dont[sic] know; if they ever slept separate I dont[sic] know it.

Q Who was the father of this first child that this woman had?

A I dont[sic] know, but we thought it was Bill Williams.

Q It was an illegitimate child?   A Yes sir.

Q Do you swear positively that there was not a dispute between Gleeson and his wife about who was the father of the second child?   A No sir, he claimed that it was his, for he come to me and asked me to raise it when he quit his wife.

Q Did you ever see the second man that this woman married?   A No sir.

Q Never saw him? A No sir.

Q You do not know what he looked like?   A No sir.

Q Do you know whether he was an Indian, a white man, or what?

A I don't know what he was.

Q Did this woman get a divorce before she married that fellow?   A I dont[sic] know whether she did or not; in them days they didn't get divorces when they separated.

Q How long did Gleeson and that woman live together?   A Something like 2 or 3 years; I dont[sic] know just how long.

Q Are you certain that they never lived together longer than 4 years?   A No sir, I know they didn't.

Q They were married, I believe, in 1873, were they not? A I dont[sic] recollect.

BY MR. HASTINGS:

Q How long did you know Gleeson before he married this woman?
A May be 5 or 6 months; not over that.

Q Did he live there in the neighborhood? A Right in our house.

Q Then he know[sic] that this woman who afterward became his wife, had this illegitimate child?   A Certainly he knew it, and I told him to treat the child right.

Q Then he knew that she had this child at the time he married her?
A Yes sir, I told him all about it.

Q Did John W. Gleeson's wife ever come to Canadian District before they separated?
A No sir.

Q You say that she lived up there at her grandmother's about a year after they separated, and that her grandmother lived about 10 miles from you?   A Yes sir.

Q And she married while at her grandmother's, and then moved to Arkansas River Bottoms?   A Yes sir.

Q Did you hear of her while she was at Arkansas Bottoms?   A Heard of her often.

Q What was this woman's second husband's name[sic] A I can't recollect it.

BY MR. LIEBER:

Q Who subpoenaed you, Mrs. Crittendon?

BY MR/[sic] HASTINGS:

    I object to that, because I believe it is irrelevant and immaterial as to who subpoenaed this witness; it does not have any bearing upon the truthfulness or untruthfulness of the statement, and tends in no way to throw any light upon the question as to whether or not the applicant, John W. Gleeson, abandoned his wife or not.

OBJECTION NOTED.

BY MR. HASTINGS:

Q Who subpoenaed you?   A Mr. Kelly
Q Lige Kelly?   A Yes sir.

BY MR. LIEBER:

Q Your family, and Lige's family are related?   A Mr. Kelly is related to my man.

Q What relation is he?   A I don't know exactly.

Q Kelly's wife was a Crittendon, wasn't she? A No sir, she was no Crittendon; Kelly's mother was a little kin to my man

Q Lige is the fellow that is trying to file on old man Gleeson's place, is he?

A I dont[sic] know nothing about it.

Q Didn't he tell you about that when he subpoenaed you?   A No sir. I thought I was told to come here about my own business, and didn't know the difference until I got her.

BY MR. HASTINGS:

Q And you have made application for enrollment today, have you?

A Yes sir.

The Cherokee Nation desires to offer here, and have quoted in this evidence, Section 667, of the Compiled Laws of the Cherokee Nation.

ON BEHALF OF THE COMMISSIONER:

The request of the Attorney for the Cherokee Nation will be granted, and said Section is as follows:

"Sec. 667: Every person who shall lawfully marry under the provisions of this act, and afterward abandon his wife shall thereby forfeit every right and priviliege[sic] of citizenship in this Nation."

BY MR. HASTINGS:

The Cherokee Nation rests.

ON BEHALF OF THE COMMISSIONER:

The representative of the applicant, and the Attorney for the Cherokee Nation announce that they have no further evidence to introduce. This case will be considered closed, and a decision rendered on evidence heretofore introduced.

The under signed, being first duly sworn, states that as stenographer to the Commission to the Five Civilized Tribes, she correctly reported the above and foregoing testimony, and that the same is a full, true and correct transcript of her stenographic notes thereof.

Sarah Waters.

Subscribed and sworn to before me this 18th day of January, 1907.
(SEAL)

B. P. Rasmus
Notary Public.

◇◇◇◇◇

E.C.M.   Cherokee 7340

DEPARTMENT OF THE INTERIOR,

COMMISSIONER TO THE FIVE CIVILIZED TRIBES.

In the matter of the application for the enrollment of John W. Gleeson as a citizen by intermarriage of the Cherokee Nation.

D E C I S I O N .

THE RECORDS OF THIS OFFICE SHOW: That at Muskogee, Indian Territory, February 21, 1901, application was received by the Commission to the Five Civilized Tribes, for the enrollment of John W. Gleeson as a citizen by intermarriage of the Cherokee Nation. Further proceedings in the matter of said application were had at Muskogee, Indian Territory, October 15, 1902 and January 17, 1907.

THE EVIDENCE IN THIS CASE SHOWS: That the applicant herein, John W. Gleeson, is a white man, and neither claims nor possesses any right to enrollment as a citizen of the Cherokee Nation, other than such right as he may have acquired by virtue of his marriage, January 21, 1873, to one Katie Gleeson, nee Crittendon, a native Cherokee, who is identified on the Cherokee Authenticated Tribal Roll of 1880, Goingsnake District, No. 331, marked "Dead". The said Katie Gleeson can not be identified on the Cherokee Authenticated Tribal Roll of 1880. It is further shown that about the year 1878, said John W. Gleeson abandoned the said Katie Gleeson and thereafter refused to live with her. Section 667, of the Cherokee Constitution, provides: "Every person who was lawfully married under the provisions of this act, and afterwards abandon his wife, should thereby forfeit every right and privilege of citizenship of this nation."

IT IS, THEREFORE, ORDERED AND ADJUDGED: That in accordance with the decision of the Supreme Court of the United States, dated November 5, 1906, in the cases of Daniel Red Bird, et al. vs. the United States, Nos. 125, 126, 127, and 128, the said applicant, John W. Gleeson, is not entitled, under the provisions of Section 21, of the Act of Congress approved June 28, 1898 (30th. Stats. 495), to enrollment as a citizen by intermarriage of the Cherokee Nation, and his application for enrollment as such is accordingly denied.

Tams Bixby
Commissioner.

Dated at Muskogee, Indian Territory,
this   FEB 9 1907

◇◇◇◇◇

Cherokee Intermarried White 1906
Volume VIII

DEPARTMENT OF THE INTERIOR,

COMMISSIONER TO THE FIVE CIVILIZED TRIBES.

Cherokee No. 7340.

In the matter of the application for the enrollment of John W. Gleason as a citizen by intermarriage of the Cherokee Nation.

BRIEF ON BEHALF OF APPLICANT.

We believe the Commissioner and the Attorney for the Cherokee Nation are entitled to know the motives which have prompted the investigation in this case. Not that we object to the investigation but to the motives which prompted it. We therefore give a brief history of the matter.

On November 30th., 1903, John W. Gleason, the applicant, died possessed of some personal property and a valuable farm located a few miles east of Muskogee, Indian Territory. He had resided on the farm continuously about twenty-five years before his death, and the Cherokees had never questioned his right as an intermarried citizen of the Nation. Some time prior to his death, he executed a will reciting that he had neither wife nor child, and bequeathing all his property, after the payment of his just debts, including his allotment in the Cherokee Nation (which he had theretofore selected) to the Catholic Church at Muskogee, of which he was a member. Some time prior to his death he came to Muskogee for medical attention, leaving his farm and all other property in charge of his neighbor, William Stranks, to whom he had rented the place for the ensuing year.

The applicant had scarcely been laid in his grave when the covetous eye of a worthless scoundrel thought it saw an opportunity to get something for nothing, and Lige Kelly, under cover of night "jumped" the applicant's farm and laid claim to it; not as an heir of the applicant, but solely on the ground that the applicant had no right to dispose of it by will, and that he (Kelly) being a Cherokee citizen, had a right to take the land in allotment. Kelly, it seems, had no trouble in getting attorneys to cooperate with him in his selfish schemes, and when Stranks demanded of him posession[sic] of the place, he refused to surrender posession, and compelled Stranks to institute suit in the United States Court for posession of the premises. Stranks obtained judgment for possession, and the case was appealed by Kelly to the Court of Appeals at South McAlester, where it was recently dismissed by that Court.

Kelly and his counsel, no doubt despairing of depriving the applicant's legatees of this property through the courts, had but one other way to deprive them of it, and that was to prevent him from being enrolled as a citizen of the Cherokee Nation This they are now attempting to do, and to hide their selfish motives they allege that the applicant abandoned his Cherokee wife, and thereby forfeited his citizenship in the Cherokee Nation. This is the only question in the case, and to prove this alleged abandonment, they have produced but one witness, who is the step-mother of the applicant's wife.

The record in this case shows that on February 21, 1901, the applicant appeared before Commissioner Needles and testified as to his right to enrollment. At that time not a word of protest was uttered by the representatives of the Cherokee Nation as to his right of enrolment[sic]. Commissioner Needles, after seeing the applicant and hearing his testify, was of opinion, and so stated in the record, that he was entitled to enrolment[sic]. On October 15, 1902, the applicant again appeared before the Commissioner and testified regarding his enrolment matters, and again we hear no word of protest from the Cherokee Nation as to his right to enrolment. But now, after a lapse of thirty years, and after the applicant's voice has been stilled in death Kelly and his coharts[sic] raise the cry of abandonment. Is it not singular that in all that thirty years the Cherokee Nation should not have found that the applicant had abandoned his wife and refused to enroll him as a citizen? There is every reason to believe that at the time of this alleged abandonment, the Cherokee authorities knew the facts regarding it, and for that reason declined to protest against this applicant's enrolment, for we find that in 1880, which was a few years after the alleged abandonment is said to have taken place, the Cherokee enrolled the applicant as one of their citizens. Again in 1896, and after Kelly and all others had had nearly twenty years in which to produce evidence regarding this alleged abandonment, we find the Cherokees enrolling this applicant as one of their citizens on their Census Roll of that date. The Cherokees, no doubt, viewed their law of abandonment in the broad legal sense, and not in the narrow minded sense which Kelly and his counsel would have the Commissioner view it. "Desertion or abandonment consists in the voluntary separation of one spouse from the other for the prescribed time, without the latter's consent, without justification, and with the intention of not returning."

(14 CYC.611.-. "The party who drives the other way by force or misconduct, and causes the separation, is guilty of desertion although the guilty party continues to reside in the matrimonial home." (9Am. & Eng. Enc. Law,-2nd Ed.-page 770.).

Misconduct causing a separation is desertion.

Morris vs Morris, 20 Ala. 168.
Levering vs Levering, 16 Md. 213.
Daeters vs Daeters, (N.J. 1897) 38 Atl. 950.

In Stocking vs Stocking, 76 Minn. 292, 79 N.W. 668, it was held that "it is a sufficient justification if the party withdrawing from the cohabitation, has reasonable grounds for believing, and does honestly believe, that by reason of the actual misconduct of the other it cannot be longer continued with health, safety or self respect."

In the case of Warner vs Warner, 54 Mich. 492, it was held that "desertion under the statute, is the wilful abandonment of one party by the other without cause, and against the will of the party abandoned, for the period of two years. If the husband's conduct is so cruel towards his wife that she cannot live and cohabit with him with safety to her health or without peril to her life, or if she has good reason to believe she cannot, and for such reason she leaves him and abandons his home, she does not thereby commit the crime of desertion. In such case she does not leave her husband or her home in consequence of any willfulness on her part, but is compelled by the cruelty of her husband, and against her will, so to do. The desertion in such case is upon his part, and not upon hers. He has completely committed the crime of desertion when, by his cruel conduct and conversation, he compels her for safety to leave him and his home, as when he wilfully and without cause leaves and abandons her."

In the case of Thompson vs Choctaw and Chickasaw Nations, 11th Annual Report of Commission to the Five Civilized Tribes, page 132, it was held by the Choctaw and Chickasaw Citizenship Court that, although Thompson left his citizen wife he was justified in doing so, and was therefore not guilty of abandonment, and did not forfeit his rights as a citizen by intermarriage.

While the evidence in this case is somewhat conflicting, it is certainly not sufficient upon which to base a finding that the applicant left his wife without just cause, and thereby forfeited his rights as a citizen by intermarriage.

The undisputed testimony shows that the applicant married his Cherokee wife in January, 1873; that prior to that time she had given birth to an illegitimate child: that the applicant and his wife lived together in Going Snake District some three or four years after their marriage, when the applicant, with the consent of his wife, went to Canadian District to establish a home: that he went back to Going Snake District to see his wife and returned to Canadian District: That about two years thereafter she married another man without having obtained a divorce from the applicant, and that all this occured[sic] prior to 1880. These are the undisputed facts of this case.

The disputed facts are as follows. The applicant testified that at the time he married this woman she was represented to him as a widow, and that he did not know that her child was illegitimate. This is denied by Mrs. Crittendon, his mother-in-law. The applicant further testified that after he went to Canadian District his wife gave birth to a negro baby, and it was for that reason that he refused to live with her. This is also denied by Mrs. Crittendon, but she is unable to give any reason why the applicant refused to live with his wife.

The following is a portion of the evidence given by the applicant before Commissioner Needles.

> Q. When you left her you did not know that she was going to have a colored baby did you? A. No, sir.
>
> Q. Then what made you leave her? A. I did not leave her: I come to make a place here in Canadian district and before she come down she had the negro baby; her and the negro come down here and she had the negro baby and she had a husband with her."

The Cherokee law does not say how long a man must live apart from his wife to be guilty of abandonment, and we are not sure that the applicant's wife was not guilty of abandonment upon the admitted facts in this case, by marrying another man within two years after the applicant refused to live with her, without first having obtained a divorce from him. But be that as it may, it is clear from the applicant's testimony that her conduct was such that he could not with self respect, continue to live with her as his wife.

We submit that under the law and the evidence in this case, the applicant was not guilty of abandonment, and that he should be enrolled as a citizen of the Cherokee Nation by intermarriage.

Respectfully submitted,

John G. Lieber, as Representa-
tive of the _____
Executors of the Last Will and
Testament of John W. Gleason, deceased.

Service of a copy of the foregoing brief is hereby acknowledged this 26" day of January, 1907.

W.W. Hastings, _____
Attorney for Cherokee Nation.
H.M.V.

◇◇◇◇◇

Cherokee Intermarried White 1906
Volume VIII

DEPARTMENT OF THE INTERIOR,
COMMISSIONER TO THE FIVE CIVILIZED TRIBES.

In the matter of the application for the enrollment of John W. Gleeson as a citizen by intermarriage of the Cherokee Nation.

Reply of the Cherokee Nation.

Counsel representing the executors of the last will and testament of John W. Gleeson, the applicant, has taken occasion to file a brief in this case in which he criticizes the motive that prompts John D. Kelley and his attorneys in contesting the enrollment of John W. Gleeson. with[sic] this the Cherokee Nation has nothing to do and is in no wise concerned and is only concerned with the question of whether or not the said John W. Gleeson under the testimony and law is entitled to be enrolled as a citizen by intermarriage of the Cherokee Nation. There is but little testimony introduced.

John W. Gleeson testifies in substance that the[sic] was married in Goingsnake District and claims to have been married to Katie, also known as Clara Crittenden. After living with her a while he admits having gone to Canadian District, as he states, for the purpose of making a place, and this is some 50 or 60 miles distant. He puts up two excuses in his testimony. At first he states that he went down to make a place in Canadian District, intending to go back for his wife, and second, he justified his desertion of his wife by saying she gave birth to a colored baby. Now these two excuse are inconsistent, and we think the second charge justified us in saying that from his testimony alone it is clear that he deserted this woman. Lets[sic] see when she was accused of having a colored baby, from his own testimony. On page 2 of his testimony given February 1, 1901, this question was asked him:

"Q. Well now how long was it after you left her until she had this colored baby? A It must have been more than a year or two."
"Q. When you left her you did not know that she was going to have a colored baby, did you? A No sir."

In the above testimony he admits leaving her, and he admits that he did not know that she was going to have an illegitimate child, and therefore of course that was not the moving cause for his leaving his wife, and brushing that aside, he gives no excuse of the desertion of his wife.

Upon the other hand, Margaret Crittenden, the stepmother of the wife of John W. Gleeson, testifies that John W. Gleeson wilfully deserted her and went off and left her and went down to Canadian District; that he used every effort to, and did finally suceed[sic] in moving her cattle down there, but that her father went down and succeeded in getting the money for them. He did pretend that he was going first down to Canadian district and was coming back, but as soon as he returned he told his wife that he was not going to live with her any more, and his wife went off to live with her grandmother. She afterwards married some one whose name was not remembered. Gleeson only testifies that they had one child, and Mrs. Crittenden this was born in lawful wedlock; that he never doubted the paternity of the child; that in fact it was never questioned.

Section 667 of the Compiled Laws of the Cherokee Nation provides

"Every person who shall lawfully marry under the provisions of this act and afterwards abandon his wife shall thereby forfeit every right and privilege of citizenship in this Nation."

We contend from the testimony of Gleeson himself that it shows that he left his wife, that he left her without cause; and that in fact there was no justification of it. He attempts to give as a reason for leaving her that she had an illegitimate child was not the moving cause for his leaving her, but that it was born some year of two afterwards. Next to the concluding line of counsel representing the applicant brief is as follows:

"But be that as it may it is clear from applicant's testimony that her conduct was such that he could not with self respect continue to live with her as his wife."

We challenge any one to show in the applicant's testimony a single line that would reflect upon his wife prior to his leaving her, but the only reflection which he attempts to cast upon his wife happened some year to two after his desertion and abandonment of her, and the testimony introduced on behalf of the Cherokee Nation is clear and conclusive that he left her, left her without cause, took her cattle and attempted to dispose of them, and came back and told his wife that he did not intend to live with her and at that time no child, except the one born to them in lawful wedlock, had been born to them; there was no dispute about the paternity of that child.

We submit under Section 667 of the Compiled Laws of the Cherokee Nation and the evidence in this case that the applicant was guilty of abandoning his wife and therefore should not be enrolled as a citizen by intermarriage of the Cherokee Nation.

Respectfully submitted.

(Signed)   W W Hastings
Attorney for the Cherokee Nation.

Muskogee, I. T., February 4, 1907.

Service of a copy of the above accepted this February 4, 1907.

> Attorney representing the executor
> of the last will and testament of
> John W. Gleeson.

DEPARTMENT OF THE INTERIOR,
Commissioner to the Five Civilized Tribes.
RECEIVED
FEB - 4 1907

◇◇◇◇◇

REFER IN REPLY TO THE FOLLOWING:
Cherokee
7340

DEPARTMENT OF THE INTERIOR,
COMMISSIONER TO THE FIVE CIVILIZED TRIBES.

Muskogee, Indian Territory, December 26, 1906.

John W. Gleeson,
Muskogee, Indian Territory.

November 6, 1906, the United States Supreme Court held that white persons who intermarried with Cherokee citizens according to Cherokee law prior to November 1, 1875, are entitled to enrollment and allotments of land as citizens of the Cherokee Nation.

You are advised that to properly determine your right to enrollment as a citizen by intermarriage of the Cherokee Nation, it will be necessary for you to appear before the Commissioner for the purpose of giving testimony as to the date of your marriage and whether or not your wife, by reason of your marriage to whom you claim the right to enrollment as a citizen of the Cherokee Nation, was a recognized citizen of the Cherokee Nation at the time of your marriage to her, and whether or not you were married to her in accordance with Cherokee laws.

You are therefore directed to appear before the Commissioner at Muskogee, Indian Territory, at 9 o'clock A. M., on Saturday, January 5, 1907, and give testimony as above indicated.

Respectfully,

Wm O. Beall
Acting Commissioner.

GHL

◇◇◇◇◇

Cherokee Intermarried White 1906
Volume VIII

Muskogee, Indian Territory, January 19, 1907.

W. W. Hastings,
Attorney for the Cherokee Nation,
Muskogee, Indian Territory.

Dear Sir:

There is enclosed herewith a copy of the testimony taken before the Commissioner to the Five Civilized Tribes, Muskogee, January 17, 1907, in the matter of the application for the enrollment of John W. Gleeson, as a citizen by intermarriage of the Cherokee Nation.

Respectfully,

Encl. HJ-50.
HJC   Commissioner.

◇◇◇◇◇

Muskogee, Indian Territory, January 21, 1907.

John G. Lieber,
Muskogee, Indian Territory.

Dear Sir:

There is enclosed herewith a copy of the testimony taken before the Commissioner to the Five Civilized Tribes, Muskogee, Indian Territory, January 17, 1907, in the matter of the application for the enrollment of John W. Gleeson, as a citizen by intermarriage of the Cherokee Nation.

Respectfully,

Encl. HJ-501
HJC   Commissioner.

◇◇◇◇◇

Cherokee 7340

Muskogee, Indian Territory, February 9, 1907.

John G. Lieber,
Administrator for the estate of John W. Gleeson.
Muskogee, Indian Territory.

Dear Sir:

There is enclosed herewith copy of the decision of the Commissioner to the Five Civilized Tribes, dated February 9, 1907, rejecting the application for the enrollment of John W. Gleeson, as a citizen by intermarriage of the Cherokee Nation.

The decision, together with the record of proceedings had in the case, has this day been transmitted to the Secretary of the Interior for his review and decision. You will be advised of the Secretary's action as soon as this office is informed of the same.

Respectfully,

Enc I-36   Commissioner.
RPI
Register.

◇◇◇◇◇

Cherokee 7340

Muskogee, Indian Territory, February 9, 1907.

W. W. Hastings,
Attorney for the Cherokee Nation,
Muskogee, Indian Territory.

Dear Sir:

There is enclosed herewith copy of the decision of the Commissioner to the Five Civilized Tribes, dated February 9, 1907, rejecting the application for the enrollment of John W. Gleeson as a citizen by intermarriage of the Cherokee Nation.

The decision, together with the record of proceedings had in the case, has this day been transmitted to the Secretary of the Interior for his review and decision. You will be advised of the Secretary's action as soon as this office is informed of the same.

Respectfully,

Enc I-37.   Commissioner.

Cherokee Intermarried White 1906
Volume VIII

◇◇◇◇◇

Muskogee, Indian Territory, February 9, 1907.

The Honorable,
     The Secretary of the Interior.

Sir:

     There is transmitted herewith the record of proceedings had in the matter of the application for the enrollment of John W. Gleeson, as a citizen by intermarriage of the Cherokee Nation, together with the decision of the Commissioner to the Five Civilized Tribes, dated February 9, 1907, rejecting said application.

Respectfully,

Enc I-38   Commissioner.
RPI
Through the Commissioner
     of Indian Affairs.

◇◇◇◇◇

COPY.

Refer in reply
to the following:
Land   DEPARTMENT OF THE INTERIOR.
15079-1907
18200-1907   OFFICE OF INDIAN AFFAIRS,

Washington, February 23, 1907.

The Honorable,
     The Secretary of the Interior.

Sir:

     There is enclosed a communication from the Commissioner to the Five Civilized Tribes, dated January 9, 1907, transmitting the record relative to the application of John W. Gleason for enrollment as an intermarried citizen of the Cherokee Nation, together with his decision of February 9, 1907, rejecting the application.

     There is also enclosed a communication from Reverend William H. Ketcham, director of the Bureau of Catholic Missions of this city, dated February 19, 1907, concerning the application.

Cherokee Intermarried White 1906
Volume VIII

Father Ketcham says that Gleason as an intermarried citizen of the Cherokee Nation bequeathed some very valuable property to the Catholic Church of Muskogee; that the Commissioner to the Five Civilized Tribes held that the applicant was not entitled to enrollment; and that this holding has caused intense feeling among the members of the congregation referred to, some of whom are the best legal talent in the Indian Territory; that they have appealed to him to do everything in his power to procure a careful and thorough consideration of the case by the Department, believing that if its merits are properly brought out by investigation a decision favorable to the church will be rendered. He expresses the opinion that a great deal can be said on such side and he says that he is anxious to do his duty as a representative of the church; and that he desires to be in a position to impress upon the Muskogee congregation that they have no grounds whatever for complaint should an adverse decision be rendered against their contention.

Father Ketcham goes on to say that he feels confident that the Department and this office will deal out even-handed justice, and that as far as he is concerned he is satisfied to leave the matter entirely to the Department and Office; but in order to avoid any chance whatsoever for resentment on the part of the people in question, in case of an adverse decision, he suggests the advisability of the record in the case being submitted to the Attorney General, with request that he render an opinion in the case, and says that in the event the opinion is unfavorable there can be no possibility of any reasonable displeasure from any quarter.

The fourth of March is now distant only eight working days, and into that brief period it will be necessary to crowd an immense amount of work, either now in this Office or to be sent here within a week, on, enrollment cases. The Congress having declined to extend the period within which the Secretary of the Interior could approve or disapprove enrollments in the Five Civilized Tribes, the only thing left for the office is to hurry through as fast as possible the disposal of this multitude of cases and trust to grouping a number, here and there, under some rule of precedent and devoting such brief time as may remain to a hasty survey of the decisions of the Commissioner to the Five Civilized Tribes in all miscellaneous cases.

The John W. Gleason case seems to belong in the miscellaneous remnant, and there would probably be left for it scant time for consideration. In view of Father Ketcham's interest in this case and his representation of the feelings of the people most concerned on one side, I have consented to transmit it to the Department without passing my judgment whatever on its merits, for the Secretary of the Interior, if he regards such course as advisable, to refer to the Attorney General as requested.

Very respectfully,

F.E. Leupp,

Commissioner.

GAW-GH.

◇◇◇◇◇

COPY.

DEPARTMENT OF JUSTICE.

Washington.

February 26, 1907.

The Secretary of the Interior.
    Sir:

    I beg to acknowledge the receipt of your letter of the 25th instant, requesting my opinion upon the Cherokee enrollment case of John W. Gleason. It appears from the record in this case that Gleason applied to the Commission to the Five Civilized Tribes on February 21, 1901, to be enrolled as a citizen by intermarriage of the Cherokee Nation. Upon the testimony adduces before him at that time, Commissioner Needles held:-

    The name of John W. Gleason appears upon the 1880 authenticated roll as well as the census roll of 1896 as an intermarried citizen. He makes satisfactory proof of his marriage to his wife, Clarry Crittendon, a Cherokee citizen by blood, in the year 1873. The testimony develops the fact that he separated from his wife after living with her some three or four years but that separation occurred before 1880. Since 1880 he has never been remarried; consequently said John W. Gleason will be duly listed for enrollment as a Cherokee citizen by intermarriage.

    Some further testimony was taken in this case on October 15, 1902, by which it appeared that Gleason had lived in the Cherokee Nation all the time since 1880.

    January 17, 1907, this case appears to have been again taken up by the Commissioner to the Five Civilized Tribes. At the hearing then had, the Cherokee Nation, by its attorney, introduced testimony tending to show that Gleason, after living with his wife two or three years, had abandoned her. Gleason, it appears, died November 30, 1903, bequeathing all his property, including the allotment in the Cherokee Nation, which he had theretofore selected, to the Catholic Church at Muskogee.

    On February 9, 1907, the Commissioner to the Five Civilized Tribes rendered the following decision:

    The records of this office show: That at Muskogee, Indian Territory, February 21, 1901, application was received by the Commission to the Five Civilized Tribes for the enrollment of John W Gleason as a citizen by intermarriage of the Cherokee Nation?[sic] Further proceedings in the matter of said application were had at Muskogee, Indian Territory, October 15, 1902, and January 17, 1907.

Cherokee Intermarried White 1906
Volume VIII

The evidence in this case shows: That the applicant herein, John W. Gleason, is a white man, and neither claims nor possessed any right to enrollment as a citizen of the Cherokee Nation other than such right as he may have acquired by virtue of his marriage, January 21, 1873, to one Katie Gleeson, nee Crittendon, a native Cherokee, who is identified on the Cherokee Authenticated Tribal Roll of 1880, Goingsnake District, No. 331, marked "Dead". The said Katie Gleeson can not be identified on the Cherokee Authenticated Tribal Roll of 1880. It is further shown that about the year 1878, said John W. Gleason abandoned the said Katie Gleeson and thereafter refused to live with her. Section 667, of the Cherokee Constitution, provides: "Every person who was lawfully married under the provisions of this act, and afterwards abandon his wife, should thereby forfeit every right and privilege of citizenship of this nation."

It is, therefore, ordered and adjudged: That in accordance with the decision of the Supreme Court of the United States, dated November 5, 1906, in the cases of Daniel Red Bird, et al. vs. the United States, Nos. 125, 126, 127, and 128, the said applicant, John W. Gleason, is not entitled, under the provisions of Section 21, of the Act of Congress approved June 28, 1898 (30th. Stats. 495), to enrollment as a citizen by intermarriage of the Cherokee Nation, and his application for enrollment as such is accordingly denied.

In the case of Red Bird v. the United States the Supreme Court affirmed the decree of the Court of Claims, which held that white persons who intermarried in the Cherokee Nation prior to November 1, 1875, were entitled to share in the distribution of the tribal property and to be enrolled for such purpose. The Supreme Court also affirmed that portion of the decree of the Court of Claims which held that white men who, having intermarried Cherokee women, subsequently abandoned their Cherokee wives were not entitled to participate in the distribution of the tribal property or to be enrolled for such purpose. It will be observed that the decision of the Commissioner is based upon the fact, found by him, that Gleason abandoned his wife. The testimony is conflicting upon this point, but the matter is immaterial from my point of view, because I think that, under the law, the Commissioner had no authority to go behind the Cherokee roll of 1880, upon which the name of Gleason appeared.

Section 21 of the Act of June 28, 1898 (30 Stat., 495, 502), provides:

That in making rolls of citizenship of the several tribes, as required by law, the Commissioner to the Five Civilized Tribes is authorized and directed to take the roll of Cherokee citizens of eighteen hundred and eighty (not including freedmen) as the only roll intended to be confirmed by this and proceding[sic] acts of Congress, and to enroll all persons now living whose names are found on said roll, and all descendants born since the date of said roll to persons whose names are found thereon; and all persons who have been enrolled by the tribal authorities who have heretofore made permanent settlement in the Cherokee Nation, whose parents by reason of their Cherokee blood, have been lawfully admitted to citizenship by the tribal authorities, and who were minors when their parents were so admitted; and they shall investigate the right of all other persons whose names are found on any other rolls and omit all such as may have been placed thereon by fraud or without authority of law, enrolling only such as may have lawful right thereto, and their descendants born since such rolls were made, with such intermarried white persons as may be entitled to citizenship under Cherokee laws.

It will be observed that the act of June 10, 1896, confirmed all the rolls of citizenship of the several tribes as then existing, and that the act of June 7, 1897, provided that the words "rolls of citizenship", as used in the act of June 10, 1896 should be construed to mean "the last authenticated rolls of each tribe which have been approved by the counsel of the Nation, and he descendants of those appearing on such rolls, and such additional names and their descendants as have been subsequently added, either by the counsel of such nation, the duly authorized courts thereof, or the Commission, under the act of June tenth, eighteen hundred and ninety-six.

The Act of June 28, 1898, limits the confirmation of Congress to the Cherokee roll of 1880, and specifically directs the Commission "to enroll all persons now living whose names are found on said roll." The authority given the Commission to eliminate from the tribal rolls those placed thereon by fraud or without authority of law is also expressly limited to "any other rolls", meaning any other than the roll of 1880, which was confirmed. It seems to me clear, therefore, that if due effect is to be given to the language used by Congress in this act, the Commissioner was bound to enroll Gleason, since his name appeared on the Cherokee roll of 1880, and he was a resident of the nation at the time of the passage of the act of June 28, 1898, as required therein.

In the Red Bird case the Supreme Court held that the confirmation given to the roll of 1880 "was not intended to create any rights which citizens of the Cherokee nation had not before enjoyed, but merely to furnish the basis for making up the roll of citizens." By this it evidently meant that although a person was upon the roll, he was not, because of that fact alone, entitled to share in the distribution of the tribal property. But where, as here, a person belonged to a class entitled to share in the distribution of the tribal property, and the only question was as to whether he had forfeited his citizenship, the fat that his name appeared on such confirmed roll must be held to remove that question from the realm of controversy, he being a resident of the Nation as required by the act of June 28, 1898. To hold that the Commission could go behind the roll of 1880 and investigate the right to citizenship of persons whose names appeared thereon would be to put that roll on exactly the same footing as the other rolls of the tribes which were not confirmed but expressly left open to investigation.

As I understand it, that part of the decree of the Court of Claims in the Red Bird case, affirmed by the Supreme Court, in regard to "married out and abandoned whites" has no reference to a case of this kind.

I am, therefore, of he[sic] opinion, that Gleason was entitled to be enrolled.

Respectfully,

Charle[sic] J. Bonaparte,

Attorney General.

◇◇◇◇◇

SPECIAL   J.P.

O.K.

DEPARTMENT OF THE INTERIOR.

I.T.D. 6252-1907   Washington,
      6472- "   March 1, 1907.
L.R.S.
Direct.

Commissioner to the Five Civilized Tribes,

    Muskogee, Indian Territory.

Sir:

The following telegram to you, of March 1, 1907, is hereby confirmed:

"It is held in opinion of Attorney-General of February 26th that John W. Gleason (see your decision of February 9th adverse to applicant), who married his Cherokee wife in 1873, and is alleged to have separated from her prior to 1880, is entitled to enrollment. He is on the 1880 roll.

The Attorney-General states: "In the Red Bird case the Supreme Court held that the confirmation given to the roll of 1880 'was not intended to create any rights which citizens of the Cherokee Nation had not before enjoyed, but merely to furnish the basis for making up the roll of citizens.' By this it evidently meant that although a person was upon the roll he was not, because of that fact alone, entitled to share in the distribution of the tribal property. But where, as here, a person belonged to a class entitled to share in the distribution of the tribal property, and the only question was as to whether he had forfeited his citizenship, the fact that his name appeared on such confirmed roll must be held to remove that question from the realm of controversy, he being a resident of the Nation as required by the act of June 28, 1898".

You will enroll Gleason. You are directed to inform the Department by wire at once of all analogous cases in which the claimants should be enrolled."

A copy hereof has been sent to the Indian Office, and the papers in the case. A copy of Indian Office letter of March 1, 1907, in the Gleason case, is enclosed, also copy of said opinion.

Respectfully,
E. A. Hitchcock,
Secretary.

2 inc. and
5 inc. to Ind. Of.
A.F. McG.
3-2-07.

◇◇◇◇◇

Cherokee 7340   COPY

Muskogee, Indian Territory, March 20, 1907.

John G. Lieber,
Muskogee, Indian Territory.

Dear Sir:

You are hereby advised of the enrollment of John W. Gleason as a citizen by intermarriage of the Cherokee Nation, in accordance with a letter from the Secretary of the Interior, dated March 1, 1907.

For your information, there is enclosed herewith a copy of Departmental letter referred to.

Respectfully,

SIGNED *Tams Bixby*
Commissioner.

Encl. H-46
JMH

◇◇◇◇◇

Cherokee 7340   COPY

Muskogee, Indian Territory, March 20, 1907.

W. W. Hastings,
      Attorney for the Cherokee Nation,
          Muskogee, Indian Territory.

Dear Sir:

      You are hereby advised of the enrollment of John W. Gleason as a citizen by intermarriage of the Cherokee Nation, in accordance with Departmental letter of March 1, 1907.

      For your information, there is enclosed herewith a copy of Departmental letter referred to.

Respectfully,

SIGNED *Jams Bixby*

Encl. H-47   Commissioner.
JMH

◇◇◇◇◇

Department of the Interior.
Commissioner to the Five Civilized Tribes,
MUSKOGEE, IND. TER.

John W. Gleason,

Muskogee, Indian Territory.

(Copy of original document from case.)

Cher IW 234

◇◇◇◇◇

Cherokee Intermarried White 1906
Volume VIII

Department of the Interior,
Commission to the Five Civilized Tribes,
Chelsea, I. T., November 26, 1900.

In the matter of the application of Mary J. Thompson for the enrollment of herself as a Cherokee citizen; being sworn and examined by Commissioner Needles she testified as follows:

Q   What is your name?   A Mary J. Thompson.
Q   What is your age?   A 62
Q   What is your post-office?   A Chelsea.
Q   In what district do you live?   A Cooweescoowee.
Q   Are you a recognized citizen of the Cherokee Nation?
A   Yes sir, I am white adopted.
Q   Who do you desire to enroll?   A Myself.
Q   Are you married?   A I am a widow; John Martin Thompson's widow.
Q   Is he living?   A No sir.
Q   When were you married to him?   A In 1877.
1880 roll page 187 #2927 as Jane M. Thompson Cooweescoowee adopted white;
1896 roll page 326 #981 Mary J. Thompson Cooweescoowee Dist.
Q   Have you married since the death of Mr. Thompson?   A No sir.
Q   You have always lived in the Cherokee Nation?   A Yes sir, ever since 1866.

Com'r Needles: The name of Mary J. Thompson is found upon the authenticated roll of 1880 as Jane M. Thompson, and upon the census roll of 1896 as Mary J. Thompson, an intermarried white person; she having been duly identified according to page and number of the roll; having made satisfactory proof as to residence said Mary J. Thompson will be duly listed for enrollment as a Cherokee citizen by intermarriage.

M.D. Green, being first duly sworn states that as stenographer to the Commission to the Five Civilized Tribes he correctly recorded the testimony and proceedings in this case and the foregoing is a true and correct transcript of his stenographic notes thereof.

M.D. Green

Subscribed and sworn to before me this 16th day of November 1900.

C R Breckinridge
Commissioner.

◇◇◇◇◇

Cherokee Intermarried White 1906
Volume VIII

CHEROKEE BY BLOOD AND ADOPTION.

Date   **NOV 16 1900**   1900.

Name .... **Chelsea IT** ....

District .... Year .... Page .... No. ....

Citizen by blood .... Mother's citizenship ....

Intermarried citizen ....

Married under what law .... Date of marriage ....

License **62** .... Certificate ....

Wife's name .... **Mary J Thompson** ✓

District .... **COOWEESCOOWEE** .... Year **1880** .... Page **187** .... No. **2927**

Citizen by blood .... **No** .... Mother's citizenship ....

Intermarried citizen .... **Yes** ....

Married under what law .... Date of marriage ....

License .... Certificate ....

      Names of Children:

	Dist.	Year	Page	No.	Age
	Dist.	Year	Page	No.	Age
	Dist.	Year	Page	No.	Age
	Dist.	Year	Page	No.	Age
	Dist.	Year	Page	No.	Age

1 on 1880 roll as Jane M. Thompson

◇◇◇◇◇

R.

DEPARTMENT OF THE INTERIOR.
Commission to the Five Civilized Tribes.
Muskogee, Indian Territory, October 6th, 1902.

    In the matter of the application of Mary J. Thompson for the enrollment of herself as a citizen by intermarriage of the Cherokee Nation.

Supplemental to #5492.

    Applicant appears in person.
               Cherokee Nation by J. C. Starr.

Cherokee Intermarried White 1906
Volume VIII

MARY J. THOMPSON, being duly sworn, testified as follows:
Examination by the Commission.

Q. What is your name?   A. Mary J. Thompson.
Q. What is your age at this time?   A. 63.
Q. What is your post office?   A. Chelsea.
Q. Are you the same Mary J. Thompson for whom application was made to this Commission for enrollment as an intermarried citizen on November 16th, 19oo[sic]?
A. Yes, sir.
Q. What was your husband's name?   A. J. M. Thompson.
Q. Is he living or dead?   A. He is dead.
Q. How long has he been dead?   A. 18 years.
Q. When were you and he married?   A. We were married in '77.
Q. Were you ever married before?   A. Yes, he was my third husband and I was his third wife.
Q. Were both your former husbands dead when you and he married?
A. Yes, sir.
Q. Were his two former wifes[sic] dead when you and he married?
A. Yes, sir.
Q. Did you and Mr. Thompson live together all the time from the time you were married up until the time he died?   A. Yes, sir.
Q. As husband and wife?   A. Yes, sir.
Q. You and he were never separated during that time?   A. No, sir; never separated.
Q. Still a widow and single on the first of September, 1902?   A. Yes, sir.
Q. How long have you lived in the Cherokee Nation?   A. Ever since the fall of '66.
Q. Have you lived in the Cherokee Nation all the time since 1880?   A. Yes, sir.
Q. Up to the present time?   A. Yes, sir.

+++

Jesse O. Carr, being first duly sworn, states that as stenographer to the Commission to the Five Civilized Tribes he reported the above entitled case and that the foregoing is a true and complete transcript of his stenographic notes thereof.

Jesse O. Carr

Subscribed and sworn to before me this 3rd day of November, 1902.

B.C. Jones
Notary Public.

◇◇◇◇◇

COPY.

DEPARTMENT OF THE INTERIOR,
Commissioner to the Five Civilized Tribes.

In the matter of the application for the enrollment, as citizens by intermarriage of the Cherokee Nation, of Frank Howard, et al.

DECISION.

THE RECORDS OF THIS OFFICE SHOW: That prior to October
31, 1902, applications were received by the Commission to the Five
Civilized Tribes for the enrollment, as citizens by intermarriage of the
Cherokee Nation, of the following named persons who are listed for
enrollment as citizens by intermarriage of the Cherokee Nation on the
Cherokee enrollment cards corresponding to the numbers following
their respective names, viz:

Frank Howard	281	Georgia A. Walker	4392
Julia A. Alberty	513	Mary A. Journeycake	4475
Angeline Oer	968	Pat Flanagan	4617
Nancy E. Twist	1028	Ethic Foster	4613
Samuel D. Harp	1556	Albert F. Johnson	4616
Marquis D. L. Dowell	1707	Alexander H. Knaggs	4617
Lindsey Wallace	2020	Jackson W. Drake	4654
Richard Southerlin	2058	James E. Burrows	4672
George W. Kirk	2273	William P. McClellan	4740
Caroline P. Waybourn	2510	Samuel A. Wells	5262
George W. Talbott	2892	Mary J. Thompson	5492
Thomas J. Jordan	2946	Jeremiah Y. Stokes	5543
Robert B. Neighbours	3002	John G. Butler	5639
James B. Smith	3483	Ora B. Downing	5699
Rachel Silverheel	3703	James W. McSpadden	5724
Frederick Fluke	3858	Jeremiah Springston	5773
David Stinger	4059	Hettie Holland	5799
Huldah Bennett	4265	Merriweather G. Reagan	5821
Amos V. Flint	4370	Bartley E. Scott	5831

(Copy of original document from case.)

143

Louvena Alberty	5891	Henry A. Frye	6664
Katie L. C. Duncan	5917	William B. Taylor	6761
William F. Roberts	5945	Sallie Runels	6764
Leonidas Dobson	5997	Thomas M. Bird	6939
James L. Guinn	6053	Eugene L. Bracken	7008
Dora Lowery	6073	Elizabeth Latta	7058
Mary E. King	6157	Stephen M. McDaniel	7068
Maggie Sevier	6198	Rebecca Miller	7135
Thomas Johnson	6262	George W. Ritchie	7293
Eliche Mathis	6278	Fannie E. Cummings	7550
Rosanna Wood	6337	Nancy Hicks	7837
Edward W. Rackleff	6342	John S. Skillman	9993
Lou McCoy	6417	Willis Davis	10019
William Sullivan	6419	Albert Shepard	10106
Kizzie Linder	6429	Charles F. McGinnis	10121
Josephine Rider	6438	Hugh Campbell	10144
Francis A. Meek	6522	Mary J. Glass	10229

THE RECORDS FURTHER SHOW: That the names of said persons appear upon the Cherokee authenticated roll of 1880; that they possess no right to enrollment as citizens of the Cherokee Nation other than by intermarriage, and that no one of said persons claims to have been married to a citizen by blood of the Cherokee Nation prior to November 1, 1875.

IT IS THEREFORE ORDERED AND ADJUDGED: That in accordance with the decision of the Supreme Court of the United States, dated November 5, 1906, in the cases of Daniel Red Bird et al. vs. the United States, Nos. 125, 126, 127 and 128, said applicants are not entitled, under the provisions of Section 21 of the Act of Congress approved June 28, 1898 (30 Stats., 495), to enrollment as citizens by intermarriage of the Cherokee Nation, and their applications for enrollment as such are accordingly denied.

SIGNED.   *Tams Bixby.*

COMMISSIONER

Dated at Muskogee, Indian Territory,

this   Jan. 10 1907

(Copy of original document from case.)

◇◇◇◇◇

C. F. B.   Cherokee 5492.

DEPARTMENT OF THE INTERIOR,
COMMISSION TO THE FIVE CIVILIZED TRIBES.
Muskogee, Indian Territory, January 11, 1907.

In the matter of the application for the enrollment of Mary J. Thompson as a citizen by intermarriage of the Cherokee Nation.

APPEARANCES:

Applicant appears in person.

Cherokee Nation represented by
W. W. Hastings, Attorney.

Mary J. Thompson being first duly sworn by B. P. Rasmus, Notary Public, testified as follows:

ON BEHALF OF COMMISSIONER.

Q   What is your name?   A   Mary J. Thompson.
Q   What is your age?   A   68.
Q   What is your post office address?
A   Chelsea.
Q   You are an applicant for enrollment as a citizen by intermarriage of the Cherokee Nation?
A   Yes sir.
Q   You have no Cherokee blood?   A   No sir.
Q   The only claim you make to the right to enrollment as a citizen of the Cherokee Nation is by virtue of your marriage to a citizen by blood?
A   Yes sir.
Q   What is the name of that citizen?
A   J. M. McNair.
Q   Is he living or dead?   A   He is dead.
Q   When were you married to him?   A   '65.
Q   Was he a recognized citizen of the Cherokee Nation at that time?
A   Yes sir.
Q   And living in the Cherokee country?
A   No, he was living in Eastern Texas. We were married in '65 and in the fall of '65 we came to the Choctaw Nation and in '66 we came to the Cherokee Nation.
A   He considered the Cherokee Nation his home?
A   Yes sir.
Q   Are you his first wife?   A   Yes sir.
Q   Was he your first husband?   A   My second.
Q   Was your former husband dead at the time of your marriage to J. M. McNair?
A   Yes sir.

Cherokee Intermarried White 1906
Volume VIII

Q   From the time of your marriage to your Cherokee husband in 1865, did you and he continuously live together as husband and wife until his death?
A   Yes sir.
Q   And live in the Cherokee Nation?
A   Yes sir.
Q   Since his death, have you re-married?
A   Yes sir; I married Martin Thompson, another Cherokee.
Q   When did you marry Martin Thompson?
A   '77 as well as I remember.
Q   Is he living at this time?   A   No sir.
Q   When did he die?   A   In '86.
Q   You and he lived together as man and wife until the time of his death?
A   Yes sir.
Q   Since his death, have you married again?
A   No sir.
Q   Your residence has been continuously in the Cherokee Nation since 1866?
A   Yes sir.

The applicant presents a certified copy of marriage license and certificate, showing that June 12, 1865, marriage license was issued in Rusk County, Texas, authorizing the marriage of John M. McNair and Mary Jane Brown, and that said parties were united in marriage on June 13, 1865, by John Adams, Minister of the Gospel. This instrument will be filed and made a part of the record in this case.

The applicant, Mary J. Thompson, is identified on the Cherokee authenticated tribal roll of 1880, Cooweescoowee District, No. 2927 The name of her deceased husband, Martin Thompson, appears on said roll immediately preceding the name of Mary J. Thompson.

James M. Keys being first duly sworn by B. P. Rasmus, Notary Public, testified as follows:

ON BEHALF OF COMMISSIONER.

Q   State your name, age and post office address.
A   James M. Keys; age 63 years; post office address, Pryor Creek, Indian Territory.
Q   Were you ever acquainted with a man by the name of John M. McNair who was a citizen by blood of the Cherokee Nation?
A   Yes sir.
Q   When did you first become acquainted with him?
A   In March, 1867. I knew of him,- knew the family at that time.
Q   He and his family were recognized citizens of the Cherokee Nation at the time you knew him?
A   Yes sir.
Q   Was he a married man?   A   Yes.

Q   Do you remember his wife's name?
A   Mary Jane McNair.
Q   Do you know when Mr. McNair died?
A   No sir: I don't remember just the year.
Q   He and his wife lived together as husband and wife in the Cherokee Nation from the time you knew them here as husband and wife, until the time of his death?
A   Yes sir.

The undersigned being first duly sworn states that as stenographer to the Commission to the Five Civilized Tribes, she recorded the testimony taken in this case and that the foregoing is a full, true and correct transcript of her stenographic notes thereof.

Myrtle Hill

Subscribed and sworn to before me this the 14th day of January, 1907.

John E. Tidwell
Notary Public.

◇◇◇◇◇

Cherokee
5492

Muskogee, Indian Territory, January 10, 1907.

Mary J. Thompson,
Chelsea, Indian Territory.

Dear Sir[sic]:

There is inclosed a copy of the decision of the Commissioner to the Five Civilized Tribes, dated January 10, 1907, rejecting, among others, the application for your enrollment as a citizen by intermarriage of the Cherokee Nation. The Commissioner's decision has this day been forwarded to the Secretary of the Interior for review. You will be advised of the Secretary's action as soon as this office is informed of same.

Respectfully,

Incl. Decn.   __B__   Commissioner.

◇◇◇◇◇

(COPY)

DEPARTMENT OF THE INTERIOR,
OFFICE OF INDIAN AFFAIRS,
WASHINGTON.

February 14, 1907.

The Honorable,
    The Secretary of the Interior.

Sir:

On January 19, 1907, the Office transmitted the decision of the Commissioner to the Five Civilized Tribes relative to applications for the enrollment of Frank Howard, et al, as citizens by intermarriage of the Cherokee Nation. The decision includes the applications of seventy-two persons found by the Commission to be not entitled to enrollment under the decision of the Supreme Court of the United States in the case of Daniel Red Bird, et al, against the United States.

It appears from the record in the case that the names of all the applicants are found on the authenticated 1880 roll of citizens of the Cherokee Nation, and the Office in transmitting the record did not consider this phase of the case. On January 31 the Department was requested to return the record in the case for further consideration by the Office. It was returned with Department letter of February 6, 1907, I.T.D. 1390.

With reference to the names of those applicants being on the 1880 roll Mr. Bixby says:

THE RECORDS FURTHER SHOW: That the names of said persons appear upon the Cherokee authenticated roll of 1880; that they possess no right to enrollment as citizens of the Cherokee Nation other than by intermarriage, and that no one of said persons claims to have been married to a citizen by blood of the Cherokee Nation prior to November 1, 1875.

As the applicants were not married to citizens by blood of the Cherokee Nation in accordance with the laws, usages and customs of the tribes prior to November 1, 1875, they are not entitled to enrollment, unless it be by virtue of their names being on the 1880 roll. By the provisions of section 21 of the Act of June 28, 1898 (30 Stat. L., 495), the roll of Cherokee citizens of 1880, not including freedmen, is confirmed, and the Commission is directed to enroll all persons whose names are found on that roll and their descendants born since the date of the roll. It is then provide that other rolls shall be examined and that the names of all persons found on the other rolls not placed thereon by fraud or without authority of law shall be enrolled.

Cherokee Intermarried White 1906
Volume VIII

The only question in the case seems to be whether a confirmation of this roll by Congress entitles a person whose name appears on said to[sic] roll to enrollment as a citizen of the Cherokee Nation who would not otherwise be entitled to such enrollment.

The Supreme Court in the case of Nofire vs. the United States (164 U.S., 657), said:

(Syllabus)
The fact that a marriage license has been issued carries with it a presumption that all statutory prerequisites thereto have been cimplied[sic] with, and one who claims to the contrary must affirmatively show the fact.
****

The evidence shows that the deceased sought, in his lifetime, to become a citizen of the Cherokee Nation, took all the steps he supposed necessary therefore, considered himself a citizen, and that the Cherokee Nation in his lifetime recognized him as a citizen and still asserts his citizenship.   Held, that, under these circumstances it must be adjudged that he was a citizen by adoption, and consequently that the jurisdiction over the offence charged is, by the laws of the United States and treaties with the Cherokee Nation, vested in the courts in of that Nation.

In the case of Daniel Red Bird; et al, vs. the United States the Supreme Court said:

The roll of 1880, made by the Cherokees, was a census roll, and its confirmation was not intended to create any rights which citizens of the Cherokee Nation had not before enjoyed, but merely to furnish the basis for making up the roll of citizens.   Section 21 was in reality a statement that no previous act of Congress was intended to confirm any other roll of the Cherokee Nation.
****

Section 31 of the Act of July 1, 1902, says that no person whose name does not appear on the roll made by the Commission to the Five Civilized Tribes "shall be entitled to in any manner participate in the distribution of the common property of the Cherokee tribe, and those whose names appear thereon shall participate in the manner set forth in this act."   In other words, the roll must be made up of citizens who under the laws of the Cherokee Nation were entitled to participation in the distribution of the common property of the Cherokee tribes.

The concluding words of section 21, "with such intermarried white persons as may be entitled to citizenship under Cherokee laws," emphatically indicate that Congress had the Indian citizen in mind in all that went before and limited enrollment of white persons to such as might be entitled to citizenship under Cherokee laws.

From the foregoing quotations it is evident that the Supreme Court makes a distinction between citizens having political rights only and those having all rights, including the right to share in the distribution of the land and other property of the

Cherokee Nation. This being true, it is evident that Congress did not intend that any persons should be given the right to share in the property of the Cherokee Nation simply because his name was on some roll of the nation that had been confirmed by Congressional action unless it is there as a full citizen and not as a citizen with political rights only.

The Office is of the opinion that the persons whose names appear in the record enclosed are not entitled to enrollment as citizens by intermarriage of the Cherokee Nation, and the approval of the Commissioner's adverse decision is recommended.

Very respectfully,

C. F. Larrabee,

GAW-GH   Acting Commissioner.

◇◇◇◇◇

D.C, 10668-1907.   DEPARTMENT OF THE INTERIOR,   LLB   JFJr
I.T.D. 3422-1907.
LRS   WASHINGTON/[sic]
Direct.

February 20, 1907.

Commissioner to the Five Civilized Tribes,
    Muskogee, Indian Territory.

Sir:

On February 14, 1907 (land 12493), the Indian Office transmitted your report dated January 10, 1907, in the matter of the application for the enrollment of Frank Howard and seventy-two others as citizens by intermarriage of the Cherokee Nation, together with your decision, adverse to said applicants.

The Indian Office concurs in your recommendation. A copy of its letter is inclosed.

It appears that the names of said persons appear upon the Cherokee authenticated roll of 1880 and that they possess no right to enrollment as citizens of the Cherokee Nation other than by intermarriage, and that no one of said persons claims to have been married to ea citizen by blood of the Cherokee Nation prior to November 1, 1875.

In view of the decision of the Supreme Court of the United States dated November 5, 1906, in the case of Daniel Red Bird et al. vs. the United States, it is considered that your decision, adverse to these persons, is correct, and it is hereby affirmed.

The papers in the case and a carbon copy hereof have been sent to the Indian Office.

Respectfully,

Thos Ryan.

First Assistant Secretary.

1 Inc and 3 to Ind. Of.

APMc
2-21-07.

◇◇◇◇◇

W.W.HASTINGS.
ATTORNEY.

OFFICE OF

H.M. VANCE.
SECRETARY.

Attorney for the Cherokee Nation,

MUSKOGEE, I. T.   February 21, 1907.

Commissioner to the Five Civilized Tribes,
    Muskogee, Indian Territory.

Sir:

I have examined the record in the matter of the application for the enrollment of Mary J. Thompson as a citizen by intermarriage of the Cherokee Nation. I do not desire to protest against the enrollment of this applicant as a citizen by intermarriage of the Cherokee Nation and I consent to her enrollment.

Respectfully,

W. W. Hastings
Attorney for the Cherokee Nation.

◇◇◇◇◇

Cherokee Intermarried White 1906
Volume VIII

Muskogee, Indian Territory, February 21, 1907.

The Honorable,
    Secretary of the Interior.

Sir:

    January 10, 1907 the Commissioner to the Five Civilized Tribes rendered his decision denying, among others, the application for the enrollment of Mary J. Thompson as a citizen by intermarriage of the Cherokee Nation. Said applicant is embraced in the case of Frank Howard, et al., transmitted January 10, 1907.

    The original record in this case shows Mary J. Thompson to have been married to her Cherokee husband in 1877. Subsequent proceedings were had in the case at the request of the applicant January 11, 1907, showing that said applicant, Mary J. Thompson claims the right to enrollment as a citizen by intermarriage of the Cherokee Nation by reason of a former marriage to a Cherokee citizen, which former marriage was not shown by the evidence received prior to the rendition of the decision in the case.

    The record shows that Mary J. Thompson, a white woman, was married in accordance with the laws of the State of Texas, June 13, 1865 to one John M. McNair, who was at the time of said marriage a recognized citizen by blood of the Cherokee Nation; that said John M. McNair was temporarily absent from the Cherokee Nation at the time of his said marriage, but removed thereto with his said wife in 1866 and continuously lived in said Nation until he time of his death. It is further shown that in 1877 the said Mary J. McNair was married to Martin Thompson, since deceased, who was at the time of said marriage a recognized citizen by blood of the Cherokee Nation, who is identified on the Cherokee authenticated tribal roll of 1880, Cooweescoowee district No. 2926 as a native Cherokee; that the said Martin Thompson and Mary J. Thompson resided together as husband and wife and continuously lived in the Cherokee Nation from the time of said marriage until the death of said Martin Thompson, which occurred in 1886; that after the death of said Martin Thompson the said Mary J. Thompson remained unmarried and continuously lived in the Cherokee Nation up to and including September 1, 1902. Said applicant is identified on the Cherokee authenticated tribal roll of 1880 and the Cherokee census roll of 1896 as an intermarried citizen of the Cherokee Nation.

    In view of the decision of the Supreme Court, dated November 5, 1906 in the cases of Daniel Red Bird, et al. vs the United States, Nos. 125, 126, 127 and 128, it is respectfully recommended that the Department reverse the decision of the Commissioner of January 10, 1907, as far as it relates to this applicant, and that the application for the enrollment of Mary J. Thompson as a citizen by intermarriage of the Cherokee Nation be granted. The record of proceedings had in the case is inclosed.

Respectfully,

Commissioner.

Through the Commissioner
of Indian Affairs.

ECM - GHC

◇◇◇◇◇

Muskogee, Indian Territory, February 22, 1907

Arthur F. McGarr,
Room 116 Department of the Interior.
Washington, D.C.

Dear Sir:

There are enclosed herewith copies of three letters addressed to the Department under dates of February 18 and 21, 1907, recommending that the Department rescind its decision of January 26, 1907, adverse to Joseph Reed, and reverse the Commissioner's decision of January 10, 1907, adverse to Mary J. Thompson and Louvena Alberty, applicants for enrollment as citizens by intermarriage of the Cherokee Nation, and that they be enrolled.

In the event the Department concurs in the Commissioner's recommendation in these cases, data from which schedules containing their names can be prepared is as follows:

Reed, Joseph,	51	M	
Alberty, Louvena	50	F	5891
Thompson, Mary J.	64	F	5492.

Respectfully,

Encl. B-37   Commissioner.

L M B

◇◇◇◇◇

153

SPECIAL

J.P.

DEPARTMENT OF THE INTERIOR,   LLB

W a s h i n g t o n .

I. T. D. 6054-1907.   March 1, 1907.
      6494- "
D.C. 12416-1907.
L R S
Direct.

Commissioner to the Five Civilized Tribes,
    Muskogee, Indian Territory.

Sir:

      There has been filed by Mr. A. F. McGarr, representing your office, a copy of your letter to the Department of the Interior February 21, 1907, in which you recommend that a decision rendered by you January 10, 1907, adverse to Mary J. Thompson, applicant for enrollment as a citizen by intermarriage of the Cherokee Nation in the case of Frank Howard et al., be rescinded, in view of Subsequent testimony submitted.

      It appears that the applicant was married in Texas to her first Cherokee husband, in 1865, a recognized and enrolled citizen by blood of the Cherokee Nation. This citizen was temporatily[sic] absent from the nation at the time of his marriage but removed thereto with his wife in 1866, and continued to live in the nation until the time of his death.

      Concurring in your recommendation, the decision of the Department in the case of Frank Howard et al., to which Mary J. Thompson was a party, is rescinded as to her, and you are authorized to enroll her as a citizen by intermarriage of the Cherokee Nation.

      Since the receipt of the copy of your letter, the Indian Office transmitted with its letter of February 28, 1907, your report and the supplemental testimony submitted therewith.

      The papers received with Indian Office letter have been returned, together with a carbon copy hereof.

                Respectfully,
                 (Signed) Jesse E Wilson
                    Assistant Secretary.

4 inc. to Ind. Of.
AFMc
3-2-07

◇◇◇◇◇

Cherokee 5492   COPY

Muskogee, Indian Territory, March 8, 1907.

Mary J. Thompson,
        Chelsea, Indian Territory.

Dear Madam:

You are hereby advised that the application for your enrollment as a citizen by intermarriage of the Cherokee Nation, was granted by the Secretary of the Interior, March 1, 1907.

Respectfully,

SIGNED *Jams Bixby*

RPI   Commissioner.

◇◇◇◇◇

Cherokee 5492   COPY

Muskogee, Indian Territory, March 8, 1907.

George E. McCulloch,
        Attorney for Mary J. Thompson,
                Vinita, Indian Territory.

Dear Sir:

You are hereby advised that the application for the enrollment of Mary J. Thompson as a citizen by intermarriage of the Cherokee Nation, was granted by the Secretary of the Interior March 1, 1907.

Respectfully,

SIGNED *Jams Bixby*

RPI   Commissioner.

◇◇◇◇◇

155

Cherokee 5492

COPY

Muskogee, Indian Territory, March 8, 1907.

W. W. Hastings,
        Attorney for the Cherokee Nation,
                Muskogee, Indian Territory.

Dear Sir:

      You are hereby advised that the application for the enrollment of Mary J. Thompson as a citizen by intermarriage of the Cherokee Nation, was granted by the Secretary of the Interior March 1, 1907.

      For your information, There is enclosed herewith a copy of Departmental letter referred to.

                          Respectfully,

                          SIGNED *Tams Bixby*
Enc I-10   Commissioner.

RPI

◇◇◇◇◇

Cherokee
I.W.

Muskogee, Indian Territory, April 16, 1907.

Mary J. Thompson,
        Chelsea, Indian Territory.

Dear Madam:

      Your marriage license and certificate filed in connection with your application for enrollment as a citizen by intermarriage of the Cherokee Nation is returned to you herewith, copies of the same being retained in the files of this office.

                          Respectfully,

Encl. W-25   Commissioner.
S.W.

Cherokee Intermarried White 1906
Volume VIII

Cher IW 235

◇◇◇◇◇

Department of the Interior,
Commission to the Five Civilized Tribes.
Tahlequah, I. T., November 27, 1900.

In the matter of the application of Cicero Johnson, for the enrollment of himself, wife and children as Cherokee citizens; he being sworn and examined by Commissioner T. B. Needles, testified as follows:

Q   What is your name?   A Cicero Johnson.
Q   What is your age?   A 57 years old.
Q   What is your postoffice address?   A Tahlequah.
Q   What district do you live in?   A Tahlequah.
Q   Are you a recognized citizen of the Cherokee Nation?   A Yes sir.
Q   By blood or intermarriage?   A By blood.
Q   What degree of blood do you claim?   A Always told me about 1/16.
Q   Who do you want to enroll?   A Myself and family.
Q   What is the name of your wife?   A Dovie.
Q   Is she a citizen by blood?   A No sir.
Q   White woman?   A White woman.
Q   When did you marry her?   A '67.
Q   How old is she?   A She's 49.
Q   What is the name of your oldest child at home and under 21?   A Allen.
Q   How old is Allen?   A 20 years.
Q   Next child?   A Mollie E.
Q   How old is she?   A 19 years old.
Q   Next one?   A Thomas, born in '83; 17 years old.
Q   Next?   A Alonzo, born in '86; 14 years old.
Q   Got any others?   A Henry, born in '88; 12 years old.
Bell, born in 1893; 7 years old.

1880 roll; page 445, #962, Cicero Johnson, Goingsnake.
1880 roll; page 445, #963, Davey[sic] Johnson,   "
1896 roll; page 1194, 1718, Cicero   "   Tahlequah.
1896 roll; page 1283, #136, Dovie   "   "
                    1194, #1719, Allen Johnson, Tahleqah[sic].
                    1194, #1720, Mollie   "
                    1194, #1721, Thomas   "
                    1194, #1722, Alonzo   "
                    1194, #1723, Henry   "
                    1194, #1724, Bell   "

Q   These children living with you at this tim[sic]?   A Yes sir.
Q   Always lived in the Cherokee Nation?   A No sir, as born in North Carolina.
Q   Been living here since 1880?   A Yes sir.

Q Your wife and you living together since your marriage? A Yes sir.
Q She's living now? A Yes sir.

Commissioner Needles-

The name of Cicero Johnson appears upon the authenticated roll of 1880 as well as the Census roll of 1896. The name of his wife Dovie, appears upon the authenticated roll of 1880 and the Census roll of 1896 as an intermarried citizen of the Cherokee Nation white. The name of his children, Allen, Mollie E., Thomas, Alonzo, Henry and Bell, appear upon the Census roll of 1896. All being duly identified according to page and number of the rolls, and having made satisfactory proof as to their residence, the said Cicero Johnson and children as enumerated herein, will be duly listed for enrollment as Cherokee citizens by blood; his wife, Dovie, as a Cherokee citizen by intermarriage.

E. G. Rothenberger, being duly sworn, states that as stenographer to the Commission to the Five Civilized Tribes, he reported correctly the testimony and proceedings in the above cause, and tat[sic] the foregoing is a full true and complete transcript of his stenographic notes in this case.

E.G. Rothenberger

Subscribed and sworn to before me this 28th day of November, 1900.

T B Needles
Commissioner.

◇◇◇◇◇

CHEROKEE-5728.

DEPARTMENT OF THE INTERIOR,
COMMISSIONER TO THE FIVE CIVILIZED TRIBES.
Muskogee, Indian Territory, January 5, 1907.

In the matter of making proof of the marriage of Dovie Johnson to her Cherokee husband, prior to November, 1875.

Dovie Johnson, being first duly sworn by John E. Tidwell, a Notary Public, testified as follows:

Commissioner:

Q. What is your name? A. Dovie Johnson.
Q. What is your afe[sic]? A. 58.

Q. What is your post office address?   A. Tahlequah.

Q. Do you claim rights as an intermarried citizen of the Cherokee Nation?   A. Yes sir.

Q. Through whom do you claim your intermarried rights?   A. Cicero Johnson.

Q. When were you married to Cicero Johnson?   A. In '67.

Q. Where?   A. In North Carolina.

Q. In 1867?   A. Yes sir.

Q. How long did you live in North Carolina after you were married to Cicero Johnson?
A. Seven years.

Q. Then where did you go?   A. To the Cherokee Nation.

Q. What time did you reach the Cherokee Nation?   A. In '73.

Q. When was your husband admitted to citizenship in the Cherokee Nation?
A. About a year after we came here.

Q. That would be in about '74?   A. Yes sir.

Q. Were you admitted by Act of Council or by a decree of the Court?
A. By the Council I reckon.

Q. Have you any documentary evidence showing that your husband was admitted to Cherokee citizenship in 1874?   A. No sir.

Q. Is he here today?   A. Yes sir.

Q. Were you ever married before you married Cicero Johnson?   A.   No sir.

Q. Was he ever married before he married you?   A. No sir.

Q. Have you lived together continuously as husband and wife since o867[sic]?
A. Yes sir.

Q. Are you living together now?   A. Yes sir.

(Commissioner -- Applicant is identified upon the 1880 Cherokee Roll, Going Snake District, opposite No. 963. Her husband, through whom she claims her right to enrollment, is identified upon said roll, said District, opposite No. 962. Her husband is also identified upon the final roll of citizens by blood of the Cherokee Nation, opposite No. 13746.)

Witness excused.

Cicero Johnson, being duly sworn by John E. Tidwell, a Notary Public, testified as follows:

COMMISSIONER:

Q. What is your name?   A. Cicero Johnson.

Q. What is your age?   A. Close to 64.

Q. What is your post office address?   A. Tahlequah.

Q. Do you know Dovie Johnson?   A. Yes sir.

Q. What relation are you to Dovie Johnson?   A. She is my wife.

Q. When were you married?   A. We were married in 1867.

Q. Where?   A. In Cherokee County, North Carolina.

Q. Were you ever married before you married your present wife?   A. No sir.

Q. Was she ever married before she married you?   A. Not that I know of.
Q. Have you lived together continuously since 1867?   A. Yes sir.
Q. How long did you stay in North Carolina after you were married?
A. We stayed there some 5 or 6 years.
Q. When did you come to the Cherokee Nation?   A. We came in 1872 I believe.
Q. When were you admitted to Cherokee citizenship after you got here?
A. I declare, I have forgotten about how long it was, but I think about a year or maybe a little over.
Q. Were you admitted by Act of Council or judgment of the Court? A. By the Court.
Q. What Court?   A. That Court that was held there -- the citizenship Court.
Q. What was the name of the Judge who admitted you? A. I will be-dogged if I remember.
Q. It will be necessary for you to furnish this office with a copy of the Act admitting you to citizenship in the Cherokee Nation before your wife can be enrolled?
A. Do you want me to bring witnesses?
Q. You might bring some witnesses, but you must show the Act admitting you?
A. I have a witness here now.
Q. What is his name?   A. Mr. Wallace.

Witness excused.

Martin Wallace, being duly sworn by John E. Tidwell, a Notary Public, testified as follows:

COMMISSIONER:

Q. What is your name?   A. Martin Wallace.
Q. What is your age?   A. 60.
Q. What is your post office address?   A. Tahlequah.
Q. Are you a citizen of the Cherokee Nation?   A. I am a white man -- an adopted citizen.
Q. How long have you lived in the Cherokee Nation? A. I come here in the fall of '71.
Q. Do you know Cicero Johnson?   A. Yes sir.
Q. Do you know anything about his admission to citizenship in the Cherokee Nation?
A. No, I wasn't present at anything of the kind, but he has always been considered a citizen.
Q. How long have you known him?   A. All my live.
Q. Did you know him in North Carolina?   A. Yes sir.
Q. Do you know when he came to the Cherokee Nation?   A. Yes sir.
Q. When was it?   A. If I remember right I think it was in the spring of '73.
Q. Do you know how soon he was admitted after he came to the Cherokee Nation?
A. No sir, I don't know exactly, but I don't think it was very long. I couldn't state the exact time.

Witness excused.

Cicero Johnson recalled.

COMMISSIONER:

Q. When was the first time you voted in the Cherokee elections, if you remember?
A. The first time I voted was just a little while back.
Q. When did you acquire your first property in the Cherokee Nation?
A. I got a place directly after I came here.
Q. How directly -- how soon after you came here?   A. About a year.

Witness excused.

Martin Wallace recalled.

COMMISSIONER:

Q. Were you present when Cicero Johnson and Dovie Johnson were married?
A. No sir.
Q. Do you know that they were married?   A. Well, I couldn't say that I know it, for I wasn't present, but I know they lived together as man and wife in North Carolina, and I heard my wife say that she was present at the wedding. I wasn't there.

Witness excused.

Eula Jeanes Branson, being sworn, states that she correctly reported the proceedings had in the above and foregoing, on the 5th. day of January, 1907.

Eula Jeanes Branson

Subscribed and sworn to before me, this the 7th. day of January, 1907.

Walter W. Chappell
Notary Public.

◇◇◇◇◇

C. F. B.   Cherokee 5728.

DEPARTMENT OF THE INTERIOR,
COMMISSION TO THE FIVE CIVILIZED TRIBES.
Muskogee, Indian Territory, January 14, 1907.

Supplemental proceedings in the matter of the application for the enrollment of Dovie Johnson as a citizen by intermarriage of the Cherokee Nation.

Adeline Ratlinggourd being first duly sworn by B. P. Rasmus, Notary Public, testified as follows:

Q   What is your name?   A   Adeline Ratlinggourd.
Q   What is your age?   A   56.
Q   What is your post office address?
A   Tahlequah.
Q   Are you acquainted with a person by the name of Dovie Johnson?
A   Yes sir.
Q   Are you related to her in any way?
A   Sister-in-law by marriage.
Q   She married a brother of your first husband?
A   Yes sir.
Q   What is his name?   A   Cicero Johnson.
Q   When was Cicero and Dovie Johnson married?
A   Cherokee County, North Carolina.
Q   When did they remove to the Cherokee Nation?
A   They came here in '73.
Q   Was Dovie Johnson, Cicero Johnson's first wife?
A   Yes sir.
Q   And he was her first husband?   A   Yes sir.
Q   Since their marriage have they continuously lived together as husband and wife?
A   Yes sir.
Q   You have lived since 1873 in the Cherokee Nation?
A   Yes sir.
Q   Did you witness their marriage?
A   But you have every reason to believe that they were married?
A   Yes sir.
Q   And you know of your own personal knowledge that they have lived together as husband and wife since 1867?
A   Yes sir.

The undersigned being first duly sworn states that as stenographer to the Commission to the Five Civilized Tribes, she recorded the testimony taken in this case and that the foregoing is a full, true and correct transcript of her stenographic notes thereof.

Myrtle Hill

Subscribed and sworn to before me this the 19th day of January, 1907.

John E. Tidwell
Notary Public.

◇◇◇◇◇

C.F.B.   Cherokee 5728.

DEPARTMENT OF THE INTERIOR,

COMMISSIONER TO THE FIVE CIVILIZED TRIBES.

In the matter of the application for the enrollment of DOVIE JOHNSON as a citizen by intermarriage of the Cherokee Nation.

D E C I S I O N

THE RECORDS OF THIS OFFICE SHOW: That at Tahlequah, Indian Territory, November 27, 1900, application was received by the Commission to the Five Civilized Tribes for the enrollment of Dovie Johnson as a citizen by intermarriage of the Cherokee Nation. Further proceedings in the matter of said application were had at Tahlequah, Indian Territory, October 22, 1902, February 17, 1905, and at Muskogee, Indian Territory, January 5 and 14, 1907.

THE EVIDENCE IN THIS CASE SHOWS: That the applicant herein, Dovie Johnson, a white woman, was married in the State of North Carolina in the year 1867 to one Cicero Johnson, who is identified on the Cherokee authenticated tribal roll of 1880, Going Snake District, Page 445, No. 962, as a native Cherokee, and whose name is included in the approved partial roll of citizens by blood of the Cherokee Nation, opposite No. 13746. It is further shown that the said Dovie Johnson neither claims nor possesses any right to enrollment as a citizen of the Cherokee Nation other than such right as she may have acquired by virtue of her marriage to the said Cicero Johnson; that the said Cicero Johnson was not at the time of said marriage a recognized citizen by blood of the Cherokee Nation, and did not become such until his admission to citizenship in said Nation by the duly constituted authorities thereof November 16, 1876. Said Dovie Johnson did not, therefore, marry a citizen by blood of the Cherokee Nation prior to November 1, 1875.

IT IS, THEREFORE, ORDERED AND ADJUDGED: That in accordance with the decision of the Supreme Court of the United States, dated November 5, 1906, in the cases of Daniel Red Bird et al. vs. the United States, Nos. 125, 126, 127, and 128, the said applicant, Dovie Johnson, is not entitled, under the provisions of Section 21, of the Act of Congress approved June 28, 1898 (30 Stats., 495), to enrollment as a citizen by intermarriage of the Cherokee Nation, and her application for enrollment as such is accordingly denied.

Tams Bixby
Commissioner.

Dated at Muskogee, Indian Territory,
this   FEB 2 1907

◇◇◇◇◇

Cherokee
 5728

Muskogee, Indian Territory, December 27, 1906.

Dovie Johnson,
    Tahlequah, Indian Territory.

Dear Madam:

November 6, 1906, the United States Supreme Court held that white persons who intermarried with Cherokee citizens according to Cherokee law prior to November 1, 1875, are entitled to enrollment and allotments of land as citizens of the Cherokee Nation.

You are advised that to properly determine your right to enrollment as a citizen by intermarriage of the Cherokee Nation, it will be necessary for you to appear before the Commissioner for the purpose of giving testimony as to the date of your marriage and whether or not your husband, by reason of your marriage to whom you claim the right to enrollment as a citizen by intermarriage of the Cherokee Nation, was a recognized Cherokee citizen at the time of your marriage to him.

You are therefore directed to appear before the Commissioner at Muskogee, Indian Territory, at 9 o'clock A. M., on Saturday, January 5, 1907, and give testimony as above indicated.

Respectfully,

S.W.   Acting Commissioner.

◇◇◇◇◇

COPY

DEPARTMENT OF THE INTERIOR,
Land   OFFICE OF INDIAN AFFAIRS,
12687-1907.   WASHINGTON.

February 25, 1907.

The Honorable,
     The Secretary of the Interior.

Sir:

There is enclosed a report from the Commissioner to the Five Civilized Tribes, dated February 2, 1907, transmitting the record relative to the application for enrollment of Dovie Johnson as a citizen by intermarriage of the Cherokee Nation. On February 2, 1907, the Commissioner held that the applicant was not entitled to enrollment.

The evidence shows that the applicant, Dovie Johnson, a white woman, was married in the State of North Carolina in the year 1867, to one Cicero Johnson, who is identified on the Cherokee authenticated tribal roll of 1880 as a native Cherokee and whose name is included in the approved partial roll of citizens by blood of the Cherokee Nation. The applicant claims no right to enrollment other than such as she acquired by virtue of her marriage to Cicero Johnson, who was not at the time of the marriage a recognized citizen by blood of the Cherokee Nation, and did not become such until his admission to citizenship in that nation by the duly constituted authorities on November 16, 1876. Therefore the applicant did not marry a citizen by blood of the Cherokee Nation prior to November 1, 1875.

Under the decision of the Supreme Court of the United States, dated November 6, 1906, the case of Daniel Red Bird, et al., vs. the United States, the applicant is not entitled to enrollment as a citizen by intermarriage of the Cherokee Nation.

It is therefore recommended that the decision of the Commissioner adverse to the applicant be approved.

Very respectfully,

C. F. Larrabee,

JPB-Y   Acting Commissioner.

◇◇◇◇◇

GAW

DEPARTMENT OF THE INTERIOR
OFFICE OF INDIAN AFFAIRS,
WASHINGTON.

I.T.   May 11, 1907.
Reference in body
of letter.

Subject: Motions for
review in certain Chero-
kee citizenship cases.

The Honorable,
        The Secretary of the Interior.

Sir:

        There are inclosed herewith motions filed by W. W. Hastings, National Attorney for the Cherokee Nation, praying for review and rehearing of Departmental decisions authorizing the enrollment as citizens by intermarriage of the Cherokee Nation of the following persons:

42893-1907,	Jacob A. Bartles,
42895- "	Osburn J. Byrd,
42886- "	Amanda Beck,
42894- "	Sarah F. Gage,
42892- "	Phirena Harris,
42888- "	Daniel Harmon,
42891- "	Emma L. Ironsides,
42896- "	Sarah A. Jordan
42881- "	Dovie Johnson,
42882- "	Andrew H. Norwood,
42887- "	Stacy E. Perry,
42885- "	Martha Randolph, now Kernan
42893- "	John W. Smith
42884- "	John J. Smith,
42890- "	Robert H. F. Thompson,
42889- "	Hattie Wright,
42883- "	Nancy Wolfe,
42880- "	E. A. Welch.

166

In view of the provisions of section 2 of the act of April 26, 1906 (34 Stat. L., 137), providing that the rolls of the Five Civilized Tribes shall be fully completed on or before March 4, 1907, there appears to be no authority in law for the reconsideration of any enrollment cases at this time, and it is recommended that the office be authorized to advise Mr. Hastings that the motions for review herewith transmitted cannot be considered.

Very respectfully,

C. F. Larrabee

Acting Commissioner.

AJW-FHE.

May 13, 1907.

Approved.

Thos Ryan

First Assistant Secretary.

◇◇◇◇◇

I. T. References
in body of letter.

DEPARTMENT OF THE INTERIOR,
OFFICE OF INDIAN AFFAIRS,
WASHINGTON.   GAW

May 15, 1907.

Commissioner to the Five Civilized Tribes,
Muskogee, Indian Territory.

Sir:

There is inclosed copy of Office letter of May 11, 1907, approved by the Department on May 13, 1907, recommending that motions filed by W. W. Hastings, National Attorney for the Cherokee Nation, praying for a review and rehearing of Departmental decisions authorizing the enrollment of the following persons as citizens by intermarriage of the Cherokee Nation, be denied, in view of the fact that there appears to be no authority in law at this time for the reconsideration of any enrollment case.

Cherokee Intermarried White 1906
Volume VIII

42893-1907	Jacob A. Bartles
42895- "	Osburn J. Byrd
42886- "	Amanda Beck
42894- "	Sarah F. Gage
42892- "	Phirena Harris
42888- "	Daniel Harmon
42891- "	Emma L. Ironsides
42896- "	Sarah A. Jordan
42881- "	Dovie Johnson
42882- "	Andrew H. Norwood
42887- "	Stacy E. Perry
42885- "	Martha Randolph, now Kernan
42893- "	John W. Smith
42884- "	John J. Smith
42890- "	Robert H. F. Thompson
42889- "	Hattie Wright
42883- "	Nancy Wolfe
42880- "	E. A. Welch

You are requested to advise the interested parties, including Mr. Hastings, of the Department's action.

Very respectfully,
C. F. Larrabee
Acting Commissioner.

AJW-FHE.

◇◇◇◇◇

Cherokee
235

Muskogee, Indian Territory, May 25, 1907.

Dovie Johnson,
Tahlequah, Indian Territory.

Dear Madam:

You are hereby advised that on May 13, 1907, the Secretary of the Interior denied a motion filed by the Attorney for the Cherokee Nation, for a review of its decision authorizing your enrollment as a citizen by intermarriage of the Cherokee Nation.

For you information, there is enclosed herewith a copy of Departmental decision referred to.

Respectfully,

Commissioner.

Encl. C-10
LMC

Cher IW 236

◇◇◇◇◇

Department of the Interior,
Commission to the Five Civilized Tribes,
Bartlesville, I. T. October, 11th 19oo[sic].

In the matter of the application of Andrew H. Norwood for the enrollment of himself as a Cherokee Citizen. He being sworn by Commissioner Breckinridge testified as follows-

Q How old are you?   A. 40.
Q What us[sic] your pot[sic] office?   A. Dewey.
Q What district. A Cooweescoowee.
Q. Who is it that you want put on the roll?   A. Myself.
Q Do you apply as a Cherokee?   A. Adopted white.
Q Have you your marriage license and certificate?   A. Yes sir.
Q. Are you on the roll of 1880?   A. Yes sir all of them since 1874 I guess.
Q. You were married in 1872 to Miss Alice R. Goard were you?   A. Yes sir.
Q Was she a Cherokee woman?   A. Yes sir.
Q Is she living?   A. She died ten months after our marriage.
Q Did you marry again?   A. Yes sir, in 1879 I married a Deleware[sic] woman, named Susan Love.
Q Is she dead?   A. Died in 1894.
Q Did you live with her from the time of your marriage until her death and in the Cherokee Nation?   A. Yes sir.
Q Have you married since her death?   A. No sir.
1880 roll, page 150, No 2123, A. H. Norwood, Cooweescoowee, Adopted white
1896 "   "   317   " 741. Andy H. Norwood,   "
The applicant is identified on the roll of 1880 and 1896 as an adopted white. On the roll of 1880 there is identified with him his Deleware[sic] wife who died in 1894. They lived together from the time of their marriage in 1897 until her death and he has not re-married since her death. He has lived continuously in the Cherokee Nation since his enrollment in 1880 and he will now be listed for enrollment as a Cherokee by intermarriage.

Chas. von Weise being sworn states that as stenographer to the Commission to the Five Civilized Tribes he reported in full all proceedings had in the above entitled cause and that the foregoing is a true, correct and full transcript of his stenographic notes in said proceedings.

Chas von Weise

Cherokee Intermarried White 1906
Volume VIII

Subscribed and sworn to before me this the 11th of October, 1900.

C R Breckinridge

Commissioner.

◇◇◇◇◇

COOWEESCOOWEE.
Statement of Applicant Taken Under Oath.

CHEROKEE BY BLOOD AND ADOPTION.

$\overline{49}$

Date **OCT 11 1900** 1900.

Name **Andrew H. Norwood** **Dewey I.T.**

District **COOWEESCOOWEE.** Year **1880** Page **155** No. **2123**

Citizen by blood **No** Mother's citizenship

Intermarried citizen **Yes** **C- Act.**

Married under what law Date of marriage **(1872) (1879)**

License Certificate

Wife's name

District Year Page No.

Citizen by blood Mother's citizenship

Intermarried citizen

Married under what law Date of marriage

License Certificate

Names of Children:

Dist. Year Page No. Age

Dist. Year Page No. Age

Dist. Year Page No. Age

Dist. Year Page No. Age

Dist. Year Page No. Age

On 1880 Roll as A. H. Norwood.

#434

◇◇◇◇◇

R.

DEPARTMENT OF THE INTERIOR.
Commission to the Five Civilized Tribes.
Muskogee, Indian Territory, September 29th, 1902.

In the matter of the application of Andrew H Norwood for the enrollment of himself as a citizen by intermarriage of the Cherokee Nation.

Supplemental to #4321.

Appearances:

Applicant appears in person.
Cherokee Nation by J. C. Starr.

ANDREW H. NORWOOD, being duly sworn, testified as follows:--
Examination by the Commission.

Q. What is your name, Mr. Norwood?   A. Andrew Norwood, or A. H.

Q. Is there an "H" in your name?   A. Yes, sir; Andrew Henry.

Q. What is your age at this time?   A. 52; will be in a short time.

Q. What is your post office?   A. Dewey, I. T.

Q. Are you the same Andrew Norwood that applied to the Commission in 1900 for enrollment as an intermarried citizen of the Cherokee Nation citizen?   A. I am.

Q. What is your wife's name?   A. Susie. I have been married twice. I first married in 1872 and my wife died in 1873. In 1878 I married again and she died in 1894

Q. You were first married in 1872?   A. Yes, sir.

Q. What was that wife's name?   A. Alice R. Gourd.

Q. Were you married under a Cherokee license?   A. Yes, sir.

Q. She was a Cherokee by blood, was she?   A. Yes, sir.

Q. When did you say she died?   A. 1873; lived only 10 months.

Q. Did you live with her from the time you were married until her death?   A. Yes, sir.

Q. You married again?   A. Yes, sir.

Q. Who did you marry the second time?   A. Susie Love.

Q. She was a citizen by blood?   A. Yes, sir. She was a Delaware. Adopted Cherokee.

Q. You lived with this second wife from the time you were married until her death?
A. Yes, sir.

Q. Have you married since her death?   A. I have not.

Q. You were never separated from either one of your wifes[sic] during their lifetime?
A. No, sir; not in any manner.

Q. You were single on the first of September, 1902, were you?   A. Yes, sir.

Q. How long have you lived in the Cherokee Nation?   A. Since '70.

Q. You lived in the Nation all the time for the last 30 years?
A. Yes, sir; never lived any where else since I come here in '70.

Jesse O. Carr, being first duly sworn, states that as stenographer to the Commission to the Five Civilized Tribes he reported the above entitled case and that the foregoing is a true and correct transcript of his stenographic notes thereof.

Jesse O. Carr

Subscribed and sworn to before me this 4th day of October, 1902.

BC Jones
Notary Public.

◇◇◇◇◇

Recommendation of
A. H. Norwood for Marriage
License.

COPY

We the undersigned citizens of the District of Tahlequah and Cherokee Nation would most respectfully recommend A. H. Norwoo[sic] a white man and citizen of the U. S. as a moral and industrious man and one calculated to make a good and useful citizen of the Cherokee Nation, such being his desire, under the law "Regulating Intermarriage With White Men."

Signers Names----

1.   Arch Miller
2   W. H. Turner
3   S. H. Coldin
4   Richard Halfbreed
5   Henry Barnes
6   Jno. L. Adair
7   Nathaniel Fish

◇◇◇◇◇

Certificate of Record

United States of America,   (
    Indian Territory   )   ss.
    Northern District   (

I, Chas. A. Davidson, Clerk of the United States Court in the Northern District, Indian Territory, do hereby certify that the instrument hereto attached is a true and correct copy of License that was filed in my office the 13 day of October 1904, at M[sic], and duly recorded in Book "C" Marriage Rccord[sic] Page 335.

Witness my hand and seal of said Court at Muskogee, in said Territory this 9 day of January A. D., 1907.
SEAL   Chas. A. Davidson, Clerk

By E. B. Davidson, Deputy.

◇◇◇◇◇

MARRIAGE LICENSE

United States of America,   (
)
    Indian Territory.   (ss.   No. 457
)
    Northern District   (

To Any Person Authorized By Law To Solemnize Marriage, Greeting:
    You are Hereby Commanded to Solemnize the Rite and publish the Banns of Matrimony between Mr. Andrew H. Norwood of Dewey, in the Indian Territory, aged 53 years and Ida M. Woodard of Dewey, in the Indian Territory, age 43 years, according to law, and do you officially sign and return this License to the parties therein named.
(SEal)[sic] Witness my hand and official seal at Vinita, Indian Territory, this 28th day of September A. D. 1904.

                                    Chas. A. Davidson
By E. B. Davidson Deputy.   Clerk of U. S. Court.

CERTIFICATE OF MARRIAGE

United States of America,   (

)

   Indian Territory.   (ss.

)

Northern District   (

I, C. B. Larrabee, a Minister of the Gospel Do Hereby Certify that on the 2nd day of October, A. D. 1904, I did duly and according to law as commanded in the foregoing License solemnize the Rite and publish the Banns of Matrimony between the parties thereing[sic] named.

    Witness my hand this 2 day of October A. D. 1904.

    My Credentials are recorded in the officer[sic] of the Clerk of the United States Court, Indian Territory Northern District, Book A., Page 75.

C. B. Larrabee
A minister of the Gospel

◇◇◇◇◇

IW 236

License of Marriage
and Certificate
granted A. H. Norwood
Recorded
W. H. Turner.

Cherokee Nation   :   Know all persons by these <u>Presents,</u> that I, W. H. Turner,
Tahlequah Dist.   :   Clerk of the District Court for the District of Tahlequah,
Cherokee Nation, <u>do</u> by virtue of the authority in me vested by law, hereby grant Mr. A. H. Norwood a White man, and Citizen of the United States, a License to marry Miss Alice R. Gourd, a Cherokee. He, the said A. H. Norwood, having complied with the law of the Cherokee Nation, "Regulating Intermarriage with Whitemen."

    Therefore--Any Ordained Minister of the Gospel, or Judge of any of the Courts of the Cherokee Nation, are hereby authorized to solemnize the rite of matrimony in accordance with the above License between the parties above named and return this Instrument with your Certificate of service attached for record.

Cherokee Intermarried White 1906
Volume VIII

Given under my hand Officially December 20th, 1872.

W. H. Turner, Clk.
D. C. F. Dist. C. N.

Dec. 25th, 1872, I do certify that I have this day solemnized the rites of matrimony between the above named parties at the residenc[sic]

W. H. Turner

T. K. B. McSpadden

P. C Tahlequah Circuit In. Miss Court.

◇◇◇◇◇

DEPARTMENT OF THE INTERIOR
COMMISSIONER TO THE FIVE CIVILIZED TRIBES
MUSKOGEE, IND. TER.
JAN. 4, 1907.

IN THE MATTER OF THE APPLICATION FOR THE
ENROLLMENT OF ANDREW H. NORWOOD AS A
CITIZEN BY INTERMARRIAGE OF THE CHEROKEE
NATION.

CENSUS CARD   NO. 4321.

ANDREW H. NORWOOD BEING FIRST DULY SWORN TESTIFIED AS FOLLOWS

EXAMINATION BY THE COMMISSIONER:

Q   What is your name.[sic] A Andrew H. Norwood
Q   How old are you. A Fifty seven.
Q   What is your post office address. A Dewey.
Q   Do you claim to be a citizen by intermarriage of the Cherokee Nation. A Yes sir.
Q   Thru whom do you claim your intermarried rights. A By marriage with a Cherokee.
Q   What is her name. A Alice R. Gourd.
Q   Is she living at the present time. A No sir
Q   How long has she been dead?   A Been dead about thirty two years.
Q   When were you married to Alice R. Gourd. A In 1872 December 25th.

175

Cherokee Intermarried White 1906
Volume VIII

Q Were you married under Cherokee license.

A Yes sir

Q Have you that license with you. A Mr. Rossen[sic] has it; he told me a minute ago he had it; they were left with him several days ago.

Q Have you ever been married a second time since the death of your wife Alice R. Gourd. I married a citizen subsequent to that, a Delaware; registered Delware[sic].

Q What is her name. A Susie Norwood.

Q Are you living with her a[sic] the present time. A No she died ten or twelve years ago and then two years ago I married

Q Have you lived in the Cherokee Nation continuously since you married your first wife Alice R. Gourd in 1872

A Yes sir

Q Were you ever married before you married Alice R. Gourd.

A No sir.

Q Did you live with Alice R. Gourd continuously from the date of your marriage to her up to the time of her death.

A Yes sir, and I'm on every roll I think since '74.

The applicant is identified on the 1880 Cherokee Roll Coo- wee- scoo-wee District opposite No. 2123.

Q Was Alice R. Gourd a recognized citizen by blood of the Cherokee Nation at the time you married her in 1872.

A She was.

Q Was she born in the Cherokee Nation. A Yes sir.

Q Her parents were citizens by blood of the Cherokee Nation

A Yes sir.

The applicant offers in evidence the petition signed by seven signers for his license filed with the District filed with the District Court of Tahlequah District in the Cherokee Nation; also the license issued to him on the 20th day of December, 1872 to marry Alice R. Gourd and the certificate of T. K. B. McSpadden showing that he performed the marriage ceremony between the applicant and Alice R. Gourd on December 25 1872.

ooOoo

Clara Mitchell Wood being first duly sworn upon her oath states that as stenographer to the Commission to the Five Civilized Tribes she reported the above and foregoing proceedings and that this is a correct transcript of her stenographic notes.

Clara Mitchell Wood

Subscribed and sworn to before me this 8th day of December 1907.

(No Signature given.)
Notary Public.

Cherokee Intermarried White 1906
Volume VIII

◇◇◇◇◇

C.F.B.   Cherokee 4321.

DEPARTMENT OF THE INTERIOR,

COMMISSIONER TO THE FIVE CIVILIZED TRIBES.

In the matter of the application for the enrollment of ANDREW H. NORWOOD as a citizen by intermarriage of the Cherokee Nation.

D E C I S I O N

THE RECORDS OF THIS OFFICE SHOW: That at Bartlesville, Indian Territory, October 11, 1900, Andrew H. Norwood appeared before the Commission to the Five Civilized Tribes, and made application for the enrollment of himself as a citizen by intermarriage of the Cherokee Nation. Further proceedings in the matter of said application were had at Muskogee, Indian Territory, September 29, 1902, and January 4, 1907.

THE EVIDENCE IN THIS CASE SHOWS: That the applicant herein, Andrew H. Norwood, who is identified on the Cherokee authenticated tribal roll of 1880, and the Cherokee census roll of 1896, as an adopted white citizen of the Cherokee Nation, was married in accordance with Cherokee law December 25, 1872, to his wife, Alice R. Norwood, nee Gourd, since deceased, who was at the time of said marriage a recognized citizen by blood of the Cherokee Nation; that from the time of said marriage until the death of the said Alcie R. Norwood, which occurred in the year 1873, the said Andrew H. and Alice R. Norwood resided together as husband and wife; that after the death of the said Alice R. Norwood the said Andrew H. Norwood married, in the year 1879, one Susan Love, since deceased, a Delaware woman, who is identified on the Cherokee authenticated tribal roll of 1880, Cooweescoowee District, No. 2124, as an adopted Delaware.

In view of the foregoing, it is considered that the applicant herein, Andrew H. Norwood, forfeited, by his marriage in the year 1879 to Susan Love, who was a person not of Cherokee blood, the right to citizenship in the Cherokee Nation acquired by his marriage to Alice R. Gourd December 24, 1872.

IT IS, THEREFORE, ORDERED AND ADJUDGED: That in accordance with the decision of the Supreme Court of the United States, dated November 5, 1906, in the cases of Daniel Red Bird et al. vs. the United States, Nos. 125, 126, 127, and 128, the said applicant, Andrew H. Norwood, is not entitled, under the provisions of Section 21, of the Act of Congress approved June 28, 1898 (30 Stats. 495), to enrollment as a citizen by intermarriage of the Cherokee Nation, and his application for enrollment as such is accordingly denied.

Cherokee Intermarried White 1906
Volume VIII

Tams Bixby

Commissioner.

Dated at Muskogee, Indian Territory,
this   FEB 2 1907

◇◇◇◇◇

Cherokee
4321

Muskogee, Indian Territory, December 27, 1906.

Andrew H. Norwood,
     Dewey, Indian Territory.

Dear Sir:

November 6, 1906, the United States Supreme Court held that white persons who intermarried with Cherokee citizens according to Cherokee law prior to November 1, 1875, are entitled to enrollment and allotments of land as citizens of the Cherokee Nation.

You are advised that to properly determine your right to enrollment as a citizen by intermarriage of the Cherokee Nation, it will be necessary for you to appear before the Commissioner for the purpose of giving testimony as to the date of your marriage and whether or not your wife, by reason of your marriage to whom you claim the right to enrollment as a citizen of the Cherokee Nation, was a recognized citizen of the Cherokee Nation at the time of your marriage to her, and whether or not you were married to her in accordance with Cherokee laws.

You are, therefore, directed to appear before the Commissioner at Muskogee, Indian Territory, at 9 o'clock A. M., on Friday, January 4, 1907, and give testimony as above indicated.

Respectfully,

J.M.H.   Acting Commissioner.

◇◇◇◇◇

Cherokee 4321

Muskogee, Indian Territory, February 2, 1907.

Andrew H. Norwood,
Dewey, Indian Territory.

Dear Sir:

There is enclosed herewith a copy of the decision of the Commissioner to the Five Civilized Tribes, dated February 2, 1907, rejecting your application for enrollment as a citizen by intermarriage of the Cherokee Nation.

The decision, together with the record of proceedings had in the case, has this day been transmitted to the Secretary of the Interior for his review and decision. The action of the Secretary will be made known to you as soon as this office is in receipt of same.

Respectfully,

Encl. H-82   Commissioner.
JJH
M
Register.

◇◇◇◇◇

Cherokee 4321

Muskogee, Indian Territory, February 2, 1907.

W. W. Hastings,
Attorney for the Cherokee Nation,
Muskogee, Indian Territory.

Dear Sir:

There is enclosed herewith a copy of the decision of the Commissioner to the Five Civilized Tribes, dated February 2, 1907, rejecting the application for the enrollment of Andrew H. Norwood as a citizen by intermarriage of the Cherokee Nation.

The decision, together with the record of proceedings had in the case, has this day been transmitted to the Secretary of the Interior for his review and decision. The action of the Secretary will be made known to you as soon as this office is in receipt of same.

Respectfully,

Encl. H-83   Commissioner.
  JMH

◇◇◇◇◇

Muskogee, Indian Territory, February 2, 1907.

The Honorable,
  The Secretary of the Interior.

Sir:

There is transmitted herewith the record of proceedings had in the matter of the application for the enrollment of Andrew H. Norwood as a citizen by intermarriage of the Cherokee Nation, together with the decision of the Commissioner, dated February 2, 1907, denying said application.

Respectfully,

Encl. H-84   Commissioner.
  JMH

Through the Commissioner
of Indian Affairs.

◇◇◇◇◇

(COPY)

DEPARTMENT OF THE INTERIOR,
Land   OFFICE OF INDIAN AFFAIRS,
12678-1907.   WASHINGTON.

February 25, 1907.

The Honorable,
  The Secretary of the Interior.

Sir:

There is enclosed a report from the Commissioner to the Five Civilized Tribes, dated February 2, 1907, transmitting the record relative to the application for enrollment of Andrew H. Norwood as a citizen by intermarriage of the Cherokee Nation. On February 2, 1907, the Commissioner held that the applicant was not entitled to enrollment.

Cherokee Intermarried White 1906
Volume VIII

The evidence shows that the applicant, Andrew H. Norwood, who is identified on the Cherokee authenticated tribal roll of 1880, and the Cherokee census roll of 1896, as an adopted white citizen of the Cherokee Nation, was married in accordance with Cherokee law on December 25, 1872, to Alice R. Norwood, nee Gourd, since deceased, who was at the time of her marriage a recognized citizen by blood of the Cherokee Nation; that from the time of the marriage until the death of Alice R. Norwood, which occurred in the year 1873, the couple lived together as husband and wife. After the death of Alice R. Norwood, the applicant, Andrew H. Norwood, married, in the year 1879, one Susan Love, since deceased, a Delaware woman who is identified on the Cherokee authenticated tribal roll of 1880, as an adopted Delaware.

In view of the evidence, it is considered that Andrew H. Norwood, the applicant, forfeited by his marriage, in the year 1879, to Susan Love, who was a person not of Cherokee blood, the right to citizenship in the Cherokee Nation, acquired by his marriage to Alice R. Gourd on December 24, 1872.

Under the decision of the Supreme Court of the United States dated November 5, 1906, the case of Daniel Red Bird, et al. vs. the United States, the applicant is not entitled to enrollment as a citizen by intermarriage of the Cherokee Nation.

It is therefore recommended that the decision of the Commissioner adverse to the applicant be approved.

Very respectfully,

C. F. Larrabee,

JPB-GH   Acting Commissioner.

◇◇◇◇◇

Muskogee, Indian Territory, February 27, 1907.

The Honorable,
    The Secretary of the Interior.

Sir:

On February 2, 1907, this office transmitted to the Department the record in the matter of the application of Andrew H. Norwood as a citizen by intermarriage of the Cherokee Nation, together with a decision denying such application. Said decision reads in part:

"That the applicant herein, Andrew H. Norwood, who is identified on the Cherokee authenticated tribal roll of 1880, and the Cherokee census roll of 1896, as an adopted white citizen of the Cherokee Nation, was married in accordance with Cherokee law December 25, 1872, to his wife, Alice R. Norwood, nee Gourd, since deceased, who was at the time of said marriage a recognized citizen by blood of the Cherokee Nation; that from the time of said marriage until the death of the said Alice R. Norwood, which occurred in the year 1873, the said Andrew H. and Alice R. Norwood resided together as husband and wife; that after the death of the said Alice R. Norwood the said Andrew H. Norwood married, in the year 1879, one Susan Love, since deceased, a Delaware woman, who is identified on the Cherokee authenticated tribal roll of 1880, Cooweescoowee District, No. 2124, as an adopted Delaware.

In view of the foregoing, it is considered that the applicant herein, Andrew H. Norwood, forfeited, by his marriage in the year 1879 to Susan Love, who was a person not of Cherokee blood, the right to citizenship in the Cherokee Nation acquired by his marriage to Alice R. Gourd December 25, 1872."

On February 9, 1907, a brief was filed in this office by Hutchings, Murphey & German and Zevely, Givens & Smith as attorneys for said applicant, in which it was contended that the decision of this office was wrong and should be reconsidered. This brief showed no service upon the attorneys for the Cherokee Nation but subsequent, and on February 27, 1907, service of the same was acknowledged as of the latter date.

The attorneys for the Cherokee Nation have informed this office that they do not care to file any reply brief in this matter.

In the brief on behalf of applicant in which this office was asked to reconsider its decision of February 2, 1907, it is contended that the language of Section 666 of the laws of the Cherokee Nation (Compilation, 1892), which Section became effective in its present form November 1, 1875, and which is as follows:

"Sec. 74. Should any man or woman, a citizen of the United States, or of any foreign country, become a citizen of the Cherokee Nation by intermarriage, and be left a widow or widower by the decease of the Cherokee wife or husband, such surviving widow or widower shall continue to enjoy the rights of citizenship, unless he or she shall marry a white man or woman, or person (as the case may be), having no rights of Cherokee citizenship by blood; in that case all of his or her rights acquired under the provisions of this Act shall cease."

did not evidence an intention to provide for a forfeiture of citizenship by a white man who had already acquired a right to citizenship by intermarriage by a subsequent marriage to a Delaware or Shawnee after November 1, 1875.

In the great amount of enrollment work which it has been necessary to perform in this office during the past month, it has been impracticable to give this matter earlier attention, or to devote to it such attention as it perhaps deserves. It is noted, however, that one of the premises, if not the main premise, upon which the argument of applicant's attorneys is based, is that in <u>1875</u> the Cherokee Nation provided for intermarriage of white men with Delawares and Shawnees so as to confer the same citizenship rights upon the white man so married as he would obtain by marriage to a Cherokee by blood. Such contention appears in the first paragraph on page 3 of said brief and practically all of the remaining argument of the brief is based upon that statement.

The act of 1875 contains, so far as this office has been able to discover, no provision for intermarriage with Delawares or Shawnees. Such provision apparently first appears in printed form in the Compilation of 1881 in which it is indicated that the act of 1875 wa amended to provide for intermarriage with Delawares and Shawnees on December 10, 1880, which was subsequent to the marriage of the applicant in this case to his second wife who was a Delaware. If this is true it certainly cannot be contended that the fact that in the act of December 10, 1880 provision was made for intermarriage with Delawares and Shawnees can throw any light upon the intent with which the language of Section 666, already quoted, was used.

The degree of the Court of Claims in the Case of Daniel Red Bird, et al, vs. Cherokee Nation is as follows:

"It is by the court ordered, adjudged, and decreed that such white persons residing in the Cherokee Nation as became Cherokee citizens under Cherokee laws by intermarriage with <u>Cherokees by blood</u> prior to the 1st day of November, 1875, are equally interested in and have equal per capita rights with Cherokee Indians by blood in the lands constituting the public domain of the Cherokee Nation, and are entitled to be enrolled for that purpose, but such intermarried whites acquired no rights and have no interest or share in any funds belonging to the Cherokee Nation except where such funds were derived by lease, sale, or otherwise from the lands of the Cherokee Nation conveyed to it by the United States by the patent of December, 1838; and that the rights and privileges of those white citizens who intermarried with Cherokee citizens subsequent to the 1st day of November, 1875, do not extend to the right of soil or interest in any of the vested funds of the Cherokee Nation, and such intermarried persons are not entitled to share in the allotment of the lands or in the distribution of any of the funds belonging to said nation, and are not entitled to be enrolled for such purpose; that those white persons who intermarried with Delaware or Shawnee citizens of the Cherokee Nation either prior or subsequent to November 1, 1875, and those who intermarried with <u>Cherokees by blood</u> and subsequently being left a widow or widower by the death of the Cherokee wife or husband, intermarried <u>with persons not of Cherokee blood,</u> and those white men who having married Cherokee women and subsequently abandoned their Cherokee wives have no part or share in the Cherokee property, and are not entitled to participate in the allotment of the lands or in the distribution of the funds of the Cherokee Nation or people, and are not entitled to be enrolled for such purpose."

Said decree, afterwards affirmed in toto by the Supreme Court, was a final judgment which is binding on this office and the Department. So far as can be determined from the decree itself, the words "persons not of Cherokee blood" as used in the last passage underscored, in the said quotation, are employed to designate all persons not included by the phrase "Cherokees by blood" as they appear in the two first passages underscored in said quotation. There is, of course, no doubt that the latter phrase was used to designate Cherokees who were possessed of citizenship in the Cherokee Nation by virtue of Cherokee blood.

While the contentions of the attorneys for applicant seem to be largely based on a mistaken premise and the Court of Claims in its decree has apparently construed Section 666, already quoted, contrary to the claims of the applicant, the questions in this case are, nevertheless, not free from doubt and difficulty. This office is, however, not convinced that its decision of February 2, 1907, is incorrect and declines to reconsider such decision or recommend that the Department not concur therein.

Said brief, however, is forwarded herewith for consideration by the Department.

Respectfully,

Enc.L.K.P.-1   Commissioner.
Through the Commissioner of Indian Affairs.

◇◇◇◇◇

COPY

Y.P.
FHE

DEPARTMENT OF THE INTERIOR
WASHINGTON.

I.T.D.   4896, 4996
             5060-1907   February 28, 1907.

L R S
DIRECT

Commissioner to the Five Civilized Tribes,
     Muskogee, Indian Territory.

Sir:

Your decisions in the following Cherokee citizenship cases adverse to the applicants are hereby affirmed, viz:

Title of case.	Date of your letter of transmittal
Janie Landrum et al.,	January 10, 1907
Andrew H. Norwood (Intermarried)	February 2, 1907
Dovie Johnson (Intermarried)	February 2, 1907.

Copies of Indian Office letters submitting your reports and recommending that the decisions be affirmed, are inclosed.

A copy hereof and the papers in the above mentioned cases have been sent to the Indian Office.

Respectfully,

3 inc. and 6 for Ind. Of.   (Signed)   JESSE E. WILSON
                                                           Assistant Secretary.

A. F. Mc.

3-1-07

◇◇◇◇◇

(COPY)

DEPARTMENT OF THE INTERIOR,

Land
21164-1907   OFFICE OF INDIAN AFFAIRS,

WASHINGTON.

March 4, 1907.

The Honorable,
    The Secretary of the Interior.

Sir:

Attention is invited to Departmental letter of February 28, 1907 (I.T.D. 4896, 4996, and 5060-1907) and the records received therewith are returned.

The record in the case of Jennie Landrum, et al., shows that her name appears upon the authenticated roll of the Cherokee Nation as an intermarried citizen of the Cherokee Nation white; that in the case of Andrew H. Norwood, the record shows that his name is on said roll as an intermarried citizen of the Cherokee Nation white; and the record in the case of Dovie Johnson shows that her name appears on the authenticated tribal roll of 1880. (See the Commission's decision of March 2, 1903.)

It is believed by this Office that under the opinion of the Attorney General of February 26, 1907, the applicants are entitled to enrollment.

Very respectfully,
C. F. LARRABEE,

GAW:LM   Acting Commissioner.

◇◇◇◇◇

D.C. 13390-1907   SPECIAL   JFJr

DEPARTMENT OF THE INTERIOR,
WASHINGTON.

I.T.D. 8000-1907.   March 4, 1907.
LRS
DIRECT.

Commissioner to the Five Civilized Tribes,
    Muskogee, Indian Territory.

Sir:

On March 4, 1907 (Land 21164), the Indian Office returned your report, dated January 10, 1907, in the matter of the application for the enrollment of Janie Landrum, et al.

It appears that on February 28, 1907, the Department rendered a decision in this case concurring in your decision.

The Indian Office returned this case and recommends that under the opinion of the Attorney General of February 26, 1907, the applicants are entitled to enrollment.

It appears that the case of the husband of this applicant, Louis W. Landrum, as a citizen by intermarriage of the Cherokee Nation has been heretofore disposed of and that the other applicants are included in a partial roll of citizens by blood of the Choctaw Nation opposite Nos. 16044, 16045 and 16046, respectively.

In view of their enrollment in the Choctaw Nation, the applicants are clearly not entitled to enrolment[sic] in the Cherokee Nation and the Department finds no reason for receding from its former decision, to which it accordingly adheres.

The papers in the case, together with a carbon copy hereof, have been sent to the Indian Office.

Respectfully,

(Signed) Jesse E. Wilson,

2 inc. to Ind. Of.   Acting Secretary.

AFMc
3-4-07

◇◇◇◇◇

Cherokee
4321

Muskogee, Indian Territory, March 11, 1907

Andrew H. Norwood,
      Dewey, Indian Territory.

Dear Sir:

There is enclosed for your information a copy of Departmental decision of February 28, 1907, affirming the decision of the Commissioner to the Five Civilized Tribes dated February 2, 1907, rejecting your application for enrollment as a citizen by intermarriage of the Cherokee Nation. There is also enclosed copy of Departmental decision of March 4, 1907, rescinding its said decision of February 28, 1907, and granting your application for enrollment as a citizen by intermarriage of the Cherokee Nation.

Respectfully,

Encl. B-22   Commissioner.

◇◇◇◇◇

Cherokee
4321.

Muskogee, Indian Territory, March 11, 1907

William T. Hutchings,
    Attorney for Andrew H. Norwood,
        Muskogee, Indian Territory.

Dear Sir:

There is enclosed for your information a copy of Departmental decision of February 28, 1907, affirming the decision of the Commissioner to the Five Civilized Tribes dated February 2, 1907, rejecting the application for the enrollment of Andrew H. Norwood, as a citizen by intermarriage of the Cherokee Nation. There is also enclosed copy of Departmental decision of March 4, 1907, rescinding its said decision of February 28, 1907, and granting his application for enrollment as a citizen by intermarriage of the Cherokee Nation.

Respectfully,

Encl. B-23   Commissioner.

<><><><><>

Cherokee
4321

Muskogee, Indian Territory, March 11, 1907

W. W. Hastings,
    Attorney for the Cherokee Nation,
        Muskogee, Indian Territory.

Dear Sir:

There is enclosed for your information a copy of Departmental decision of February 28, 1907, affirming the decision of the Commissioner to the Five Civilized Tribes dated February 2, 1907, rejecting the application for the enrollment of Andrew H. Norwood, as a citizen by intermarriage of the Cherokee Nation. There is also enclosed copy of Departmental decision of March 4, 1907, rescinding its said decision of February 28, 1907, and granting his application for enrollment as a citizen by intermarriage of the Cherokee Nation.

Respectfully,

Encl. B-24   Commissioner.

<><><><><>

GAW

DEPARTMENT OF THE INTERIOR
OFFICE OF INDIAN AFFAIRS,
WASHINGTON.

May 11, 1907.

I.T.
Reference in body
of letter.

Subject: Motions for
review in certain Chero-
kee citizenship cases.

The Honorable,
The Secretary of the Interior.

Sir:

There are inclosed herewith motions filed by W. W. Hastings, National Attorney for the Cherokee Nation, praying for review and rehearing of Departmental decisions authorizing the enrollment as citizens by intermarriage of the Cherokee Nation of the following persons:

42893-1907,	Jacob A. Bartles,
42895- "	Osburn J. Byrd,
42886- "	Amanda Beck,
42894- "	Sarah F. Gage,
42892- "	Phirena Harris,
42888- "	Daniel Harmon,
42891- "	Emma L. Ironsides,
42896- "	Sarah A. Jordan
42881- "	Dovie Johnson,
42882- "	Andrew H. Norwood,
42887- "	Stacy E. Perry,
42885- "	Martha Randolph, now Kernan
42893- "	John W. Smith
42884- "	John J. Smith,
42890- "	Robert H. F. Thompson,
42889- "	Hattie Wright,
42883- "	Nancy Wolfe,
42880- "	E. A. Welch.

In view of the provisions of section 2 of the act of April 26, 1906 (34 Stat. L., 137), providing that the rolls of the Five Civilized Tribes shall be fully completed on or before March 4, 1907, there appears to be no authority in law for the reconsideration of any enrollment cases at this time, and it is recommended that the office be authorized to advise Mr. Hastings that the motions for review herewith transmitted cannot be considered.

Very respectfully,

C. F. Larrabee

Acting Commissioner.

AJW-FHE.

May 13, 1907.

Approved.

Thos Ryan

First Assistant Secretary.

◇◇◇◇◇

DEPARTMENT OF THE INTERIOR,
I.T. References   OFFICE OF INDIAN AFFAIRS?[sic]   GAW
in body of letter.   WASHINGTON.

May 15, 1907.

Commissioner to the Five Civilized Tribes,
    Muskogee, Indian Territory.

Sir:

There is inclosed copy of Office letter of May 11, 1907, approved by the Department on May 13, 1907, recommending that motions filed by W. W. Hastings, National Attorney for the Cherokee Nation, praying for a review and rehearing of Departmental decisions authorizing the enrollment of the following persons as citizens by intermarriage of the Cherokee Nation, be denied, in view of the fact that there appears to be no authority in law at this time for the reconsideration of any enrollment case.

42893-1907	Jacob A. Bartles
42895- "	Osburn J. Byrd
42886- "	Amanda Beck

42894-	"	Sarah F. Gage
42892-	"	Phirena Harris
42888-	"	Daniel Harmon
42891-	"	Emma L. Ironsides
42896-	"	Sarah A. Jordan
42881-	"	Dovie Johnson
42882-	"	Andrew H. Norwood
42887-	"	Stacy E. Perry
42885-	"	Martha Randolph, now Kernan
42893-	"	John W. Smith
42884-	"	John J. Smith
42890-	"	Robert H. F. Thompson
42889-	"	Hattie Wright
42883-	"	Nancy Wolfe
42880-	"	E. A. Welch

You are requested to advise the interested parties, including Mr. Hastings, of the Department's action.

Very respectfully,
C. F. Larrabee
Acting Commissioner.

AJW-FHE.

◇◇◇◇◇

Cherokee
I.W. 236.

Muskogee, Indian Territory, May 25, 1907.

Andrew H. Norwood,
Dewey, Indian Territory.

Dear Sir:

You are hereby advised that on May 13, 1907, the Secretary of the Interior denied a motion filed by the Attorney for the Cherokee Nation, for a review of its decision authorizing your enrollment as a citizen by intermarriage of the Cherokee Nation.

Respectfully,

Commissioner.

LMC

◇◇◇◇◇

Cherokee
I.W. 236.

Muskogee, Indian Territory, May 25, 1907.

W. T. Hutchings,
    Attorney for Andrew H. Norwood,
      Muskogee, Indian Territory.

Dear Sir:

    You are hereby advised that on May 13, 1907, the Secretary of the Interior denied a motion filed by the Attorney for the Cherokee Nation, for a review of its decision authorizing the enrollment of Andrew H. Norwood, as a citizen by intermarriage of the Cherokee Nation.

    For your information, there is enclosed herewith a copy of Departmental decision referred to.

Respectfully,

Commissioner.

Encl. C-11
  LMC

◇◇◇◇◇

Cherokee
  253 et al.

Muskogee, Indian Territory, May 25, 1907.

W. W. Hastings,
    Attorney for the Cherokee Nation,
      Muskogee, Indian Territory.

Dear Sir:

    You are hereby advised that on May 13, 1907, the Secretary of the Interior denied the motion filed by you for a review of its decision authorizing the enrollment of Jacob A. Bartles, et al., as citizens by intermarriage of the Cherokee Nation.

    For your information, there is enclosed herewith a copy of Departmental decision referred to.

Respectfully,

Commissioner.

Encl. C-20
  LMC

Cherokee Intermarried White 1906
Volume VIII

Cher IW 237

◇◇◇◇◇

COPY

Cherokees by blood and intermarriage:

Department of the Interior,
Commission to the Five Civilized Tribes,
Vinita, I.T., May 14, 1901.

In the matter of the application of James Wright for the enrollment of himself, wife and five children as Cherokee citizens, his wife by intermarriage and himself and children by blood; being sworn and examined by Commissioner Needles, he testified as follows:

Simon R. Walkingstick, Interpreter:

Q   What is your name ?   [sic] James Wright.
Q   How old is he ?   A Says over 50 years old.
Q   What is her post-office?   A South-west City, Missouri.
Q   What district?   A Delaware District.
Q   Is he a Full-blood Cherokee?   A Yes sir.
Q   Who does he want to enroll besides himself?   A Himself, wife and about seven children.
Q   What is his wife's name?   A Hattie.
Q   How old is Hattie?   A About 47.
Q   Is she a full-blood?   A No, I think she is a white woman.
Q   What are the names of his children under 21?   A Sarah is the first one, 15 years old; Thomas is next, nine or ten years old, don't know exactly; Josie is the next one, eight years old.
"[sic] She a girl?   A Yes sir. Annie is the next one, five years old. Lizzie is the next one, three years old; that's all.

> 1880 authenticated roll of citizens of the Cherokee Nation examined and applicants identified thereon as follows:
> page 339 #2960 James Wright, Delaware District
> page 339 #2961 Hattie Wright, Delaware District.

> 1896 census roll of citizens of the Cherokee Nation examined and applicants identified thereon as follows:
> page 556 #3517 James Wright, Delaware District.
> page 593 #561 Hattie Wright, Delaware District;
> page 556 #3520 Sarah Wright, Delaware District;
> 1896 roll page 556 #3521 Thomas Wright, Delaware District;
> page 556 #3522 Josie Wright, Delaware District;
> page 556 #3523 Annie Wright, Delaware District.

Q   Has he got any paper made out for Lizzie?   A No sir
Q   Are these children all living at this time?   A Yes sir.
Q   Has he always lived in the Cherokee Nation himself?   A Yes sir.
"   Him and his wife been living together since they were married?
A   Yes sir.
Q   Is his present wife, Hattie, the mother of these children?
A   Yes sir.

> Commissioner Needles: James Wright applies for the enrollment of himself and his wife, Hattie and five children, to-wit; Sarah, Thomas, Josie, Annie and Lizzie;   said applicant and his wife Hattie are duly identified upon the authenticated roll of 1880 and on the census roll of 1896; he as a full-blood Indian and she as an intermarried citizen of the Cherokee Nation white;   the names of his children, Sarah, Thomas, Josie and Annie are found upon the census roll of 1896; they are all duly identified according to page and number of roll; he makes satisfactory proof as to residence, consequently said James Wright, and his children enumerated herein will be listed for enrollment as Cherokee citizens by blood, and his wife, Hattie will be listed for enrollment as a Cherokee citizen by intermarriage; the name is his child, Lizzie, does not appear upon the census roll of 1896 consequently, it will be necessary for him to file with this Commission satisfactory proof of its birth.

-------------___--------------

M.D. Green, being first duly sworn, states that as stenographer to the Commission to the Five Civilized Tribes he correctly recorded the testimony and proceedings in this case and the foregoing is a true and complete transcript of his stenographic notes thereof.

(Signed) M.D. Green

Subscribed and sworn to before me this May 14, 1901.

(Signed) C.N[sic]. Breckinridge
Commissioner.

◇◇◇◇◇

JOR.
Cher. 7482.

Department of the Interior,
Commission to the Five Civilized Tribes.
Tahlequah, I. T., October 27, 1902.

SUPPLEMENTAL TESTIMONY in the matter of the application for the enrollment of HATTIE WRIGHT as a citizen by intermarriage of the Cherokee Nation.

Cherokee Intermarried White 1906
Volume VIII

HATTIE WRIGHT, being first duly sworn, and being examined, testified as follows:

BY COMMISSION: What is your name?   A Harriet Wright. Some calls me Hattie, but I always sign it Harriet.

Q Is your name Harriet or Hattie?   A For a short name they call me Hattie.

Q Did your husband make application for your enrollment?   A Yes sir

Q He gae[sic] your name as Hattie. Do you want to be enroled[sic] as Hattie or Harriet?
A It don't make any difference with me. They call me Hattie, and I would just as soon be called Hattie.

Q Do you want to be enrolled under your name of Hattie?   A He has got it that way, and I reckon might just let it go that way.

Q How old are you?   A I am about forty-seven, as well as I can remember.

Q What is your post office address?   A Grove.

Q You are a white woman, are you?   A Yes sir.

Q Has application been made for your enrollment as a citizen by intermarriage of the Cherokee Nation?   A Yes sir.

Q What is the name of your husband?   A James Wright.

Q Is he living?   A Yes sir.

Q Is he a Cherokee by blood?   A Yes sir.

Q Do you claim your right to enrollment by reason of your marriage to him? A Yes sir.

Q When were you and he married?   A We have been married about twenty-nine years.

Q Does your name appear upon the roll of 1880?   A Yes sir.

Q With his?   A Yes sir.

Q Were you ever married before you married him?   A No sir.

Q Was he ever married before he married you?   A Yes sir.

Q What was the name of his first wife?   A Awy Muskrat.

Q Is she living?   A No sir.

Q Was she living when you were married?   A No sir.

Q Is that the only time you were ever married?   A Yes sir.

Q He is your first husband, and you are his second wife?   A Yes sir

Q Have you and he lived together continuously since your marriage?   A Yes sir.

Q Were you living together on the 1st day of September, 1902?   A Yes sir.

Q Never been separated at all?   A No sir.

Q Have you resided in the Cherokee Nation continuously since you married him about twenty-nine years ago?   A Yes sir, lived together ever since. we[sic] were married, never been parted.

Q Have you lived in the Cherokee Nation continuously?   A Yes sir, that is all I know. I don't know anything but the Cherokee Nation.

Q How long has your husband resided in the Cherokee Nation? A All his life, I reckon.

Q Born and raised here and lived here continuously all his life?   A Yes sir.

Q Have either of you been outside the Cherokee Nation for any purpose within the past five years?   A No sir.

Q You have how many minor children that application was made for?   A Five.

Q Are all of these children living at this time? A Yes sir.

Q You had no children die since you were enrolled?   A No sir.

This testimony will be filed with and made a part of the record in the matter of the application for the enrollment of Hattie Wright as a citizen by intermarriage of the Cherokee Nation, Cherokee straight card field No. 7482.

Wm. Hutchinson, being first duly sworn, states that as stenographer to the Commission to the Five Civilized Tribes he correctly recorded the testimony and proceedings in this case, and that the foregoing is a true and complete transcript of the stenographic notes thereof.

Wm Hutchinson

Subscribed and sworn to before me this 13th day of November, 1902.

BC Jones
Notary Public.

◇◇◇◇◇

COPY

FCM

DEPARTMENT OF THE INTERIOR
COMMISSIONER TO THE FIVE CIVILIZED TRIBES.
Muskogee, Indian Territory,
February 20, 1907.
Cherokee 7482.

In the matter of the application for the enrollment of Hattie Wright as a citizen by intermarriage of the Cherokee Nation.

(Applicant appeared in person.
APPEARANCES: (Cherokee Nation represented by W. W. Hastings.
(Commissioner.

HATTIE WRIGHT, being duly sworn by Walter Chappel[sic], a Notary Public, testified as follows:

ON BEHALF OF THE COMMISSIONER:

Q   What is your name?
A   Hattie Wright.

196

Q   What is your age?

A   Well, I haven't got any education and I can't tell you exactly my age, I think I was about six years old when the war first begun; it is pretty hard to tell, I have no education.

Q   Mrs. Wright, you appear here to-day for the purpose of giving testimony relative to your right to enrollment as a citizen by intermarriage of the Cherokee Nation?

A   Yes.

Q   Are you a white woman, Mrs. Wright?

A   Yes sir.

Q   What was the name of your father?

A   Hall was his name, I don't remember my father; my father was gone before I can remember him.

Q   What was the name of you[sic] mother?

A   Annie Walker.

Q   Then she was married to a white man before she married her Cherokee husband Walker?

A   I guess so.

Q   What is the name of the husband through whom you claim you[sic] right to be enrolled as a citizen of the Cherokee Nation?

A   James Wright.

Q   Is he a Cherokee by blood?

A   Yes sir.

Q   Is he a full blood?

A   Yes sir.

Q   When were you married to James Walker[sic]?

A   Well, it has been about 32 years ago.

Q   About 32 years ago?

A   Yes sir, as good as I can remember.

Q   You don't remember what month you were married in?

A   No sir, I don't remember.

Q   Was it in the winter?

A   It was between Christmas and New Years[sic], about the last of December, I think.

Q   In about the last of December 32 years ago you were married?

A   Yes sir.

Q   Have you any children, Mrs. Wright?

A   Yes, sir.

Q   How many?

A   Eight living.

Q   What is the name of your oldest child?

A   Ailcy Wright.

Q   Do you remember when she was born, Mrs. Wright?

A   No, I cannot remember that.

Q   How long after you were married?

A   About two years, I believe.

Q   About two years?

A   Yes.

Cherokee Intermarried White 1906
Volume VIII

Examination by W. W. Hastings, attorney for Cherokee Nation:

Q   About how old is Ailcy now?
A   I can't just exactly tell you; I can tell you just the way I counted it she would be thirty years old the 27th of next month, I may be mistaken, though.
Q   The 27th of next month?
A   Yes sir, March, I can't say exactly, we lost her age, we had it down but I lost it, it is pretty hard for anyone without any education to tell all these things.
Q   Now then, your best judgment is that you had been married about two years when Ailcy was born?
A   Yes sir.
Q   She was your oldest child by your husband James Walker[sic]?
A   Yes sir, the oldest one living.
Q   Did you have one child born before Ailcy was born?
A   Yes sir, the oldest one died.
Q   Did it die while it was an infant?
A   Yes sir, it died when it was about three weeks old.
Q   Then Ailcy was born only about two years from your marriage?
A   Yes sir.
Q   And you think Ailcy was born in March?
A   Yes sir, the 27th of March, I couldn't tell you exactly, I am just a guessing at it.
Q   Then she may not be thirty years old in March?
A   Why, no, I couldn't tell, I am just a guessing at it.
Q   You are just guessing at it?
Q[sic] Yes sir.
Q   Now where were you and him married?
A   Where were we.
Q   Yes
A   There on Honey Creek.
Q   Who married you?
A   Ben Hilderbrand.
Q   Is he living?
A   No sir, he is dead.
Q   Is he that preacher that used to preach near Beaty's?
A   Yes sir.
Q   Was he a preacher that early?
A   No sir, we were married by what they call old Cherokee laws, and after the new laws come in we were lawfully married by Mr. Hilderbrand.
Q   When were you lawfully married?
A   I couldn't tell you that exactly.
Q   About how long ago?
A   About eight or nine years ago.
Q   You never were married by a preacher until 8 or 9 years ago?
A   No sir.
Q   In other words you took up together and lived together before Ailcy was born?
A   Yes sir.

Q   And you were married by a preacher eight or nine years ago?
A   Yes sir.
Q   Did you get a license from the United States Court eight or nine years ago?
A   I don't know, I don't know anything about a license or nothing about it at all.
Q   Where were you married?
A   Over on Honey Creek at home.
Q   Where was Ben Hilderbrand then living?
A   Living on Pawoaw[sic].
Q   That is out west there?
A   Yes sir, he goes down in there preaching.
Q   He didn't commence preaching until ten or fifteen years ago?
A   I guess not, I don't remember.
Q   The first time that you were lawfully married by a preacher to Jim Wright through whom you claim citizenship, was eight or nine years ago?
A   Yes sir.
Q   And that was by Ben Hilderbrand?
A   Yes sir.
Q   And he was a regular preacher?
A   Yes sir.
Q   And before that time you and Jim just lived together and these children were born to you?
A   Yes sir.

ON BEHALF OF THE COMMISSIONER:

1880 examined, Page 339, Delaware District, opposite No. 2961, Hattie Wright, adopted white, 19 years of age; opposite No. 2962 Ailcy Wright, native Cherokee, two years of age.

WITNESS EXCUSED.

JOE FOX, being duly sworn by Walter Chappel[sic], a Notary Public, testified as follows:

ON BEHALF OF THE COMMISSIONER:

Q   What is your name?
A   Joe Fox
Q   What is your age?
A   Let's see---be 61 in next month.
Q   What is your postoffice address?
A   Grove.
Q   Mr. Fox, you appear here to-day for the purpose of giving testimony relative to the right of Hattie Wright to enrollment as a citizen by intermarriage of the Cherokee Nation?
A   Yes sir.

Q   Is she a white woman?
A   Well, been adopted.
Q   She is a white woman?
A   Yes sir, she is white.
Q   How long have you been acquainted with her?
A   Well, she come up before the war.
Q   Are you acquainted with her husbank[sic]?
A   Oh, yes.
Q   What is his name?
A   Jim Wright.
Q   Is he a Cherokee by blood?
A   Yes sir, a full blood.
Q   Mr. Fox, do you remember when these people were married?
A   The way I know it, it must be about 32 years ago.
Q   Thirty-two years ago?
A   Yes sir, near as I know, just about that.
Q   What time in the year were they married?
A   I believe somewhere in January, I think.
Q   January, Thirty-two years ago?
A   Yes, 32 years ago, or close in there.
Q   Since their marriage have they continuously resided together as husband and wife and remained in the Cherokee Nation?
A   Ye sir.
Q   Never been separated?
A   No.
Q   Were they married by a minister?
A   Yes sir, a preacher.

By W. W. Hastings, attorney for the Cherokee Nation:

Q   What preacher married them?
A   It was Hilderbrand.
Q   Ben Hilderbrand?
A   Yes sir.
Q   How far do you live from where they were married?
A   Why about two miles.
Q   About two miles?
A   Yes.
Q   Were you over there when they were married?
A   Yes, I was there.
Q   And you witnessed their marriage?
A   I wasn't a witness no sir.
Q   That is, you saw them married?
A   Yes sir.
Q   You saw Ben Hilderbrand marry them?
A   Yes sir.

Q   That was about thirty-two years ago?
A   Yes.
Q   How many children did they have when Ben Hilderbrand married them, any?
A   No.
Q   What kind of a house were they living in?
A   Just a little old log house.
Q   Whose house was it?
A   Jim Wright's.
Q   Where was this woman living at this time?
A   She used to stay with her mother before she married Jim Wright.
Q   Did she go over to Jim Wright's house to get married?
A   Yes sir.
Q   I want to know at whose house they were married?
A   They were married right down at the Quah-la-tah place.
Q   Who was living there?
A   Quah -la-tah.
Q   They were married at Quah -la-tah's house?
A   Yes sir.
Q   Who was living there at the time they were married?
A   Quah -la-tah.
Q   How long has Quah -la-tah been dead?
A   I couldn't tell you.
Q   Now, you know Ben Hilderbrand was not a preacher 32 years ago, he used to live right next to me?
A   I don't know.
Q   You know he wasn't a preacher 32 years ago?
A   He had been preaching.
Q   Well, was he a preacher 32 years ago.
A   He was preaching I was informed for some time, I don't know how long he been preaching.
Q   Where was Ben Hilderbrand living when he married these people?
A   I couldn't tell you where abouts, I used to know.
Q   Where was Quah-la-tah living, down there by old man Milton's on Honey Creek?
A   Yes sir.
Q   There was where he was living, was it?
A   Yes sir, where Nan Muskrat used to live.
Q   And you were there and saw them married, were you?
A   Yes sir.
Q   About 32 years ago?
A   Yes sir.
Q   What makes you remember it was in January?
A   Well, the way we talked about it, me and Jim Wright decided it was.
Q   You and him got to talking about it between youselves[sic], when it was?
A   Yes sir, and couldn't tell just hardly exactly just when it was.
Q   Well, not say, Joe, this woman was on the stand just now and she has already been examined and she gave some testimoney[sic] and she swore that Ben Hilderbrand

married them about eight or nine years ago, and she swore that she was not married to him 32 years ago and that they took up and lived together and that Ben Hilderbrand didn't marry them until eight or nine years ago; and you been on the stand and you are swearing that Ben Hilderbrand married them 32 years ago, now how are you going to account for her statement as I have told you she has testified in the record?

A   Well, I know that Ben did marry them.

Q   She stated that they were not married by Ben Hilderbrand until eight or nine years ago, and she said they lived together a number of years before this marriage by the preacher, now are you going to deny that?

A   Well - - - - - (witness mumbles something unintelligible).

Q   Are you going to deny that they lived together a long time before Ben Hilderbrand married them?

A   They were married, that's all.

Q   Don't you know that they lived together a long time before Ben Hilderbrand married them?

A   I expect they did.

Q   Why don't you tell it then?

A   Well, I know he was married to her.

Q   Yes, but you are telling that he married her thirty-two years ago, now I want to know the truth; about how many years ago did this preacher marry them, you are a preacher now, you ought to be more careful?

A   Just about to forget that.

Q   Now since you come to remember you know they had lived together a long time before they were married by the preacher?

A   Yes.

Q   And they had some children?

A   Yes sir.

Q   Before they were married?

A   Yes sir, they got eight.

Q   I don't want to excit[sic] you I want to know the truth, tell me the truth about it?

A   I expect they lived together a while anyhow.

Q   Did they live together a while before they were married?

A   Yes.

Q   Did they have some children before they were married?

A   Yes sir.

Q   How many children now, did they have before they were married?

A   Somewhere two, or three, or four, I guess.

Q   Well, now since you come to think about it, how many years ago do you think it was that Ben Hilderbrand married them?

A   Well, I - - - somewhere along ten years, somewhere along there.

Q   About ten years ago?

A   Yes sir.

WITNESS EXCUSED.

Cherokee Intermarried White 1906
Volume VIII

SARAH MORGAN, being duly sworn by Walter Chappell, a Notary Public, testified as follows:

ON BEHALF OF THE COMMISSIONER:

Q   What is your name?
A   Sarah Morgan.
Q   Your age?
A   I guess my age is about 71 or 72.
Q   What is your postoffice addres[sic], Mrs. Morgan?
A   Grove.
Q   Mrs. Morgan, you appear here to-day for the purpose of giving testimony relative to the right of Hattie Wright as a citizen by intermarriage of the Cherokee Nation?
A   Yes sir.
Q   Is she a white woman?
A   Well, I cant[sic] tell you that, what kind of blood she has got.
Q   She has always been regarded as a white woman, has she?
A   Yes sir.
Q   What is the name of her husband?
A   Jim Wright.
Q   Is he a Cherokee?
A   Yes sir.
Q   How long have you known them?
A   Well, I have known Jim Wright and his wife about 32 or 32 years.
Q   You remember when they were married?
A   I don't know anything about that, I know they were living together.
Q   About how long ago has it been since you first know them?
A   About thirty-one or two years ago, somewhere along there.
Q   How do you account for it being about thirty-one or two years ago?
A   I know by studying and thinking these things over.
Q   What time in the year did you become acquainted with them?
A   I don't know.
Q   Don't you know whether it was in the winter or the summer?
A   I don't know, I didn't think that was necessary.
Q   If you didn't keep time as to anything, how do you know it has been thirty-one years ago?
A   I just know, that's all.
Q   Have you any idea how old Hattie Wright is?
A   No, I don't know, she must be somewhere in forty or fifty-one, somewhere along there, I don't know exactly.
Q   Did they have any children when you first became acquainted with them?
A   No sir.
Q   Didn't have any at all?
A   No sir.
Q   How long after you became acquainted with them before they had any children?
A   About a year, I think.

Q   Then you became acquainted with them about 31 years ago and it was about a year after you became acquainted with them before they had any children?

A   Well, I think it was that long.

Q   Since you became acquainted with them have they continuously resided together as man and wife and resided in the Cherokee Nation?

A   Yes sir.

WITNESS EXCUSED.

Mabelle Cohenour, stenographer to the Commissioner to the Five Civilized Tribes, states on oath that she reported the proceedings had in the above entitled cause on the above named date and that the foregoing is a true and correct transcript of her stenographic notes in said cause on said date.

(Signed) Mabelle Cohenour

Subscribed and sworn to before me this 21st day of February, 1907.

(Signed) B.P. Rasmus
Notary Public.

◇◇◇◇◇

F.R.   Cherokee 7484.

DEPARTMENT OF THE INTERIOR,

COMMISSIONER TO THE FIVE CIVILIZED TRIBES.

In the matter of the application for the enrollment of Hattie Wright as a citizen by Intermarriage of the Cherokee Nation.

D E C I S I O N

THE RECORDS OF THIS OFFICE SHOW: That at Vinita, Indian Territory, May 14, 1901, application was received by the Commission to the Five Civilized Tribes for the enrollment of Hattie Wright as a citizen by intermarriage of the Cherokee Nation. Further proceedings in the matter of said application were had at Tahlequah, Indian Territory, October 27, 1902, and at Muskogee, Indian Territory, February 20, 1907.

Cherokee Intermarried White 1906
Volume VIII

THE EVIDENCE IN THIS CASE SHOWS: That the applicant herein, Hattie Wright, is a white woman and neither claims nor possesses any right to enrollment as a citizen of the Cherokee Nation other than such rights as she may have acquired by virtue of her marriage to one James Wright a recognized citizen by blood of the Cherokee Nation who is identified on the Cherokee authenticated tribal roll of 1880, Delaware District No. 2960, as a native Cherokee, and whose name is included on the approved partial roll of citizens by blood of the Cherokee Nation opposite No. 17701.

It is alleged on the part of the applicant that she and the said James Wright cohabited and lived together as husband and wife in the Cherokee Nation from about the year 1875, and that in the year 1897, they were married by a duly authorized minister, which affirmed their prior common law marriage.

Hattie Wright testified before the Commissioner to the Five Civilized Tribes at Muskogee, Indian Territory, on February 20, 1907, that she and the said James Wright had been living together for a period of about two years when their oldest child Ailcy Wright was born.

The said Ailcy Wright is identified on the Cherokee authenticated tribal roll of 1880, Delaware District, Page 339, opposite No. 2962, as a native Cherokee.

It also appears from examination of said rolls that the said Ailcy Wright was two years of age at the date of the making of said roll.

The applicant, Hattie Wright, is identified on the Cherokee authenticated tribal roll of 1880, as an adopted white, nineteen years old, showing that she was fourteen years of age at the time it is alleged she became the wife of said James Wright.

In view of the foregoing, it is considered that the evidence in this case is not sufficient to support a finding that the said James Wright and Hattie Wright were married prior to November 1, 1875.

IT IS, THEREFORE, ORDERED AND ADJUDGED: That in accordance with the decision of the Supreme Court of the United States, dated November 5, 1906, in the cases of Daniel Red Bird, et al. vs. the United States, Nos. 125, 126, 127, and 128, the said applicant, Hattie Wright, is not entitled under the provisions of Section Twenty-one of the Act of Congress approved June 28, 1898 (30 Stats., 495), to enrollment as a citizen by intermarriage of the Cherokee Nation, and her application for enrollment as such is accordingly denied.

Tams Bixby
Commissioner.

Dated at Muskogee, Indian Territory,
this   FEB 28 1907

◇◇◇◇◇

Form No. 260.

THE WESTERN UNION TELEGRAPH COMPANY.
INCORPORATED
23,000 OFFICES IN AMERICA.   CABLE SERVICE TO ALL THE WORLD.

ROBERT C. CLOWRY, President and General Manager.

Receiver's No.	Time Filed	Check
		Cherokee 8-10-7462

SEND the following message subject to the terms on back hereof, which are hereby agreed to.

W.C.M.

Muskogee, Indian Territory, February 12, 1907

C. W. Kellam,

Grove, Indian Territory.

Answering yours eighth proof of marriage necessary to complete intermarried case of Annie Walker. Case of Hattie Wright in same status. Have witnesses appear immediately.

Rixby,

Commissioner.

O.T.T.R.Paid

☞ READ THE NOTICE AND AGREEMENT ON BACK. ☜

(Copy of original document from case.)

(Copy of original document from case.)

◇◇◇◇◇

COPY

Muskogee, Indian Territory, February 28, 1907.

The Honorable,
    The Secretary of the Interior.

Sir:

There is transmitted herewith the record of proceedings had in the matter of the application for the enrollment of Hattie Wright, as a citizen by intermarriage of the Cherokee Nation, together with the decision of the Commissioner, dated February 28, 1907, rejecting said application.

Respectfully,

SIGNED *Jams Bixby*

Encl. F-38.   Commissioner.

Through the Commissioner of
    Indian Affairs.

◇◇◇◇◇

Cherokee 7484   COPY

Muskogee, Indian Territory, February 28, 1907.

W. W. Hastings,
        Attorney for the Cherokee Nation,
                Muskogee, Indian Territory.

Dear Sir:

There is enclosed herewith a copy of the decision of the Commissioner to the Five Civilized Tribes, dated February 28, 1907, rejecting the application for the enrollment of Hattie Wright, as a citizen by intermarriage of the Cherokee Nation.

The decision, together with the record of proceedings had in the case, has this day been transmitted to the Secretary of the Interior for his review and decision. You will be advised of the Secretary's action as soon as this office is informed of the same.

Respectfully,

SIGNED *Jams Bixby*

Encl. F-39.   Commissioner.

◇◇◇◇◇

Cherokee Intermarried White 1906
Volume VIII

Cherokee 7484   COPY

Muskogee, Indian Territory, February 28, 1907.

Hattie Wright,
     Southwest City, Missouri.

Dear Madam:

There is enclosed herewith a copy of the decision of the Commissioner to the Five Civilized Tribes, dated February 28, 1907, rejecting the application for your enrollment as a citizen by intermarriage of the Cherokee Nation.

The decision, together with the record of proceedings had in the case, has this day been transmitted to the Secretary of the Interior for his review and decision. You will be advised of the Secretary's action as soon as this office is informed of the same.

Respectfully,

SIGNED *Jams Bixby*
Commissioner.

Encl. F-40.
Register.

◇◇◇◇◇

~~D.C. 15276-1907~~.
I.T.D. 8022-1907

SPECIAL

DEPARTMENT OF THE INTERIOR,   FHE JfJr[sic].

WASHINGTON.

DIRECT.

LRS   March 4, 1907.

Commissioner to the Five Civilized Tribes,
     Muskogee, Indian Territory.

Sir:

Your decisions in the following Cherokee enrollment cases adverse to the applicants, received with Indian Office letter of March 4, 1907 (Land 21844-07) copy inclosed, are hereby affirmed, viz:

     Will E. Linton   (Intermarried)

208

Franklin Andrews (Intermarried)

Relative to the Cherokee intermarried case of Hattie Wright, also received with said Indian Office letter, you are advised that in view of the opinion of the Attorney-General in the John W. Gleason case, your decision adverse to her is hereby reversed, and you are directed to enroll said Hattie Wright as a citizen by intermarriage of the Cherokee Nation.

The papers in the cases have been sent to the Indian Office with a copy hereof.

Respectfully,

Jesse E. Wilson,

1 inc and Acting Secretary.
__ for Ind Of. with
copy hereof.

AFMc
3-4-07

◇◇◇◇◇

I. T. References in
body of letter.

DEPARTMENT OF THE INTERIOR,
OFFICE OF INDIAN AFFAIRS,
WASHINGTON.   GAW

May 15, 1907.

Commissioner to the Five Civilized Tribes,
        Muskogee, Indian Territory.

Sir:

There is inclosed copy of Office letter of May 11, 1907, approved by the Department on May 13, 1907, recommending that motions filed by W. W. Hastings, National Attorney for the Cherokee Nation, praying for a review and rehearing of Departmental decisions authorizing the enrollment of the following persons as citizens by intermarriage of the Cherokee Nation, be denied, in view of the fact that there appears to be no authority in law at this time for the reconsideration of any enrollment case.

42893-1907	Jacob A. Bartles
42895- "	Osburn J. Byrd
42886- "	Amanda Beck
42894- "	Sarah F. Gage

42892-	"	Phirena Harris
42888-	"	Daniel Harmon
42891-	"	Emma L. Ironsides
42896-	"	Sarah A. Jordan
42881-	"	Dovie Johnson
42882-	"	Andrew H. Norwood
42887-	"	Stacy E. Perry
42885-	"	Martha Randolph, now Kernan
42893-	"	John W. Smith
42884-	"	John J. Smith
42890-	"	Robert H. F. Thompson
42889-	"	Hattie Wright
42883-	"	Nancy Wolfe
42880-	"	E. A. Welch

You are requested to advise the interested parties, including Mr. Hastings, of the Department's action.

Very respectfully,
C. F. Larrabee
Acting Commissioner.

AJW-FHE.

◇◇◇◇◇

Cherokee
253   etal

Muskogee, Indian Territory, May 25, 1907.

W. W. Hastings,
Attorney for the Cherokee Nation,
Muskogee, Indian Territory.

Dear Sir:

You are hereby advised that on May 13, 1907, the Secretary of the Interior denied the motion filed by you for a review of its decision authorizing the enrollment of Jacob A. Bartles, et al., as citizens by intermarriage of the Cherokee Nation.

For your information, there is enclosed herewith a copy of Departmental decision referred to.

Respectfully,

Commissioner.

Encl. C-20
LMC

◇◇◇◇◇

Cherokee
237

Muskogee, Indian Territory, May 25, 1907.

Hattie Wright,
Southwest City, Missouri.

Dear Madam:

You are hereby advised that on May 13, 1907, the Secretary of the Interior denied a motion filed by the Attorney for the Cherokee Nation, for a review of its decision authorizing your enrollment as a citizen by intermarriage of the Cherokee Nation.

For your information, there is enclosed herewith a copy of Departmental decision referred to.

Respectfully,

Commissioner.

Encl. C-17
LMC

Cher IW 238

◇◇◇◇◇

(No information given.)

Cher IW 239

◇◇◇◇◇

(No information given.)

Cher IW 240 Amanda Beck

◇◇◇◇◇

Cherokee 5462.

Department of the Interior,
Commission to the Five Civilized Tribes,
Muskogee, I. T., October 3, 1902.

In the matter of the application of David M. Beck for the enrollment of himself and children, Osborn A., Wesley C., David M. Jr., Martha A., Walter F., George L., and Birtha[sic] Beck, as citizens by blood of the Cherokee Nation, and for the enrollment of his wife, Amanda Beck, as a citizen by intermarriage of the Cherokee Nation:
he being sworn and examined by the Commission, testified as follows:

Q What is your name?   David M. Beck.
Q Are you a citizen by blood of the Cherokee Nation?   A Yes sir.
Q What is your wife's name?   A Amanda.
Q She claims to be a citizen by intermarriage of the Cherokee Nation, does she?
A Yes sir.
Q Is she the same Amanda Beck for whom application was made to the Commission for enrollment as an intermarried citizen on November 16, 1900?   A I couldn't tell you.
Q Has she made application?   A Yes sir, she went on the roll all right.
Q What is her age at this time?   A 44.
Q When were you and your wife Amanda married, Mr. Beck?   A I couldn't tell you that either.
Q How long ago about?   A About twenty years ago. It was about in '79.
Q Where were you married, Mr. Beck, to your wife, Amanda, here in the Cherokee Nation?   A Yes sir.
Q Were you ever married prior to your marriage to Amanda?   A Yes sir.
Q How many times had you been married before that?   A Twice.
Q Were your two first wives Cherokees?   A My first wife was a Cherokee and the second was a white woman.
Q Was your first wife dead when you married your wife Amanda?   A Yes sir.
Q Was your second wife dead when you married Amanda?   A No, she run away from me.
Q Did you ever get a divorce?   A Yes sir.
Q You filed a copy of the divorce with the Commission when you made your original application did you?   A I don't know whether I did or not; I didn't take any notice of it at all.
Q You married your wife Amanda before the 1880 roll was made?   A Yes sir.
Q Have you and your wife Amanda Beck, lived together as husband and wife ever since your marriage up until the present time?   A Yes, only I would get mad some time and go away for a day or two.
Q You never actually have been separated?   A No sir, never have been and aint[sic] going to be if I can help it.
Q And you and she were living together on the first day of September, 1902?   A Yes sir.
Q How long has your wife, Amanda, lived in the Cherokee Nation?   A All her life.
Q Have you lived in the Cherokee Nation ever since the 1880 roll was made?   A Yes.

Cherokee Intermarried White 1906
Volume VIII

Q Lived here all the time for the last twenty years? A Yes.

Q Are these children, Osborn A., Wesley C., David M. Jr., Martha A., Walter F., George L. and Birtha your children by your wife Amanda?

A Yes sir, these are all my children by Amanda.

Q Are all these children whom I have named living at this time? A Except one, the last one.

Q Birtha is dead is she? A Yes sir.

Q When did she die? A The 2nd day of last August, about two months ago.

Q Have all these children lived in the Cherokee Nation ever since they were born up to the present time? A Never were anywhere else.

The undersigned, being duly sworn, states that as stenographer to the Commission to the Five Civilized Tribes he correctly recorded the testimony and proceedings in this case, and the foregoing is a true and correct transcript of his stenographic notes thereof.

E.G. Rothenberger

Subscribed and sworn to before me this 17th day of October, 1902.

BC Jones
Notary Public.

◇◇◇◇◇

C.F.B.   Cherokee 5462

DEPARTMENT OF THE INTERIOR,

COMMISSIONER TO THE FIVE CIVILIZED TRIBES.

In the matter of the application for the enrollment of Amanda Beck as a citizen by intermarriage of the Cherokee Nation.

D E C I S I O N

THE RECORDS OF THIS OFFICE SHOW: That at Chelsea, Indian Territory, November 16, 1900, application was received by the Commission to the Five Civilized Tribes for the enrollment of Amanda Beck as a citizen by intermarriage of the Cherokee Nation. Further proceedings in the matter of said application were had at Muskogee, Indian Territory, October 3, 1902.

THE EVIDENCE IN THIS CASE SHOWS: That the applicant herein, Amanda Beck, who is identified on the Cherokee authenticated tribal roll of 1880, page 227, No.

303, Delaware District, as an intermarried citizen of the Cherokee Nation, is a white woman, and neither claims nor possesses any right to enrollment as a citizen of the Cherokee Nation other than such right as she may have acquired by reason of her marriage to her husband, David M. Beck, a citizen by blood of the Cherokee Nation. The evidence further shows that said Amanda Beck was married prior to her marriage to the said David M. beck, and fails to show that her former husband was dead, but affirmatively shows that she had not been divorced from him at the time of her marriage to the said David M. Beck. It is shown by a preponderance of the evidence that the marriage of said applicant to the said David M. beck did not occur until 1879, and it is considered that granting that said marriage did occur prior to November 1, 1875, by reason of the invalidity of said marriage, the said Amanda Beck would have acquired no right to enrollment as a citizen by intermarriage of the Cherokee Nation.

IT IS, THEREFORE, ORDERED AND ADJUDGED: That in accordance with the decision of the Supreme Court of the United States, dated November 5, 1906, in the cases of Daniel Red Bird, et al., vs. the United States, Nos. 125, 126, 127, and 128, the said applicant, Amanda Beck, is not entitled, under the provisions of Section twenty-one of the Act of Congress approved June 28, 1898 (30 Stats. 495), to enrollment as a citizen by intermarriage of the Cherokee Nation, and her application for enrollment as such is accordingly denied.

Tams Bixby
Commissioner.

Dated at Muskogee, Indian Territory,
this   FEB 19 1907

◇◇◇◇◇

Cherokee
5462.

Muskogee, Indian Territory, December 29, 1906.

Amanda Beck,
       Chelsea, Indian Territory.

Dear Madam:

November 6, 1906, the United States Supreme Court held that white persons who intermarried with Cherokee citizens according to Cherokee law prior to November 1, 1875, are entitled to enrollment and allotments of land as citizens of the Cherokee Nation.

You are advised that to properly determine your right to enrollment as a citizen by intermarriage of the Cherokee Nation, it will be necessary for you to appear before the Commissioner for the purpose of giving testimony as to the date of your marriage and whether or not your husband, by reason of your marriage to whom you claim the right to enrollment as a citizen by intermarriage of the Cherokee Nation, was a recognized Cherokee citizen at the time of your marriage to him.

You are, therefore, directed to appear before the Commissioner at Muskogee, Indian Territory, at 9 o'clock A. M., on Friday, January 4, 1907, and give testimony as above indicated.

Respectfully,

H.J.C. Commissioner.

◇◇◇◇◇

Cherokee 5462.

Muskogee, Indian Territory, February 19, 1907.

Amanda Beck,
        Chelsea, Indian Territory.

Dear Madam:

There is enclosed herewith a copy of the decision of the Commissioner to the Five Civilized Tribes, dated February 19, 1907, rejecting the application for your enrollment as a citizen by intermarriage of the Cherokee Nation.

The decision, together with the record of proceedings had in the case, has this day been transmitted to the Secretary of the Interior for his review and decision. You will be advised of the Secretary's action as soon as this office is informed of same.

Respectfully,

Enc I-112 Commissioner.

RPI

Register.

◇◇◇◇◇

Cherokee 5462

Muskogee, Indian Territory, February 19, 1907.

W. W. Hastings,
     Attorney for the Cherokee Nation,
          Muskogee, Indian Territory.

Dear Sir:

There is enclosed herewith copy of the decision of the Commissioner to the Five Civilized Tribes, dated February 19, 1907, rejecting the application for the enrollment of Amanda Beck as a citizen by intermarriage of the Cherokee Nation.

The decision, together with the record of proceedings had in the case, has this day been transmitted to the Secretary of the Interior for his review and decision. You will be advised of the Secretary's action as soon as this office is informed of same.

Respectfully,

Enc I-111   Commissioner.

RPI

◇◇◇◇◇

Muskogee, Indian Territory, February 19, 1907.

The Honorable,
     The Secretary of the Interior.

Sir:

There is transmitted herewith the record of proceedings had in the matter of the application for the enrollment of Amanda Beck as a citizen by intermarriage of the Cherokee Nation, together with the decision of the Commissioner, dated February 19, 1907, rejecting said application.

Respectfully,

Enc I-113   Commissioner.

RPI

Through the Commissioner
     of Indian Affairs.

◇◇◇◇◇

(C O P Y)

D.C. 13260-1907.   FHE. JFJr.

SPECIAL

DEPARTMENT OF THE INTERIOR,

I.T.D.

7618, 7674, 7824, 78028,   WASHINGTON.

8030-07.   March 4, 1907.

L.R.S.

DIRECT.

Commissioner to the Five Civilized Tribes,
    Muskogee, Indian Territory.

Sir:

The Department, in view of the opinion of the Attorney-General in the John W. Gleason case, and that of the Assistant-Attorney-General in the Jacob Bartles case, hereby reverses your decisions adverse to the applicants in the following Intermarried Cherokee enrollment cases, and their applications for enrollment are granted. You are directed to enroll all of such applicants as citizens by intermarriage of the Cherokee Nation:

| | Date of your |
Title of case?[sic]	letter of transmittal
Amanda Beck	February 19, 1907.
Osburn J. Byrd,	February 4, 1907.
Rufus M. Allen,	February 4, 1907
Daniel Harmon,	February 28, 1907
Nancy Wolfe,	February 28, 1907

Copies of Indian Office letters submitting your reports are inclosed. The papers in the various cases mentioned have been sent to the Indian Office with a copy hereof.

Respectfully,

Jesse E. Wilson

5 inc. and   Acting Secretary.

___ for Ind. Of. with copy hereof.

217

<u>A.F.Mc.</u>
3-4-07
(No encls. R.H.)

◇◇◇◇◇

GAW

DEPARTMENT OF THE INTERIOR,
I. T. references   OFFICE OF INDIAN AFFAIRS,
in body of letter.   WASHINGTON.

May 15, 1907.

Commissioner to the Five Civilized Tribes,
        Muskogee, Indian Territory.

Sir:

There is inclosed copy of Office letter of May 11, 1907, approved by the Department on May 13, 1907, recommending that motions filed by W. W. Hastings, National Attorney for the Cherokee Nation, praying for a review and rehearing of Departmental decisions authorizing the enrollment of the following persons as citizens by intermarriage of the Cherokee Nation, be denied, in view of the fact that there appears to be no authority in law at this time for the reconsideration of any enrollment case.

42893-1907	Jacob A. Bartles
42895- "	Osburn J. Byrd
42886- "	Amanda Beck
42894- "	Sarah F. Gage
42892- "	Phirena Harris
42888- "	Daniel Harmon
42891- "	Emma L. Ironsides
42896- "	Sarah A. Jordan
42881- "	Dovie Johnson
42882- "	Andrew H. Norwood
42887- "	Stacy E. Perry
42885- "	Martha Randolph, now Kernan
42893- "	John W. Smith
42884- "	John J. Smith
42890- "	Robert H. F. Thompson
42889- "	Hattie Wright
42883- "	Nancy Wolfe
42880- "	E. A. Welch

You are requested to advise the interested parties, including Mr. Hastings, of the Department's action.

Very respectfully,
C. F. Larrabee
Acting Commissioner.

AJW-FHE.

◇◇◇◇◇

DEPARTMENT OF THE INTERIOR
OFFICE OF INDIAN AFFAIRS,
WASHINGTON.   GAW

I.T.   May 11, 1907.
Reference in body
of letter.

Subject: Motions for
review in certain Chero-
kee citizenship cases.

The Honorable,

     The Secretary of the Interior.

Sir:

There are inclosed herewith motions filed by W. W. Hastings, National Attorney for the Cherokee Nation, praying for review and rehearing of Departmental decisions authorizing the enrollment as citizens by intermarriage of the Cherokee Nation of the following persons:

42893-1907,	Jacob A. Bartles,
42895- "	Osburn J. Byrd,
42886- "	Amanda Beck,
42894- "	Sarah F. Gage,
42892- "	Phirena Harris,
42888- "	Daniel Harmon,
42891- "	Emma L. Ironsides,
42896- "	Sarah A. Jordan
42881- "	Dovie Johnson,
42882- "	Andrew H. Norwood,
42887- "	Stacy E. Perry,
42885- "	Martha Randolph, now Kernan
42893- "	John W. Smith

219

42884-	"	John J. Smith,
42890-	"	Robert H. F. Thompson,
42889-	"	Hattie Wright,
42883-	"	Nancy Wolfe,
42880-	"	E. A. Welch.

In view of the provisions of section 2 of the act of April 26, 1906 (34 Stat. L., 137), providing that the rolls of the Five Civilized Tribes shall be fully completed on or before March 4, 1907, there appears to be no authority in law for the reconsideration of any enrollment cases at this time, and it is recommended that the office be authorized to advise Mr. Hastings that the motions for review herewith transmitted cannot be considered.

Very respectfully,

C. F. Larrabee

Acting Commissioner.

AJW-FHE.

     May 13, 1907.

Approved.

     Thos Ryan

       First Assistant Secretary.

◇◇◇◇◇

Cherokee
   253 et al.

Muskogee, Indian Territory, May 25, 1907.

W. W. Hastings,
    Attorney for the Cherokee Nation,
        Muskogee, Indian Territory.

Dear Sir:

You are hereby advised that on May 13, 1907, the Secretary of the Interior denied the motion filed by you for a review of its decision authorizing the enrollment of Jacob A. Bartles, et al., as citizens by intermarriage of the Cherokee Nation.

For your information, there is enclosed herewith a copy of Departmental decision referred to.

Respectfully,

Commissioner.

Encl. C-20
LMC

<><><><><>

Cherokee
240

Muskogee, Indian Territory, May 25, 1907.

Amanda Beck,
Chelsea, Indian Territory.

Dear Madam:

You are hereby advised that on May 13, 1907, the Secretary of the Interior denied a motion filed by the Attorney for the Cherokee Nation, for a review of its decision authorizing your enrollment as a citizen by intermarriage of the Cherokee Nation.

For your information, there is enclosed herewith a copy of Departmental decision referred to.

Respectfully,

Commissioner.

Encl. C-4
LMC

Cher IW 241

<><><><><>

DEPARTMENT OF THE INTERIOR,
COMMISSION TO THE FIVE CIVILIZED TRIBES,
VINITA, I.T., OCTOBER 1st, 1900:

In the matter of the application of Osburn J. Byrd for the enrollment of himself and children as citizens of the Cherokee Nation; said Byrd being sworn by Commissioner T.B. Needles, testified as follows:

Q   What is your name?   A Osburn J. Byrd.
Q   What is your age?   A 53.
Q   What is your post office address?   A Fairland.

Cherokee Intermarried White 1906
Volume VIII

Q   What district do you live in?   A Delaware.
Q   Are you a recognized citizen of the Cherokee Nation?   A Yes, sir.
Q   You are a Shawnee by blood are you?   A Yes, sir.
Q   By blood?   A No, sir.
Q   By intermarriage?   A Yes, sir.
Q   What is the name of your wife?   A Julia Ann Elick, was her maiden name.
Q   What is her age?   A She is deceased, she died in 1891, her age then was 42.
Q   What was her father's name?   A I do not know, I could ascertain.
Q   Do you know her mothers'[sic] name?   A No, sir I do not, they were indian[sic] names.
Q   Are they living?   A No, sir, they are dead.
Q   Have you a certificate of marriage?   A No, sir, I have not; I had but I lost it. I was married in 1874.
Q   Have you any children? A Seven.
Q   Please give me the names of the oldest one at home?   A Susan P.; 19 years of.
Q   The next one?   A Annie D.
Q   How old is Annie D? A 17.
Q   The namce[sic] of the next one?   A Eva R., 15.
Q   Next one?   A Fitzhugh Lee.
Q   How old is Fitzhugh?   A She is 11.
Q   These children are all alive and living with you?   A Yes, sir.
Q   How long have you lived in the Cherokee Nation?   A I have lived here, sir, ever since before I was married.
Q   Living here now are you?   A Yes, sir.
Q   Your wife died in 1892?   A 1891.
Q   Have you been married since?   A No, sir.

     1880 enrollment; page 220, #135, Osburn Bird[sic], Delaware.
     1896 enrollment; page 598, #64, Susan P.   "   "
     1896 enrollment; page 598, #65, Annie D.   "   "
     1896 enrollment; page 598, #66, Eva R.   "   "
     1896 enrollment; page 598, #69, Fitzhugh L. Bird,   "
Q   These children are all residents of the Cherokee Nation?   A Yes, sir, always have been.
Q   You are not a citizen by blood?   A No, sir.

     Com'r Needles:--The name of Osburn J. Byrd appears upon the authenticated roll of 1880 as an intermarried white. His name is also found upon the census roll of 1896. The names of his children, Susan P., Annie D., Eva R. Fitzhugh Lee, are found upon the census roll of 1896. They all being duly identified according to the page and number of the rolls as indicated in the testimony and having made satisfactory proof as to their residence, the said Osburn J. Byrd will be duly listed for enrollment as a Cherokee citizen by intermarriage, and his childre[sic] as enumerated in the testimony, will be duly listed as Cherokee citizens by blood.

---oooOOO --[sic]

Cherokee Intermarried White 1906
Volume VIII

J. O. Rosson, being first duly sworn, states that as stenographer to the Commission to the Five Civilized Tribes, he correctly recorded the testimony and proceedings in this case, and the foregoing is a true and complete transcript of his stenographic notes thereof.

JO Rosson

Subscribed and sworn to before me this third day of October, 1900.

T.B. Needles
Commissioner.

◇◇◇◇◇

Cherokee 3866

DEPARTMENT OF THE INTERIOR,
COMMISSION TO THE FIVE CIVILIZED TRIBES,
MUSKOGEE, IND. TER., SEPT. 23, 1902.

In the matter of the application for the enrollment of Osburn J. Byrd et al. as citizens of the Cherokee Nation:

SUPPLEMENTAL STATEMENT.

An examination of the 1880 authenticated Cherokee roll shows that Julia A. Byrd, deceased wife of the applicant, Osburn J. Byrd, is identified on said roll as an adopted Shawnee, Oklahoma page 220, Delaware District, #136, as Julia Bird.

It is ordered that copies of this statement be filed with the testimony in this case.

Tams Bixby
Commissioner.

◇◇◇◇◇

R.

DEPARTMENT OF THE INTERIOR.
Commission to the Five Civilized Tribes.
Muskogee, Indian Territory, September 30th, 1902.

———————————

In the matter of the application of Osburn J. Byrd for the enrollment of himself as a citizen by intermarriage of the Cherokee Nation and for the enrollment of is children Annie D., Eva R., Fitzhugh L. and Susan P. Byrd as citizens by blood of the Cherokee Nation.

———————————

Supplemental to #3866.

———————————

Appearances:

Applicant appears in person.
J. C. Starr for Cherokee Nation.

———————————

OSBURN J. BYRD, being duly sworn, testified as follows:
Examination by the Commission.

Q. What is your name, Mr. Byrd?   A. Full name?
Q. Yes. A. Osburn J. Byrd.
Q. What is your age at this time?   A. I am about 55, sir.
Q. What is your post office?   A. It is Vinita now. It was Fairland at the time I gave the-----
Q. Are you the same Osburn J. Byrd that applied to this Commission on October 1st, 1900, for enrollment as an intermarried citizen?   A. Yes, sir.
Q. What is your wife's name?   A. Julia Ann. It was her name. She has been dead a good many years.
Q. Is your wife living or dead?   A. Dead.
Q. What was her name before you married her?   A. Julia Elick.
Q. Is she a citizen by blood?   A. Yes, sir.
Q. When were you married? A. In 1874, sir. Early in 1874.
Q. Married under a Cherokee license?   A. Yes, sir.
Q. When did she die?   A. In September or October, 1891.
Q. Did you and she live together from the time of your marriage up to the time of her death all the time?   A. Yes, sir, all the time.
Q. Never was separated?   A. No, sir.
Q. Have you married any other woman since you married her?   A. No, sir.
Q. Have you married since her death?   A. No, sir.
Q. Were you single on the first of September, 1902?   A. Yes, sir.
Q. How long have you lived in the Cherokee Nation, Mr. Byrd?

A. Lets[sic] see, sir. I have lived in here ever since I was married; I believe I was in here a year or two prior to that.

Q. Have you lived in the Cherokee Nation all the time since 1880? A. Yes, sir.

Q. Are these children, Annie D., Eva R., Fitzhugh L. and Susan R., your children by your Cherokee wife? A. Yes, sir.

Q. Living with you at home? A. Yes, sir.

Q. At Vinita? A. Yes, sir.

Q. Have they lived in the Cherokee Nation all their lives? A. Yes, sir.

Q. Born and raised here? A. Boan[sic] and raised here; yes, sir.

Jesse O. Carr, being first duly sworn, states that as stenographer to the Commission to the Five Civilized Tribes he reported the above entitled case and that the foregoing is a true and complete transcript of his stenographic notes thereof.

Jesse O. Carr

Subscribed and sworn to before me this 10th day of October, 1902.

BC Jones
Notary Public.

◇◇◇◇◇

Cherokee 3866.

DEPARTMENT OF THE INTERIOR,
COMMISSIONER TO THE FIVE CIVILIZED TRIBES.
MUSKOGEE, I. T., January 7, 1907.

In the matter of the application for the enrollment of Osburn J. Byrd as a citizen by intermarriage of the Cherokee Nation.

Osburn J. Byrd being first duly sworn by Frances R. Lane, a Notary Public for the Western District of Indian Territory, testified as follows:

By the Commissioner:

Q What is your name? A Osburn J. Byrd.

Q Your age? A Sixty years.

Q And your postoffice address? A Fairland, I. T.

Q You claim to be a citizen of the Cherokee nation by intermarriage? A Yes sir.

Q Through whom do you claim citizenship? A By intermarriage with Julia Ann Choteau, whose maiden name was Julia Ann Aleck[sic].

Q Is she living at this time? A No sir.

Q What time did she die? A In 1891.

Q When were you married to her? A I was married in 1874; January, and really, I have forgotten the date. It was the latter part of January, though.

Q   You are positive of the year are you?   A Yes sir. Either the latter part of January or the first days of February, but I am satisfied it was in January. And I want to say right here--it looks very funny too. She was a widow. Her maiden name was Julia Ann Aleck and her husband only lived three or four months I think it was, and she didn't go by the name of Mrs. Choteau but very little, and whether I married her under the name of Choteau or Aleck I forget, but I think it was Choteau.

Q   Where were you married to her?   A South of Chetopa six miles.

Q   Was that under a license of the Cherokee Nation?   A Yes sir

Q   Have you the license with you?   A No, I havn't[sic], nor the certificate either, but I have evidence; plenty of it.

Q   You have no documentary evidence?   A No, unless it is in the Delaware records.

Q   Has[sic] you ever married prior to your marriage to Mrs. Choteau[sic]

A   No sir.

Q   Was she ever married prior to her marriage to you?   A Yes, to Frank Choteau.

Q   Was he living at the time you married her?   A No sir.

Q   From the time of your marriage in 1874, did you and your wife live together continuously as husband and wife up until the time of her death in 1891?   A Yes, up to her death.

Q   And lived in the Cherokee nation[sic] did you during that time?   *(No answer given.)*

Q   She was a citizen of the Cherokee nation and recognized as such at the time of your marriage to her?   A Yes sir.

Q   In what district were you married? A Delaware District.

Q   You have no documentary evidence at all?   A No, I had, but I lost it after so many years.

Q   Was the license filed for record? A Yes sir.

Q   Where?   A In Delaware District, with the clerk.

Q   Have you married since the death of your wife?   A No.

Q   You still reside in the Cherokee Nation?   A Yes sir.

Q   And have all the time since her death?   A Yes sir.

Q   You say you have no documentary evidence of your marriage Were you ever in possession of any such?   A I sent my license to the clerk and he kept telling me that he would send it back, but he never did. I have a certificate from the minister to marry me, but I lost that.

Q   Is that minister living at this time?   A I don't know; he was at Chetopa, Kansas, and he moved away.

Q   Is anybody present here at this time who was present at your marriage?

A   Jackson Mills and Johnny Choteau and Edmund Choteau.

Q   What are their postoffice addresses?   A Mills is Welch and the Choteaus are Vinita.

Q   Did you ever make application to any of the commissions of the Cherokee nation[sic] for enrollment as a citizen?   A Yes, and I am on all the rolls since that time.

Q   Did you ever personally appear before the Adair court or any of those tribunals, and have any formal action taken admitting you?   A The only way I could be admitted was by intermarriage according to the Cherokee law.

The name of the applicant, Osburn J. Byrd, appears on Cherokee Field Card No. 3866, and is included in the 1880 authenticated roll of citizens of the Cherokee Nation, Delaware District opposite No. 135.

The name of the applicant is also found on the 1896 Cherokee roll, opposite No. 32.

Edmund Choteau, being first duly sworn by Frances R. Lane, a Notary Public for the Western District of Indian Territory, testified as follows:

By the Commissioner:

Q   What is your name?   A Edmund Choteau.

Q   Your age? A Forty.

Q   Postoffice address?   A Vinita, I. T.

Q   Are you related to Osburn J. Byrd, the applicant in this case either by blood or marriage?   A By marriage is about all; His wife was related to be[sic] once.

Q   Were you present at his marriage to Julia Ann Choteau?   A Yes sir.

Q   Where were they married?   A They were married about six miles from Chetopa, Kansas, in the Territory.

Q   What was the date of the marriage?   A Along in January. The middle of January or last of the month, in 1874.

Q   Were they married under a license of the Cherokee Nation?

A   It was performed by a minister, and of course he got the necessary signers.

Q   Was this marriage under a license of the Cherokee Nation?

A   It was according to the requirements of getting up signers, if that is the idea.

Q   You are a citizen of the Cherokee nation[sic] by blood?   A Yes.

Q   Were you one of the signers to Mr. Byrd's petition?

A   I was not; my father was.

Q   You do not know by whom the marriage license was issued?

A   No, I don't know who issued it.

Q   You don't know to whom they presented this petition?

A   No sir.

Q   How old were you at the time of the marriage?   A About eight years old.

Q   Then of your own knowledge you wouldn't know very much regarding this license.

A No, not that part. I remember getting up the signers and that my father signed it.

Q   Did Mr. Byrd and his wife live together continuously in the Cherokee nation; from the time of their marriage up until her death in 1891?   A Yes sir.

Q   Held themselves out as man and wife and were so regarded in the community?

A   Yes sir.

Witness excused.

Thomas J. McGhee, being first duly sworn by Frances R. Lane, a Notary Public for the Western District of Indian Territory, testified as follows:

By the Commissioner:

Q   What is your name?   A Thomas J. McGhee.

227

Cherokee Intermarried White 1906
Volume VIII

Q Your age? A Sixty-two.

Q And your postoffice address? A Afton, I. T.

Q Do you know Osburn J. Byrd? A Yes sir.

Q How long have you know[sic] him? A I have known him I guess thirty years.

Q Did you know his wife? A No sir.

Q Do you know anything with reference to the marriage license being issued to Osburn J. Byrd and Julia Ann Choteau in the year 1874[sic]

A Mr. Milton issued them their license. Milton was acting as clerk when I was judge of that district.

Q Of your own knowledge you don't know anything about the issuance of this particular license do you? A No, I don't. Milton made a record of what he did, and the record would show of itself.

> In Marriage record, Delaware District, Book S. appears the record showing that Osburn J. Byrd, a citizen of the United States, was licensed to marry _____ Choteau, a citizen of the Cherokee nation, said license having been issued January 9, 1874. The license was returned executed January 23, 1874. Said record is signed by S. N. Melton, Clerk of Delaware District.

John Choteau, being first duly sworn by Frances R. Lane, a Notary Public for the Western District of Indian Territory, testified as follows:

By the Commissioner:

Q What is your name? A John Choteau.

Q What is your age? A Forty-six.

Q Your postoffice address? A Vinita, I. T.

Q Do you know Osburn J. Byrd? A Yes sir.

Q How long have you know[sic] him? A Since I was about 6 years old.

Q Do you know anything about his marriage to Mrs. Choteau? A Yes sir.

Q When were they married? A They were married along in January, 1874, at my grandmothers[sic] on Mud Creek.

Q Do you know whether or not they were married under a license issued by the Cherokee nation[sic]? A Yes, my father signed the petition.

Q He was one of the signers of Mr. Byrd's petition? A Yes

Q Is Mrs. Byrd living at this time? A No sir.

Q From the time of the marriage of Osburn J. Byrd and his wife, Julia Ann Choteau, did they live together continuously in the Cherokee nation from their marriage until the time of her death? A Yes sir.

Q What was the date of her death? A I can't tell you.

Q Has Mr. Byrd married since her death? A No sir.

Q You saw Osburn J. Byrd and Julia Ann Choteau married, did you? A Yes sir.

Q And you know that it was under a Cherokee license? A Yes sir.

-------   ---   ----

228

Cherokee Intermarried White 1906
Volume VIII

Frances R. Lane upon oath states that as stenographer to the Commissioner to the Five Civilized Tribes she reported the testimony in the above entitled cause and that the foregoing is an accurate transcript of her stenographic notes thereof.

Frances R Lane

Subscribed and sworn to before me this January 8, 1907.

Edward Merrick
Notary Public.

◇◇◇◇◇

E.C.M.   Cherokee 3866

DEPARTMENT OF THE INTERIOR,

COMMISSIONER TO THE FIVE CIVILIZED TRIBES.

In the matter of the application for the enrollment of OSBURN J. BYRD as a citizen by intermarriage of the Cherokee Nation.

D E C I S I O N

THE RECORDS OF THIS OFFICE SHOW: That at Vinita, Indian Territory, October 1, 1900, application was received by the Commission to the Five Civilized Tribes for the enrollment of Osburn J. Byrd, as a citizen by intermarriage of the Cherokee Nation. Further proceedings in the matter of said application were had at Muskogee, Indian Territory, September 23, 1902, September 30, 1902 and January 7, 1907.

THE EVIDENCE IN THIS CASE SHOWS: That the applicant herein, Osburn J. Byrd, who is identified on the Cherokee authenticated tribal roll of 1880 and the Cherokee census roll of 1896, is a white man and neither claims nor possesses any right to enrollment as a citizen of the Cherokee Nation other than such right as he may have acquired by virtue of his marriage in January, 1874, to one Julia Ann Byrd; that said Julia Ann Byrd, nee Ellick[sic], who is identified on the Shawnee Register, page 41, opposite No. 316, was a member of the Shawnee tribe of Indians and acquired her right to enrollment as a citizen of the Cherokee Nation by virtue of her compliance with the provisions of the agreement entered into by the Cherokee and Shawnee tribes of Indians on June 7, 1869. In view of the foregoing, it is considered that said applicant acquired no right to enrollment as a citizen by intermarriage of the Cherokee Nation by reason of his said marriage to Julia Ann Byrd, nee Ellick, in January, 1874, who is not a citizen of the Cherokee Nation of Cherokee blood.

229

IT IS, THEREFORE, ORDERED AND ADJUDGED: That in accordance with the decision of the Supreme Court of the United States, dated November 5, 1906, in the cases of Daniel Red Bird et al., vs. the United States, Nos. 125, 126, 127, and 128, the said applicant, Osburn J. Byrd, by reason of his marriage to his said Shawnee wife, is not entitled, under the provisions of Section twenty-one of the Act of Congress approved June 28, 1898 (30 Stats. 495), to enrollment as a citizen by intermarriage of the Cherokee Nation, and his application for enrollment as such is accordingly denied.

Tams Bixby
Commissioner.

Dated at Muskogee, Indian Territory,
this   FEB 4 1907

◇◇◇◇◇

3866 Cherokee
In Re Osburn J Byrd

―――――

Motion to dismiss
petition for Review &
Rehearing
Copy

DEPARTMENT OF THE INTERIOR,
Commissioner to the Five Civilized Tribes,
Muskogee, Indian Territory,

Cherokee 3866,
Citizenship of Osburn J. Byrd.

Motion to Dismiss.

Comes now the respondent herein, Osburn J. Byrd, and respectfully moves the Honorable Secretary of the Interior, for the purposes of this motion and no other, that the motion for review and reconsideration be dismissed for the following reason, to wit:-

That under the act of Congress approved April 26th., 1906, entitled " An act to provide for the final disposition of the Affairs of the Five Civilized Tribes in the Indian Territory, and for other purposes," that motion filed by the attorney for the Cherokee Nation, As under section two (2) of the above named Act, the Rolls of the said Indian Tribes affected by said Act shall be completely closed on March 4th., 1907, and the said Honorable Secretary has no jurisdiction to hear any matter of citizenship concerning any of the matters of the Five Civilized Tribes.

Respectfully Submitted,
Osburn J. Byrd,
By Geo E. McCulloch
His Attorney.

◇◇◇◇◇

Cherokee
3866

Muskogee, Indian Territory, December 26, 1906.

Osburn J. Byrd,
Fairland, Indian Territory.

Dear Sir:

November 6, 1906, the United States Supreme Court held that white persons who intermarried with Cherokee citizens according to Cherokee law prior to November 1, 1875, are entitled to enrollment and allotments of land as citizens of the Cherokee Nation.

You are advised that to properly determine your right to enrollment as a citizen by intermarriage of the Cherokee Nation, it will be necessary for you to appear before the Commissioner for the purpose of giving testimony as to the date of your marriage and whether or not your wife, by reason of your marriage to whom you claim the right to enrollment as a citizen of the Cherokee Nation, was a recognized citizen of the Cherokee Nation at the time of your marriage to her, and whether or not you were married to her in accordance with Cherokee laws.

You are, therefore, directed to appear before the Commissioner at Muskogee, Indian Territory, at 9 o'clock A. M., on Friday, January 4, 1907, and give testimony as above indicated.

Respectfully,

JMH

Acting Commissioner.

◇◇◇◇◇

Cherokee 3866

Muskogee, Indian Territory, February 4, 1907.

Osburn J. Byrd,
    Fairland, Indian Territory.

Dear Sir:

There is inclosed a copy of the decision of the Commissioner to the Five Civilized Tribes, dated February 4, 1907, denying the application for your enrollment as a citizen by intermarriage of the Cherokee Nation.

The decision, together with the record of proceedings had in the case, has this day been transmitted to the Secretary of the Interior for his review and decision. You will be advised of the Secretary's action as soon as this office is informed of same.

Respectfully,

Commissioner.

N-72

◇◇◇◇◇

Cherokee 3866

Muskogee, Indian Territory, February 4, 1907.

W. W. Hastings,
    Attorney for the Cherokee Nation,
        Muskogee, Indian Territory.

Dear Sir:

There is inclosed a copy of the decision of the Commissioner to the Five Civilized Tribes, dated February 4, 1907, denying the application for the enrollment of Osburn J. Byrd, as a citizen by intermarriage of the Cherokee Nation.

The decision, together with the record of proceedings had in the case, has this day been transmitted to the Secretary of the Interior for his review and decision. You will be advised of the Secretary's action as soon as this office is informed of same.

Respectfully,

N-72   Commissioner.

◇◇◇◇◇

Muskogee, Indian Territory, February 4, 1907.

The Honorable,
    The Secretary of the Interior.

Sir:

There is transmitted herewith, the record of proceedings had in the matter of the application for the enrollment of Osburn J. Byrd, as a citizen by intermarriage of the Cherokee Nation, together with the decision of the Commissioner, dated February 4, 1907, denying said application.

Respectfully,

Commissioner.

Through the Commissioner
    of Indian Affairs.
N-72

◇◇◇◇◇

DEPARTMENT OF THE INTERIOR
OFFICE OF INDIAN AFFAIRS,
WASHINGTON.   GAW

I.T.   May 11, 1907.
References in body
of letter.

Subject: Motions for
review in certain Chero-
kee citizenship cases.

The Honorable,
    The Secretary of the Interior.

Sir:

There are inclosed herewith motions filed by W. W. Hastings, National Attorney for the Cherokee Nation, praying for review and rehearing of Departmental decisions authorizing the enrollment as citizens by intermarriage of the Cherokee Nation of the following persons:

Cherokee Intermarried White 1906
Volume VIII

42893-1907,	Jacob A. Bartles,
42895- "	Osburn J. Byrd,
42886- "	Amanda Beck,
42894- "	Sarah F. Gage,
42892- "	Phirena Harris,
42888- "	Daniel Harmon,
42891- "	Emma L. Ironsides,
42896- "	Sarah A. Jordan
42881- "	Dovie Johnson,
42882- "	Andrew H. Norwood,
42887- "	Stacy E. Perry,
42885- "	Martha Randolph, now Kernan
42893- "	John W. Smith
42884- "	John J. Smith,
42890- "	Robert H. F. Thompson,
42889- "	Hattie Wright,
42883- "	Nancy Wolfe,
42880- "	E. A. Welch.

In view of the provisions of section 2 of the act of April 26, 1906 (34 Stat. L., 137), providing that the rolls of the Five Civilized Tribes shall be fully completed on or before March 4, 1907, there appears to be no authority in law for the reconsideration of any enrollment cases at this time, and it is recommended that the office be authorized to advise Mr. Hastings that the motions for review herewith transmitted cannot be considered.

Very respectfully,

C. F. Larrabee

Acting Commissioner.

AJW-FHE.

May 13, 1907.

Approved.

Thos Ryan

First Assistant Secretary.

◇◇◇◇◇

Cherokee
I.W. 241.

Muskogee, Indian Territory, May 13, 1907.

Chief Clerk,
Cherokee Land Office.

Dear Sir:

You are advised that a motion has been filed by the Attorney for the Cherokee Nation for a review of the Cherokee intermarried case of Osburn J. Byrd.

Until this motion shall have been acted on by the Department you are instructed to withhold the preparation of any allotment certificates and deeds describing the land heretofore selected by this applicant as an allotment in the Cherokee Nation.

Respectfully,

S.W.   Acting Commissioner.

◇◇◇◇◇

Muskogee, Indian Territory, May 13, 1907.

The Honorable,
The Secretary of the Interior.

Sir:

Referring to Departmental letter of March 4, 1907 (I.T.D. 7618, 7674, 7824, 8024, 8030-1907), granting, among others, the application for the enrollment of Osburn J. Byrd as a citizen by intermarriage of the Cherokee Nation, there is enclosed a motion filed May 9, 1907, by George E. McCulloch, of Vinita, Indian Territory, Attorney for applicant, to dismiss the "motion for review and reconsideration" of this case filed by the Attorney for the Cherokee Nation.

The records of this office fail to show that any motion to reopen or reconsider this case has been filed with it by the Attorney for the Cherokee Nation.

Respectfully,

Through the   Acting Commissioner.
    Commissioner of Indian Affairs.

Encl. W-1.
S.W.

◇◇◇◇◇

Cherokee
I. W. 241.

Muskogee, Indian Territory, May 13, 1907.

George E. McCulloch,
    Attorney for Osburn J. Byrd,
        Vinita, Indian Territory.

Dear Sir:

Referring to your letter of May 8, 1907, transmitting a motion to dismiss the motion for review and reconsideration of the Cherokee citizenship case of Osburn J. Byrd filed by the Attorney for the Cherokee Nation, you are advised your said motion has this day been forwarded to the Department for its consideration.

Respectfully,

S.W.   Acting Commissioner.

◇◇◇◇◇

                                                    GAW
                    DEPARTMENT OF THE INTERIOR,
I. T. references   OFFICE OF INDIAN AFFAIRS,
in body of letter.   WASHINGTON.

                                        May 15, 1907.

Commissioner to the Five Civilized Tribes,
    Muskogee, Indian Territory.

Sir:

There is inclosed copy of Office letter of May 11, 1907, approved by the Department on May 13, 1907, recommending that motions filed by W. W. Hastings, National Attorney for the Cherokee Nation, praying for a review and rehearing of Departmental decisions authorizing the enrollment of the following persons as citizens by intermarriage of the Cherokee Nation, be denied, in view of the fact that there appears to be no authority in law at this time for the reconsideration of any enrollment case.

        42893-1907   Jacob A. Bartles
        42895- "   Osburn J. Byrd

42886-	"	Amanda Beck
42894-	"	Sarah F. Gage
42892-	"	Phirena Harris
42888-	"	Daniel Harmon
42891-	"	Emma L. Ironsides
42896-	"	Sarah A. Jordan
42881-	"	Dovie Johnson
42882-	"	Andrew H. Norwood
42887-	"	Stacy E. Perry
42885-	"	Martha Randolph, now Kernan
42893-	"	John W. Smith
42884-	"	John J. Smith
42890-	"	Robert H. F. Thompson
42889-	"	Hattie Wright
42883-	"	Nancy Wolfe
42880-	"	E. A. Welch

You are requested to advise the interested parties, including Mr. Hastings, of the Department's action.

Very respectfully,
C. F. Larrabee
Acting Commissioner.

AJW-FHE.

◇◇◇◇◇

Cherokee
I. W. 241.

Muskogee, Indian Territory, May 25, 1907.

Chief Clerk,
Cherokee Land Office.

Dear Sir:

You are hereby advised that on May 13, 1907, the Secretary of the Interior denied a motion filed by the Attorney for the Cherokee Nation, for a review of its decision authorizing the enrollment of Osburn J. Byrd as a citizen by intermarriage of the Cherokee Nation.

Respectfully,

Commissioner.

LMC

◇◇◇◇◇

Cherokee
241

Muskogee, Indian Territory, May 25, 1907.

Osburn J. Byrd,
   Fairland, Indian Territory.

Dear Sir:

You are hereby advised that on May 13, 1907, the Secretary of the Interior denied a motion filed by the Attorney for the Cherokee Nation, for a review of its decision authorizing your enrollment as a citizen by intermarriage of the Cherokee Nation.

Respectfully,

Commissioner.

LMC

◇◇◇◇◇

Cherokee
241

Muskogee, Indian Territory, May 25, 1907.

Geo. E. McCulloch,
   Attorney for Osburn J. Byrd,
      Vinita, Indian Territory.

Dear Sir:

You are hereby advised that on May 13, 1907, the Secretary of the Interior denied a motion filed by the Attorney for the Cherokee Nation, for a review of its decision authorizing the enrollment of Osburn J. Byrd, as a citizen by intermarriage of the Cherokee Nation.

For your information, there is enclosed herewith a copy of Departmental decision referred to.

Respectfully,

Commissioner.

Encl. C-3
   LMC

◇◇◇◇◇

238

Cherokee Intermarried White 1906
Volume VIII

Cherokee
253 et al.

Muskogee, Indian Territory, May 25, 1907.

W. W. Hastings,
Attorney for the Cherokee Nation,
Muskogee, Indian Territory.

Dear Sir:

You are hereby advised that on May 13, 1907, the Secretary of the Interior denied the motion filed by you for a review of its decision authorizing the enrollment of Jacob A. Bartles, et al., as citizens by intermarriage of the Cherokee Nation.

For your information, there is enclosed herewith a copy of Departmental decision referred to.

Respectfully,

Commissioner.

Encl. C-20
LMC

Cher IW 242

◇◇◇◇◇

(jacket missing)

Cher IW 243

◇◇◇◇◇

DEPARTMENT OF THE INTERIOR.
COMMISSION TO THE FIVE CIVILIZED TRIBES.
FT. GIBSON, I. T. AUGUST 30th, 1900.

IN THE MATTER OF THE APPLICATION OF Daniel Harmon, wife and children, for enrollment as citizens of the Cherokee Nation, and he being sworn by Commissioner, T.B. Needles, testified as follows:

Q What is your name?   A Daniel Harmon.
Q What is your age?   A Sixty one.
Q What is your Postoffice?   A Webbers Falls.

Cherokee Intermarried White 1906
Volume VIII

Q Are you a recognized citizen of the Cherokee Nation?
A I am an adopted citizen.
Q For whom do you apply?   A Myself and family
Q Wife and children?   A Yes sir.
Q What district do you live in? A Canadian.
Q How long have you lived in the Cherokee Nation?
A Since 1866.
Q Continuously?   A Yes sir.
Q What is the name of your father?   A Joshuaway Harmon.
Q What is the name of your mother?   A Henrietta Harmon.
Q Both non citizens?   A Yes sir.
Q What is the name of your wife?   A Cuntha[sic] Harmon.
Q What was her name before you married her?   A Pack[sic].
Q When did you marry her?   A 1865.
Q Have you been living with her ever since?   A Yes sir.
Q Do you know the name of her father? A Thomas J. Pack.
Q Is he living?   A No sir.
Q Did he died[sic] before 1880?   A Yes sir.
Q What is the name of her mother?   A Jane Pack.
Q Is she living?   A No sir.
Q Did she died[sic] before 1880? A Yes sir.
Q What are the names of your children; the oldest at home, under twenty one years of age?   A McGilbray Harmon.
Q How old is McGilbray?   A Twenty.
Q What is the name of the next one?   A Benjamin Harmon.
Q How old is Benjamin?   A Nineteen.
Q Go on?   A Rena.
Q How old is Rena?   A Fourteen.
Q Next?   A That is all.
Q Are these three children living, and living with you?   A Yes sir.
Q At this time?   A Yes sir.
Q Born and raised in the Cherokee Nation?   A Yes sir.

(1880 Roll, Page 23, #636, Richard Harmon, Canadian District)
(1880 Roll, Page 23, #636, Cyntha Harmon, Canadian District)
     (1896 Roll, Page 88, #112, Daniel Harmon, Canadian District)
(1896 Roll, Page 33, #896, Cyntha Harmon, Canadian District)
Identification of applicant's children:
(1896 Roll, page 33, #900, Mack D. Harmon, Canadian District)
(1896 Roll, page 33, #901, Benjamin Harmon, Canadian District)
(1896 Roll, page 33, #902, Lena Harmon, Canadian District)

The name of Daniel Harmon appears on the authenticated roll of 1880, as Richard Harmon, and upon the roll of 1896, as Daniel Harmon: His wifes[sic] name appears on the authenticated roll of 1880, as well as the census roll of 1896: His children, McGilbray, Benjamin and Rena[sic] also appear upon the census roll of 1896, they all

Cherokee Intermarried White 1906
Volume VIII

being duly identified according to the page and number of the rolls, and having made satisfactory proof of their residence, said Daniel Harmon will be duly listed for enrollment by this Commission as a Cherokee citizen by intermarriage, and his wife and children as Cherokees by blood.

The undersigned, being sworn, states that as stenographer to the Commission to the Five Civilized Tribes, he correctly recorded the testimony and proceedings in this case, and the foregoing is a true and complete transcript of his stenographic notes thereof.

R R Cravens

Subscribed and sworn to before
me this 11th day of September, 1900.

C R Breckinridge
COMMISSIONER.

◇◇◇◇◇

(Copy of original document from case.)

241

Cherokee 2291

DEPARTMENT OF THE INTERIOR,
COMMISSION TO THE FIVE CIVILIZED TRIBES,
MUSKOGEE, IND. TER., SEPT. 17, 1902.

In the matter of the application of Daniel Harmon et al. as citizens of the Cherokee Nation:

SUPPLEMENTAL STATEMENT.

It appears from the testimony that the child listed for enrollment as Lena is given therein as Tena, and also in the field judgment as Rena; but, from an examination and investigation of the memorandum made from personal testimony and also from its enrollment, that the child is properly listed now as Lena, and should be enrolled as such.

It is ordered that copies of this statement be filed with the testimony in this case.

TB Needles
Commissioner.

◇◇◇◇◇

DEPARTMENT OF THE INTERIOR.
COMMISSION TO THE FIVE CIVILIZED TRIBES.
AUXILIARY CHEROKEE LAND OFFICE.

Muskogee, Indian Territory, April 7, 1905.

In the matter of the application of Daniel Harmon to select an allotment in the Cherokee Nation for his wife Cynthia Harmon, Cherokee citizen roll No. 5950, Field Card No. 2291.

Daniel Harmon, non-citizen husband, being first duly sworn testified as follows:

Examination by the Commission:
Q   What is your name?   A Daniel Harmon.
Q   What is your post office address?   A Webbers Falls.
Q   What is your age?   A 66.
Q   Are you a citizen of the Cherokee Nation?   A Yes, adopted.

Q Is your object in appearing here today to select an allotment for your wife Cynthia Harmon? A Yes sir.

Q Is she living? A Yes.

Q Why is it that she cannot appear and select this in person?
A I thought I could file for her.

Q Is the land that you desire to select for your wife under improvement? A Yes sir, mostly.

Q Have you sufficient land for her to make a complete allotment? A Yes sir.

Q Does this land lie west of the Grand river[sic]? A It is in the Canadian district.

Q Has either your wife or anyone else ever applied at either the Vinita or Tahlequah Office for an allotment for her? A No sir.

Witness offers power of attorney executed by Cynthia Harmon to Dan W. Harmon, authorizing him to select an allotment for her in the Cherokee Nation dated April 3, 1905.

WITNESS EXCUSED.

Blanch Ashton upon oath states that as stenographer to the Commission to the Five Civilized Tribes she accurately recorded the testimony in the above entitled cause and that the foregoing is a correct transcript of her stenographic notes thereof.

Blanch Ashton

Sworn and subscribed to before me this 7th day of April, 1905.

W.S. Hawkins
Notary Public.

◇◇◇◇◇

Cherokee 2291.

DEPARTMENT OF THE INTERIOR,
COMMISSIONER TO THE FIVE CIVILIZED TRIBES.
Muskogee, I. T., January 3, 1907.

In the matter of the application for the enrollment of Daniel Harmon as a citizen by intermarriage of the Cherokee Nation.

Daniel Harnon[sic], being first duly sworn by Walter W. Chappele[sic], a Notary Public for the Western District, Indian Territory, testified as follows:

By the Commissioner:

Q What is your name? A Daniel Harmon.

Q What is your age? A Sixty-seven.

Q   Your postoffice address?   A Webbers Falls, I.T.

Q   You claim to be a citizen by intermarriage of the Cherokee Nation?   A Yes sir.

Q   Through whom do you claim that right?   A My wife.

Q   What was her name?   A Cyntha Peck.

Q   Is she living at the present time?   A Yes sir.

Q   What is her citizenship?   A Cherokee by blood.

Q   When were you and Cyntha Peck married?   A Married in 1865, the 23rd of February.

Q   Where were you married?   A Choctaw Nation.

Q   Were you married under Cherokee license?   A No sir.

Q   Under what law were you married?   A Got married by a minister.

Q   In the Choctaw nation[sic]?   A Yes sir.

Q   What citizenship was your wife at the time you were married?   A She was Cherokee; She left the nation on account of the war.

Q   And was residing in the Choctaw nation at the time of your marriage?   A Yes sir.

Q   How long did you continue to live in the Choctaw nation after you were married?
A   I think we moved up here in 1866 or 1867.

Q   After your removal to the Cherokee Nation were you remarried under a Cherokee license?   A No, Indians didn't have to to marry an Indian; we didn't have to marry under a license. I am an Indian myself-- a Creek.

Q   Have you made application for enrollment in the Creek Nation?   A Yes sir.

Q   Has your application been disposed of?   A I was admitted by the House of Kings and they told me that they would get me on the roll and then they said it was not lawful, that it should have gone through both houses.

Q   Have you made application to this commission for enrollment as a citizen of the Creek Nation?   A Yes sir.

Q   Has that application been disposed of?   A They couldn't admit me as a Creek.

Q   They refused to admit you as a Creek citizen, this Commission did?   A Yes sir.

Q   And you and your wife removed to the Cherokee Nation in 1866 where you have since lived?   A Yes, near Webbers Falls.

Q   And you have lived here continuously since that time?   A Yes sir.

Q   The only marriage ceremony performed between you and your wife was the ceremony performed in the Choctaw nation?   A Yes sir.

Q   Had either you or your wife ever been married prior to your marriage in the Choctaw Nation?   A No sir.

The applicant Daniel Harmon is identified on the authenticated Cherokee tribal roll of 1880, and Cherokee Census roll of 1896, Canadian District, No. 635 and 112 respectively, as an intermarried white. The records of this office show that Cyntha Harmon, nee Peck is included in an approved partial roll of citizens by blood of the Cherokee Nation, opposite No. 5950.

Cherokee Intermarried White 1906
Volume VIII

Frances R. Lane being first duly sworn, states that as stenographer to the Commission to the Five Civilized Tribes she reported the testimony in the above entitled cause and that the foregoing is an accurate transcript of her stenographic notes thereof.

Frances R Lane

Subscribed and sworn to before me this January 4, 1907.

Edward Merrick
Notary Public.

◇◇◇◇◇

E C M   Cherokee 2291.

COPY

DEPARTMENT OF THE INTERIOR,
COMMISSIONER TO THE FIVE CIVILIZED TRIBES.

In the matter of the application for the enrollment of DANIEL HARMON as a citizen by intermarriage of the Cherokee Nation.

D E C I S I O N

THE RECORDS OF THIS OFFICE SHOW: That at Fort Gibson, Indian Territory, August 30, 1900 application was received by the Commission to the Five Civilized Tribes for the enrollment of Daniel Harmon as a citizen by intermarriage of the Cherokee Nation. Further proceedings in the matter of said application were had at Muskogee, Indian Territory, October 14, 1902 and January 3, 1907.

THE EVIDENCE IN THIS CASE SHOWS: That the applicant herein, Daniel Harmon, is a non-citizen of the Cherokee Nation and possesses no right to enrollment as a citizen of said Nation other than such right as he may have acquired by virtue of his marriage February 23, 1865 to one Cynthia Harmon, nee Pack, who is identified on the Cherokee authenticated tribal roll of 1880, Canadian District No. 636 as a native Cherokee, and whose name is included on the approved partial roll of citizens by blood of the Cherokee Nation opposite No. 5950. It is further shown that said marriage was not in accordance with Cherokee law, the said Daniel Harmon having failed to secure a license as required by the laws of the Cherokee Nation. It is also shown that said Daniel Harmon was not at the time of said marriage a citizen of the Creek Nation and has never been recognized as such, his name not being identified on any of the Creek tribal rolls now in possession of this office. Said applicant is identified on the Cherokee authenticated tribal roll of 1880 and the Cherokee census roll of 1896 as an intermarried citizen of the Cherokee Nation.

IT IS, THEREFORE, ORDERED AND ADJUDGED: That in accordance with the decision of the Supreme Court of the United States, dated November 5, 1906, in the cases of Daniel Red Bird, et al. vs. the United States, Nos. 125, 126, 127, and 128, the said

Cherokee Intermarried White 1906
Volume VIII

applicant, Daniel Harmon, is not entitled, under the provisions of Section Twenty-one of the Act of Congress approved June 28, 1898 (30 Stats. 495), to enrollment as a citizen by intermarriage of the Cherokee Nation, and his application for enrollment as such is accordingly denied.

SIGNED *James Bixby*
Commissioner.

Dated at Muskogee, Indian Territory,
this   FEB 28 1907

◇◇◇◇◇

Cherokee 2291

Vinita, Indian Territory, March 10, 1903.

Commission to the Five Civilized Tribes,
    (Creek Enrollment Division),
        Muskogee, Indian Territory.

Gentlemen:

        On August 30, 1900, Daniel Harmon applied to this Commission for the enrollment of himself as a citizen by intermarriage, and for the enrollment of his wife, Cyntha, and three children, McGilbry, Benjamin and Lena, as citizens by blood of the Cherokee Nation. A note on this card in this case is to the effect that Daniel Harmon is listed on old Creek census card #1618.

        I respectfully request to be advised if any of the persons named above are applicants for enrollment as citizens of the Creek Nation, and if so, what disposition has been made of their applications.

Respectfully,

Clerk in Charge.

GRS

◇◇◇◇◇

Cherokee Intermarried White 1906
Volume VIII

J.J.B.

REFER IN REPLY TO THE FOLLOWING

COMMISSIONERS:
TAMS BIXBY,
THOMAS B. NEEDLES,
C. R. BRECKINRIDGE,
W. E. STANLEY.

ALLISON L. AYLESWORTH,
SECRETARY.

DEPARTMENT OF THE INTERIOR,
COMMISSION TO THE FIVE CIVILIZED TRIBES.

ADDRESS ONLY THE
COMMISSION TO THE FIVE CIVILIZED TRIBES.

Muskogee, Indian Territory, March 12, 1903.

P. G. Reuter,
   Clerk in Charge Cherokee Land Office,
      Vinita, Indian Territory.

Dear Sir:

Receipt is acknowledged of your letter of the 10th instant, in which it is stated that on August 30, 1900, Daniel Harmon applied to the Commission for the enrollment of himself as a citizen by intermarriage, and for the enrollment of his wife, Cyntha and their three minor children, McGilbry, Banjamin[sic] and Lena Harmon, as citizens by blood, of the Cherokee Nation, and that a note on the card in the case is to the effect that Daniel Harmon is listed on old Creek census care No. 1618.

You request to be advised if any of the persons named above are applicants for enrollment as citizens of the Creek Nation, and, if so, what disposition has been made of their applications.

In reply you are advised that an examination of the records of the Creek Enrollment Division shows that no application has been made for the enrollment of Daniel, Cyntha, McGilbry, Benjamin and Lena Harmon, or either of them, as citizens of the Creek Nation.

The name of Daniel Harmon appears upon old Creek census care No. 1618, and a note on that card is to the effect that the name of Daniel Harmon appears on the 1880 Cherokee roll as Richard Harmon, and his wife and family, and that he is enrolled on Cherokee card No. 2291.

Respectfully,

Tams Bixby
Chairman.

◇◇◇◇◇

Cherokee
2291

Muskogee, Indian Territory, December 24, 1906.

Daniel Harmon,
    Webbers Falls, Indian Territory.

Dear Sir:

    November 6, 1906, the United States Supreme Court, held that white persons who intermarried with Cherokee citizens according to Cherokee law prior to November 1, 1875, are entitled to enrollment and allotments of land as citizens of the Cherokee Nation.

    You are advised that to properly determine your right to enrollment as a citizen by intermarriage of the Cherokee Nation, it will be necessary for you to appear before the Commissioner for the purpose of giving testimony as to the date of your marriage and whether or not your wife, by reason of your marriage to whom you claim the right to enrollment as a citizen of the Cherokee Nation, was a recognized citizen of the Cherokee Nation at the time of your marriage to her, and whether or not you were married to her in accordance with Cherokee laws.

    You are, therefore, directed to appear before the Commissioner at Muskogee, Indian Territory, at 9 o'clock A. M., on Thursday, January 3, 1907, and give testimony as above indicated.

                      Respectfully,

JMH   Acting Commissioner.

◇◇◇◇◇

(The letter below typed as given.)

2291

COPY

D.C. 1649-1907.

Webbers Falls Ind Ter Jam 7 1907.

Commishions of the Five Civilized Tribes

Dear Sirs:

I will take the liberty of trying to state my case to you as the Cherokees have put me on the roll as white intermaried citizen I would like to have the right to prove that I am a Creek Indian please allow me that privelge   I will make a statement of my case in the first place I was brought to the Creek Nation from Mobile Alabama by the Agents of United States goverment with a good many other Creeks Indians by Wm McMaston & Ward Coachman in 1847   We lived there I also went to school at old North Fork Creek Nation at the mission School known as the A. M. L. the greater part of three ten months terms boarded there drew clothing with the other Creek children which I could not have done had I not been a Creek Indian.   When this allotment question came up I went to the Creek Councils to be readmited in 1897 there I found some of my old school mates one was George Alexander chairman of the house of Kings another John Francis town chief they put my case through the house of Kings and George Alixander turned to me and saide Dick John Francis will put your name on the roll and when I went before Mr Needles for the purpose of enroleing in the Creek Nation the attorney for the Creeks said it was not leagal it ought to have gone through bothe houses I will give the names of my mother Henreitta Harmon by brothers Benjamin Harmon William Harmon and myself My name Daniel Harmon they always called me Dick.   we all cam to Creek Nation together when I was a small boy.   I have some strong evidence that is my nephews Ben and Dan Harmon bothe have filed on land in the Creek Nation my grand children also filed up there whos names are as follows Fred Boles.   Holland Boles Pearl Boles Cherokee Boles Ruby Boles Henrietta Boles.   They live near Broken Arrow their Monther's name was Jennie Boles who was my daughter   My wife has no Creek blood neather has Frank Boles the farther of my grandchildren then where did they get their right by me as a matter of fact I beg your pardon for writing so much but the Cherokee authorities have put my name on the roll as a white man I dont remember ever telling any one that I was a white man will you please reply and let me hear from you as soon as possable and greatly oblige

Yours resp
(Signed Daniel Harmon
Webbers Falls
Ind. Ter.

◇◇◇◇◇

Cherokee
2291

Muskogee, Indian Territory, January 14, 1907.

Chief Clerk,
Creek Enrollment Division.

Dear Sir:

You are requested to advise this office the status of the case of Daniel Harmon, Creek Enrollment number 63. As this matter is important you are requested to give it your immediate attention.

Respectfully,

Commissioner.

LMC

◇◇◇◇◇

Muskogee, Indian Territory, January 19, 1907.

Chief Clerk,
Creek Enrollment Division.

Dear Sir:

You were requested on January 14, 1907 to advise this office the status of the case of Daniel Harmon, Creek enrollment number 63. You are again requested to give this your immediate attention.

Respectfully,

Commissioner.

LMC

◇◇◇◇◇

(COPY)   H G H

Cherokee 2291

DC 62   DEPARTMENT OF THE INTERIOR

COMMISSIONER TO THE FIVE CIVILIZED TRIBES.

Muskogee, Indian Territory, January 19, 1907.

Chief Clerk,

Cherokee Enrollment Division,

Muskogee, Indian Territory.

Dear Sir:

Replying to your letter of January 14, 1907, you are advised that application was made for the enrollment of Daniel Harmon, as a citizen of the Creek Nation, to the Commission to the Five Civilized Tribes in 1896 (Dawes Commission Number 62) and that said application was rejected and no appeal taken from the decision of said Commission.

Respectfully,

Tams Bixby.

Commissioner.

◇◇◇◇◇

SPECIAL.

D.C. 13260-1907.   FHE. JFJr.

DEPARTMENT OF THE INTERIOR,

WASHINGTON.

I.T.D.

7618, 7674, 8028, 8030-07.   March 4, 1907.

LRS.

DIRECT.

Commissioner to the Five Civilized Tribes,

Muskogee, Indian Territory.

Sir:

The Department, in view of the opinion of the Attorney-General in the John W. Gleason case, and that of the Assistant-Attorney-General in the Jacob Bartles case, hereby reverses your decisions adverse to the applicants in the following Intermarried Cherokee enrollment cases, and their applications for enrollment are granted. You are directed to enroll all of such applicants as citizens by intermarriage of the Cherokee Nation:

Title of case.	Date of your letter of transmittal.
Amanda Beck	February 19, 1907.
Osburn J. Byrd,	February 4, 1907.
Rufus M. Allen,	February 4, 1907
Daniel Harmon,	February 28, 1907
Nancy Wolfe,	February 28, 1907

Copies of Indian Office letters submitting your reports are inclosed. The papers in the various cases mentioned have been sent to the Indian Office with a copy hereof.

Respectfully,

Jesse E. Wilson

5 inc. and   Acting Secretary.
    for Ind. Of. with copy hereof.
AFMc
3-4-07.
            (No encls. RH.)

◇◇◇◇◇

Cherokee 2291

Muskogee, Indian Territory, March 21, 1907.

Daniel Harmon,
        Webbers Falls, Indian Territory.

Dear Sir:

You are hereby advised that the decision of the Commissioner to the Five Civilized Tribes, dated February 28, 1907, rejecting your application for enrollment as a citizen by intermarriage of the Cherokee Nation, was reversed by the Secretary of the Interior, March 4, 1907, and said application granted.

For your information, there is enclosed herewith a copy of Departmental decision referred to.

Respectfully,

Encl. H-92 1/2   Commissioner.
    JMH

◇◇◇◇◇

Cherokee Intermarried White 1906
Volume VIII

Cherokee 5462,
3866, 4509, 2291,   COPY
8915.

Muskogee, Indian Territory, March 21, 1907.

W. W. Hastings,
    Attorney for the Cherokee Nation,
        Muskogee, Indian Territory.

Dear Sir:

You are hereby advised that the decisions of the Commissioner to the Five Civilized Tribes, rejecting the applications for the enrollment of the following named persons, as citizens by intermarriage of the Cherokee Nation, were reversed by the Secretary of the Interior, March 4, 1907.

        Amanda Beck
        Osburn J. Byrd
        Rufus M. Allen
        Daniel Harmon
        Nancy Wolfe.

For your information, there is enclosed herewith a copy of Departmental decision referred to.

Respectfully,

SIGNED *Jams Bixby*
Encl. H-95   Commissioner.
JMH

Cher IW 244

◇◇◇◇◇

G.

C.

Department of the Interior.
Commission to the Five Civilized Tribes.
Eucha, I. T., May 28, 1902.

In the matter of the application of NANCY WOLFE for the enrollment of herself as a citizen by intermarriage of the Cherokee Nation.

253

Cherokee Intermarried White 1906
Volume VIII

BEN O'FIELD, being first duly sworn, and being examined, testified as follows, through sworn interpreter Henry C. Ross:

BY COMMISSION: What is your name?   A Ben O'Field.
Q How old are you?   A Forty-six.
Q What is your post office address?   A Mayesville, Arkansas.
Q What district do you live in?   A Delaware District.
W[sic] You are a citizen by blood of the Cherokee Nation?   A Yes sir.
Q You are one of the witnesses before the Commission at this place?   A Yes sir.
Q Do you know Nancy Wolfe, a white woman?   A Yes sir.
Q She is living now?   A Yes sir.
Q About how old is she?   A About ninety or more.
Q What is her post office address?   A Cherokee City, Arkansas.
Q She lives in Delaware District?   A Yes sir.
Q She is very old and feeble and could not come and enroll herself?
A I think she could not come.
Q With whom is she living now?   A Living with her daughter.
Q Elam Foreman's wife?   A Yes sir.
Q Nancy is a widow now, is she?   A Yes sir.
Q How long has her husband, Wolfe, been dead?   A He has been dead a good while, could not say how lojg[sic].
Q What was his name?   A Daniel Wolfe.
Q Do you think this Nancy was married to him about 1880 or before?
A Married probably before 1880.
Q Did she live with Daniel Wolfe continuously from the time she married him until his death?   A Yes sir.
Q Did she ever marry any other person after the death of Daniel Wolfe?   A No sir.
Q Has she always lived in the Cherokee Nation since she married Daniel Wolfe?
A Yes sir.
Q Did she sometimes go by the name of Anna Wolfe?   A Never have heard that name.
Q Daniel Wolfe never had any other wife named Anna about 1880, did he, who was a white woman?   A I don't know of any. He only lived with Nancy, so far as I know. I suppose that was her English name, Anna.
Q Do you know the name of Nancy's father and mother?   A No sir.
Q They have been dead for a number of years?   A I believe they have been dead for a number of years.
Q They were non-citizens?   A Yes sir.
Q Nancy is considered to be a white woman, is she?   A Yes sir.

1880 authenticated roll of citizens of the Cherokee Nation examined, and applicant identified as follows:

Page 341, #3036, Anna Wolfe, Delaware District, age 80.
Intermarried white.

Cherokee Intermarried White 1906
Volume VIII

1896 census roll of citizens of the Cherokee Nation examined, and applicant identified as follows:

Page 593, #576, Anna Wolfe, Delaware District, age 86.
Intermarried white.

Q You know that Nancy Wolfe is living now and living in Delaware District, Cerokee[sic] Nation, and makes her home with her son-in-law, Elam Foreman?
A Yes sir.

Nancy Wolfe will be listed for enrollment upon straight care.

Wm. Hutchinson, being first duly sworn, states that as stenographer to the Commission to the Five Civilized Tribes, he correctly recorded the testimony and proceedings in this case, and that the foregoing is a true and complete transcript of the stenographic notes thereof.

Wm Hutchinson

Subscribed and sworn to before me this 29th day of May, 1902.

MD Green
Notary Public.

◇◇◇◇◇

Statement of Applicant Taken Under Oath.

Eucha I. T. 4-279

CHEROKEE BY BLOOD AND ADOPTION.

Date **May 28** 1902.

Name

District .... Year .... Page .... No. ....
Citizen by blood .... Mother's citizenship ....
Intermarried citizen ....
Married under what law .... Date of marriage ....
License .... Certificate ....

Wife's name **Nancy Wolfe, Cherokee City, Ark.**
District **Delaware** Year **1880** Page **341** No. **3036**
Citizen by blood ‾‾ Mother's citizenship **US non citz** ‾‾
Intermarried citizen **Yes**
Married under what law .... Date of marriage ....
License .... Certificate ....

Names of Children:

	Dist.	Year	Page	No.	Age
	Dist.	Year	Page	No.	Age
	Dist.	Year	Page	No.	Age
	Dist.	Year	Page	No.	Age

255

Cherokee Intermarried White 1906
Volume VIII

On 1880 Roll as Anna Wolfe
" 1896 " " p 593 #576 as Anna Wolfe Delaware Dist

◇◇◇◇◇

F.R. Cherokee 8915.

DEPARTMENT OF THE INTERIOR,

COMMISSIONER TO THE FIVE CIVILIZED TRIBES.

In the matter of the application for the enrollment of Nancy Wolfe as a citizen by intermarriage of the Cherokee Nation.

D E C I S I O N

THE RECORDS OF THIS OFFICE SHOW: That at Eucha, Indian Territory, May 28, 1902, application was received by the Commission to the Five Civilized Tribes for the enrollment of Nancy Wolfe as a citizen by intermarriage of the Cherokee Nation.

THE EVIDENCE IN THIS CASE SHOWS: That Nancy Wolfe, the applicant in this case. is alleged to have married one Daniel Wolfe, a recognized citizen by blood of the Cherokee Nation prior to 1880, who is identified on the Cherokee authenticated tribal roll of 1880, Delaware District, No. 3036, as a native Cherokee, with whom she lived until his demise.

On February 23, 1907, notice was sent to the applicant to appear immediately with witnesses to establish her marriage to a recognized citizen by blood of the Cherokee Nation prior to November 1, 1875. This said applicant failed to do.

It is considered that there is not sufficient evidence in this case to support a finding that the applicant was married to her Cherokee husband prior to November 1, 1875, or that the said applicant was living on September 1, 1902, although the said Nancy Wolfe is identified on the Cherokee authenticated tribal roll of 1880 and the Cherokee Census Roll of 1896 as an intermarried citizen of the Cherokee Nation.

IT IS, THEREFORE, ORDERED AND ADJUDGED: That in accordance with the decision of the Supreme Court of the United States, dated November 5, 1906, in the cases of Daniel Red Bird et al. vs. the United States, Nos. 125, 126, 127, and 128, the said applicant, Nancy Wolfe, is not entitled, under the provisions of Section Twenty-one of the Act of Congress approved June 28, 1898 (30 Stats. 495), to enrollment as a citizen by intermarriage of the Cherokee Nation, provisions of Section 21 of the Act of Congress

Cherokee Intermarried White 1906
Volume VIII

approved June 28, 1898 (30 Stats. 495), to enrollment as a citizen by intermarriage of the Cherokee Nation, and her application for enrollment as such is accordingly denied.

Tams Bixby

Commissioner.

Dated at Muskogee, Indian Territory,
FEB 28 1907

◇◇◇◇◇

(Copy of original document from case.)

◇◇◇◇◇

(Copy of original document from case.)

257

Cherokee Intermarried White 1906
Volume VIII

◇◇◇◇◇

(Copy of original document from case.)

◇◇◇◇◇

Cherokee 8915

Special   Muskogee, Indian Territory, February 12, 1907

Nancy Wolfe,
    Mayesville, Arkansas.

Dear Madam:

The Commissioner sent you this day a telegram as follows:

"Intermarried case incomplete. Appear
immediately to establish marriage to
Daniel Wolfe."

The Act of Congress approved April 26, 1906, provides that the Secretary of the Interior shall have no jurisdiction to approve the enrollment of any person as a citizen of the Cherokee Nation after March 4, 1907.

This matter, therefore, demands your immediate attention.

Respectfully,

MMP   Commissioner.

◇◇◇◇◇

Cherokee 8915.

ECM   Muskogee, Indian Territory, February 23, 1907.

SPECIAL.

   Nancy Wolfe,
      Cherokee City, Arkansas.

  Dear Madam:

     The Commission sent you this day a telegram as follows:

     "Intermarried case incomplete. Appear
     immediately to establish marriage to
     Daniel Wolfe."

    The Act of Congress approved April 26, 1906 provides that the Secretary of the Interior shall have no jurisdiction to approve the enrollment of any person as a citizen of the Cherokee Nation after March 4, 1907. This matter, therefore, demands your immediate attention.

              Respectfully,

GHC   Commissioner.

◇◇◇◇◇

THE WESTERN UNION TELEGRAPH COMPANY.
24,000 OFFICES IN AMERICA. CABLE SERVICE TO ALL THE WORLD.

RECEIVED at

21 KS GN E 715 pm,

Muskogee, I.T.

Youre date Wolfe signed Bixby hung up at Siloam until am account
no phone to Cherokee city to-day.

         Siloam Springs, Ark. Feb24

MONEY TRANSFERRED BY TELEGRAPH.   CABLE OFFICE.

(Copy of original document from case.)

◇◇◇◇◇

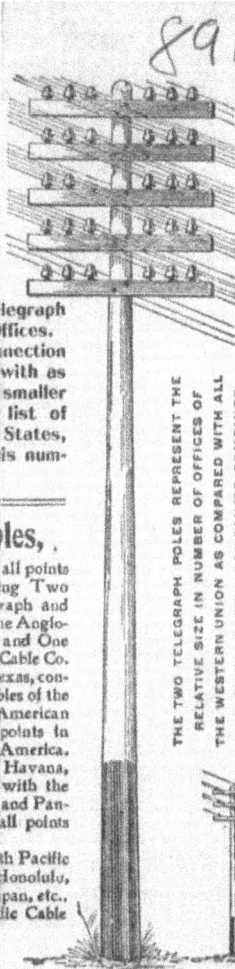

(Copy of original document from case.)

Cherokee Intermarried White 1906
Volume VIII

◇◇◇◇◇

Muskogee, Indian Territory, February 28, 1907.

The Honorable,
    The Secretary of the Interior.

Sir:

There is transmitted herewith the record of proceedings had in the matter of the application for the enrollment of Nancy Wolfe, as a citizen by intermarriage of the Cherokee Nation, together with the decision of the Commissioner to the Five Civilized Tribes dated February 28, 1907, denying said application.

Respectfully,

SIGNED *Jams Bixby*
Commissioner.

Encl. A-31
    RA

Through the Commissioner
    of Indian Affairs.

◇◇◇◇◇

Cherokee 8915

Muskogee, Indian Territory, February 28, 1907.

W. W. Hastings,
    Attorney for the Cherokee Nation,
        Muskogee, Indian Territory.

Dear Sir:

There is enclosed herewith a copy of the decision of the Commissioner to the Five Civilized Tribes, dated February 28, 1907, denying the application for the enrollment of Nancy Wolfe, as a citizen by intermarriage of the Cherokee Nation.

The decision, together with the record of proceedings had in the case, has this day been transmitted to the Secretary of the Interior for his review and decision. You will be advised of the Secretary's action as soon as this office is informed of same.

261

Respectfully,

SIGNED *Jams Bixby*
Commissioner.

Encl. A-30
RA

◇◇◇◇◇

Cherokee 8915

COPY

Muskogee, Indian Territory, February 28, 1907.

Nancy Wolfe,
      Mayesville, Arkansas.

Dear Sir[sic]:

      There is enclosed herewith a copy of the decision of the Commissioner to the Five Civilized Tribes, dated February 28, 1907, rejecting the application for your enrollment as a citizen by intermarriage of the Cherokee Nation.

      The decision, together with the record of proceedings had in the case, has this day been transmitted to the Secretary of the Interior for his review and decision. You will be advised of the Secretary's action as soon as this office is informed of same.

Respectfully,

SIGNED *Jams Bixby*
Commissioner.

Encl. A-29
RA

Register.

◇◇◇◇◇

SPECIAL.

D.C. 13260-1907.   FHE. JFJr.

DEPARTMENT OF THE INTERIOR,

WASHINGTON.

I.T.D.

7618, 7674, 8028, 8030-07.   March 4, 1907.

LRS.

DIRECT.

Commissioner to the Five Civilized Tribes,
   Muskogee, Indian Territory.

Sir:

    The Department, in view of the opinion of the Attorney-General in the John W. Gleason case, and that of the Assistant-Attorney-General in the Jacob Bartles case, hereby reverses your decisions adverse to the applicants in the following Intermarried Cherokee enrollment cases, and their applications for enrollment are granted. You are directed to enroll all of such applicants as citizens by intermarriage of the Cherokee Nation:

| | Date of your |
Title of case.	letter of transmittal.
Amanda Beck	February 19, 1907.
Osburn J. Byrd,	February 4, 1907.
Rufus M. Allen	February 4, 1907
Daniel Harmon,	February 28, 1907
Nancy Wolfe,	February 28, 1907

    Copies of Indian Office letters submitting your reports are inclosed. The papers in the various cases mentioned have been sent to the Indian Office with a copy hereof.

Respectfully,

(Signed)   Jesse E. Wilson

5 inc. and   Acting Secretary.

   for Ind. Of. with copy hereof.

AFMc

3-4-07.

              (No encls. RH.)

◇◇◇◇◇

COPY

Cherokee 8915

Muskogee, Indian Territory, March 21, 1907.

Nancy Wolfe,
Cherokee City, Arkansas.

Dear Madam:

You are hereby advised that the decision of the Commissioner to the Five Civilized Tribes, dated February 28, 1907, rejecting your application for enrollment as a citizen by intermarriage of the Cherokee Nation, was reversed by the Secretary of the Interior, March 4, 1907, and said application granted.

For your information, there is enclosed herewith a copy of Departmental decision referred to.

Respectfully,

SIGNED *Tams Bixby*
Commissioner.

Encl. H-91
JMH

◇◇◇◇◇

Cherokee 5462,
3866, 4509, 2291,   COPY
8915.

Muskogee, Indian Territory, March 21, 1907.

W. W. Hastings,
Attorney for the Cherokee Nation,
Muskogee, Indian Territory.

Dear Sir:

You are hereby advised that the decisions of the Commissioner to the Five Civilized Tribes, rejecting the applications for the enrollment of the following named persons, as citizens by intermarriage of the Cherokee Nation, were reversed by the Secretary of the Interior, March 4, 1907.

Amanda Beck
Osburn J. Byrd
Rufus M. Allen
Daniel Harmon
Nancy Wolfe.

For your information, there is enclosed herewith a copy of Departmental decision referred to.

Respectfully,

SIGNED *Tams Bixby*

Encl. H-95   Commissioner.

JMH

◇◇◇◇◇

I. T. references in
body of letter.   GAW

DEPARTMENT OF THE INTERIOR,
OFFICE OF INDIAN AFFAIRS,
WASHINGTON.

May 15, 1907.

Commissioner to the Five Civilized Tribes,
Muskogee, Indian Territory.

Sir:

There is inclosed copy of Office letter of May 11, 1907, approved by the Department on May 13, 1907, recommending that motions filed by W. W. Hastings, National Attorney for the Cherokee Nation, praying for a review and rehearing of Departmental decisions authorizing the enrollment of the following persons as citizens by intermarriage of the Cherokee Nation, be denied, in view of the fact that there appears to be no authority in law at this time for the reconsideration of any enrollment case.

42893-1907	Jacob A. Bartles
42895- "	Osburn J. Byrd
42886- "	Amanda Beck
42894- "	Sarah F. Gage
42892- "	Phirena Harris
42888- "	Daniel Harmon
42891- "	Emma L. Ironsides
42896- "	Sarah A. Jordan
42881- "	Dovie Johnson
42882- "	Andrew H. Norwood
42887- "	Stacy E. Perry
42885- "	Martha Randolph, now Kernan
42893- "	John W. Smith

265

42884-	"	John J. Smith
42890-	"	Robert H. F. Thompson
42889-	"	Hattie Wright
42883-	"	Nancy Wolfe
42880-	"	E. A. Welch

You are requested to advise the interested parties, including Mr. Hastings, of the Department's action.

Very respectfully,
C. F. Larrabee
Acting Commissioner.

AJW-FHE.

◇◇◇◇◇

DEPARTMENT OF THE INTERIOR
OFFICE OF INDIAN AFFAIRS,
WASHINGTON.   GAW

I.T.   May 11, 1907.
Reference in body
of letter.

Subject: Motions for
review in certain Chero-
kee citizenship cases.

The Honorable,
     The Secretary of the Interior.

Sir:

There are inclosed herewith motions filed by W. W. Hastings, National Attorney for the Cherokee Nation, praying for review and rehearing of Departmental decisions authorizing the enrollment as citizens by intermarriage of the Cherokee Nation of the following persons:

42893-1907,		Jacob A. Bartles,
42895-	"	Osburn J. Byrd,
42886-	"	Amanda Beck,
42894-	"	Sarah F. Gage,
42892-	"	Phirena Harris,
42888-	"	Daniel Harmon,
42891-	"	Emma L. Ironsides,
42896-	"	Sarah A. Jordan

42881-	"	Dovie Johnson,
42882-	"	Andrew H. Norwood,
42887-	"	Stacy E. Perry,
42885-	"	Martha Randolph, now Kernan
42893-	"	John W. Smith
42884-	"	John J. Smith,
42890-	"	Robert H. F. Thompson,
42889-	"	Hattie Wright,
42883-	"	Nancy Wolfe,
42880-	"	E. A. Welch.

In view of the provisions of section 2 of the act of April 26, 1906 (34 Stat. L., 137), providing that the rolls of the Five Civilized Tribes shall be fully completed on or before March 4, 1907, there appears to be no authority in law for the reconsideration of any enrollment cases at this time, and it is recommended that the office be authorized to advise Mr. Hastings that the motions for review herewith transmitted cannot be considered.

Very respectfully,

C. F. Larrabee

Acting Commissioner.

AJW-FHE.

May 13, 1907.

Approved.

Thos Ryan

First Assistant Secretary.

◇◇◇◇◇

Cherokee
244

Muskogee, Indian Territory, May 25, 1907.

Nancy Wolfe,
    Cherokee City, Arkansas.

Dear Madam:

You are hereby advised that on May 13, 1907, the Secretary of the Interior denied a motion filed by the Attorney for the Cherokee Nation, for a review of its decision authorizing your enrollment as a citizen by intermarriage of the Cherokee Nation.

267

For your information, there is enclosed herewith a copy of Departmental decision referred to.

Respectfully,

Commissioner.

Encl. C-18
LMC

◇◇◇◇◇◇

Cherokee
253. et al

Muskogee, Indian Territory, May 25, 1907.

W. W. Hastings,
Attorney for the Cherokee Nation,
Muskogee, Indian Territory.

Dear Sir:

You are hereby advised that on May 13, 1907, the Secretary of the Interior denied the motion filed by you for a review of its decision authorizing the enrollment of Jacob A. Bartles, et al., as citizens by intermarriage of the Cherokee Nation.

For your information, there is enclosed herewith a copy of Departmental decision referred to.

Respectfully,

Commissioner.

Encl. C-20
LMC

◇◇◇◇◇◇

Department of the Interior.
Commissioner to the Five Civilized Tribes,
MUSKOGEE, IND. TER.

Jam. Wolfe,
Haynville, Arkansas.

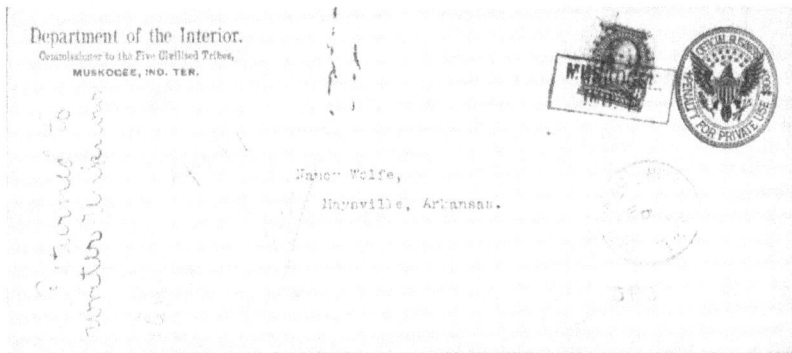

(Copy of original document from case.)

268

Cher IW 245

◇◇◇◇◇

DOUBTFUL

> Department of the Interior,
> Commission to the Five Civilized Tribes,
> Claremore, I. T. October, 25th 1900.

In the matter of the application of Robert L. Wayburn, for the enrollment of his aunt as a Cherokee Citizen. He being sworn testified before the Commission as follows-

Q What is your name?   A. Robert L. Wayburn.
Q How old are you?   A. 33.
Q What is your post office address?   A. Pryor Creek.
Q What district do you live in?   A. Cooweescoowee.
Q Who is it you want enrolled now?   A. Mrs. Sarah F. Gage.
Q This is an aunt of yours you say?   A. Yes sir.
Q How old is she?   A. 53.
Q What is her post office?   A. Claremore.
Q Is Cooweescoowee her district?   A. Yes sir.
Q Why does she not apply for herself?   A. She is sick and cannot come; I have a certificate from the doctor that she cannot come.
Q Is she just temporarily ill or permanently ill?   A. She has not been sick very long, she fell down cellar steps and hurt her back.
Q Is she living with you?   A. No sir.
Q Is she white?   A. Yes sir.
Q Is she a Cherokee by blood?   A. No sir she is a white woman.
Q Through whom does she claim her right to enrollment?   A. Her husband, John Gage.
Q He was a Cherokee was he?   A. Yes sir.
Q Is John Gage dead?   A. Yes sir.
Q When did he die?   A. In 1883 or 1884.
Q Is he on the roll of 1880[sic]?   A. Yes sir.
Q Did he live here from 1880 until he died?   A. Yes sir.
Q Was his wife married to him in 1880?   A. Yes sir.
Q After the death of John Gage was your aunt ever re-married?   A. No sir.
Q Has she continued to live in the Cherokee Nation since her husbands[sic] death?
A. Yes sir.
Q Never lived any where else?   A. No sir not that I know of, and she says she never has.

1880 roll, page 111, No. 1286, Sarah F. Gage, Cooweescoowee, Ad. White
1880   111   1285, John Gage   "   N. C.
1896   306   406 Sarah F. Gage,   "

269

Q You have not been here yourself since 1880 have you?   A. No sir.

Q Has she ever been living with any other man as his wife since her husband died?   A. No sir.

Q Has she ever lived with a man named Henry Malone?   A. He has been working there tending to her business, and is living on her farm now.

Q She stays there on the farm and this man Henry Malone lives there?   A. Yes sir.

Q Has he any family?   A. No sir.

Q How long has he been living that way?   A. I dont[sic] know.

Q Who else lives there besides them?   A. She has got a boy there and has a girl working for her.

Q Neither of them are her children are they?   A. No sir.

Q Has she always had this boy and girl living there?   A. No sir, she has had first one girl and then another.

Q How long has Malone lived there looking after her business?   A. 8 or 10 years.

Q He occupies the same house that she does?   A. Yes sir.

Q Is Henry Malone a white man?   A. Yes sir.

The applicant applies for the enrollment of an aunt whom he states is sick and cannot apply for her self. She is identified with her Cherokee husband, then living, on the roll of 1880, she being a white woman. He is said to have died in 1883. She is identified on the roll of 1896. It is said that she has lived in the Cherokee Nation ever since 1880, and that she has not re-married since the death of her Cherokee husband, it appears, however, that she has lived for the last ten years in somewhat questionable relations with a white man named Henry Malone and it may be that she has virtually contracted marriage relations with this white man and that she has lost her Cherokee rights. She is desired to appear in person before the Commission in connection with her application and at present she will be placed on a doubtful card as a Cherokee by adoption.

§§*§*§*§*§*§*§*§*§*§*§*§*§*§*

Chas. von Weise being sworn states that as stenographer to the Commission to the Five Civilized Tribes he reported in full all the proceedings in the above entitled cause and that the foregoing is a full, true and correct transcript of his stenographic notes in said proceedings.

Chas von Weise

Subscribed and sworn to before me this the 26th of October, 1900.

MD Green
Notary Public.

◇◇◇◇◇

COOWEESCOOWEE.
Statement of Applicant Taken Under Oath.

CHEROKEES BY BLOOD AND ADOPTION.

Date OCT 25 1900 ....1900.

Name .... _Clarence D.,_

District .... Year .... Page .... No.

Citizen by blood .... Mother's citizenship ....

Intermarried citizen ....

Married under what law .... Date of marriage ....

License .... Certificate ....

Wife's name _Sarah F. Gage_

District COOWEESCOOWEE. .... Year _84_ Page _111_ No. _1286_

Citizen by blood _No_ Mother's citizenship ....

Intermarried citizen _Yes_

Married under what law .... Date of marriage ....

License .... Certificate ....

Names of Children:

	Dist.	Year	Page	No.	Age
	Dist.	Year	Page	No.	Age
	Dist.	Year	Page	No.	Age
	Dist.	Year	Page	No.	Age
	Dist.	Year	Page	No.	Age
	Dist.	Year	Page	No.	Age
	Dist.	Year	Page	No.	Age
	Dist.	Year	Page	No.	Age
	Dist.	Year	Page	No.	Age
	Dist.	Year	Page	No.	Age

Applicant to appear in person

(Copy of original document from case.)

◇◇◇◇◇

271

Cherokee Intermarried White 1906
Volume VIII

SUPPLEMENTAL: D 701

Department of the Interior,
Commission to the Five Civilized Tribes,
Claremore, I.T., November 9, 1900.

In the matter of the application of Sarah Frances Gage for the enrollment of herself as a Cherokee citizen; being sworn and examined by Commissioner Breckinridge she testified as follows:

Q   Give your full name?   A Sarah Frances Gage.
Q   How old are you?   A 52.
Q   What is your post-office address?   A Claremore.
Q   You live in Cooweescoowee District do you?   A Yes sir.
Q   Do you apply for enrollment as a Cherokee by blood?   A No sir, as adopted.
Q   As an intermarried citizen?   A Yes sir.
Q   How often have you been married?   A Twice, but to the same man; I was married in Texas to my husband and then I was married here also, under Cherokee law.
Q   Never married to any other man?   A No sir.
Q   Was he ever married previous to his marriage to you?   A No sir.
Q   Your husband is dead?   A Yes sir.
Q   When did he die?   A 16 years ago last October, last month.
Q   What was your husband's full name?   A John Jackson Gage.
Q   Was he a Native of the Cherokee Nation?   A Yes sir.
Q   Did he live here all his life?   A No sir; he lived in Texas part of his life; he lived here when he was quite a boy, and then they moved to Texas and he lived there until he was a grown man.
Q   How old was he when he left Texas?   A I can't tell you; we came to the Chickasaw Nation and from the Chickasaw Nation here.- it was after his marriage.
Q   When did you come to the Cherokee Nation after leaving Texas?
A   I think it was in 1872.
Q   Is his name on the 1880 roll?   A Yes sir, I think it is.
Q   And yours is there with him?   A Yes sir.
Q   And now you came in 1872?   A I think it was 1872.
Q   Or there abouts?   A Yes sir, to the best of my recollection.
Q   Do you know whether the Cherokee Council or Commission ever admitted or re-admitted him to Cherokee citizenship?   A The Cherokee Council did.
Q   And you and he lived together as husband and wife until he died? A Yes sir.
Q   You have never re-married since he died?   A No sir.
Q   Give me the name of his father. A David Gage.
Q   He is dead, I suppose?   A Yes sir.
Q   And the name of his mother?   A Lucy.
Q   And she is dead?   A Yes sir
Q   You have no children?   A No sir.

Com'r Breckinridge:

This testimony will be supplementary to that taken in a former application for the enrollment of the applicant, card D 701. In the original application it was required that she appear before the Commission in person; because of her enormous weight and crippled condition this was found to be practically impossible, and this testimony was taken at her house, notice having been duly given to the Cherokee representative. The intimation of re-marriage is contradicted by this testimony, and apart from the strictly legal aspects of the case it appears entirely improbably that there can be any form of union between the applicant and the young man who lives at her house and attends to her farm and business.

M.D. Green, being first duly sworn, states that as stenographer to the Commission to the Five Civilized Tribes he correctly recorded the testimony and proceedings in this case and the foregoing is a true and complete transcript of his stenographic notes thereof.

MD Green

Subscribed and sworn to before me this November 10, 1900.

CR Breckinridge
Commissioner.

◇◇◇◇◇

JJB

Cherokee D -701.

Department of the Interior,
Commission to the Five Civilized Tribes.

In the matter of the application of Robert L. Wayburn for the enrollment of Sarah F. Gage as a Cherokee citizen.

-----0-----

On the 25th day of October, 1900, Robert L. Wayburn appeared before the Commission to the Five Civilized Tribes and made application for the enrollment of his aunt, Sarah F. Gage, as a citizen by intermarriage of the Cherokee Nation.

At the conclusion of the evidence offered at that time the name of Sarah F. Gage was placed upon a doubtful card awaiting personal testimony of the said Sarah F. Gage.

Further evidence in the case has been submitted to this Commission and the following decision is rendered:

Cherokee Intermarried White 1906
Volume VIII

DECISION.

From all the evidence of record in this case it appears that Sarah F. Gage is the widow of John Gage, a Cherokee by blood; that her name appears upon the 1880 authenticated tribal roll of the Cherokee Nation and upon the 1896 census roll; that she has continuously resided in the Cherokee Nation since the preparation of said roll of 1880 and that she has not remarried since the death of her late husband. She is a white woman.

In making rolls of citizenship of the Cherokee Nation this Commission is governed by the following provisions of the Act of Congress approved June 28, 1898 (30 Stats., 495):

"That in making rolls of citizenship of the several tribes as required by law, the Commission to the Five Civilized Tribes is authorized and directed to take the roll of Cherokee citizens of eighteen hundred and eighty (not including freedmen) as the only roll intended to be confirmed by this and proceding[sic] Acts of Congress, and to enroll all persons now living whose names are found on said roll, and all descendants born since the date of said roll to persons whose names are found thereon; and all persons who have been enrolled by the tribal authorities who have heretofore made permanent settlement in the Cherokee Nation whose parents, by reason of their Cherokee blood, have been lawfully admitted to citizenship by the tribal authorities, and who were minors when their parents were so admitted; and they shall investigate the right of all other persons whose names are found on any other rolls and omit all such as may have been placed thereon by fraud or without authority of law, enrolling only such as may have lawful right thereto, and their descendants born since such rolls were made, with such intermarried white persons as may be entitled to citizenship under Cherokee law."

Under the facts and the law in this case it is considered that Sarah F. Gage is entitled to enrollment as a citizen by intermarriage of the Cherokee Nation, and it is so ordered.

Tams Bixby

TB Needles

C. R. Breckinridge

Dated at Muskogee, Indian Territory,
MAY 27 1902

◇◇◇◇◇

Cherokee 9629.

Department of the Interior,
Commission to the Five Civilized Tribes,
Muskogee, I. T., October 9, 1902.

In the matter of the application of Sarah F. Gage for the enrollment of herself as a citizen by intermarriage of the Cherokee Nation; she being sworn and examined by the Commission, testified as follows:

Q Your name is Sarah F. Gage?   A Yes sir.
Q How old are you?   A Fifty-three years old or fifty-four.
Q What is your postoffice?   A Claremore.
Q You are a white woman are you?   A Yes sir.
Q On the authenticated tribal roll of 1880?   A Yes sir.
Q What was the name of your husband at that time?   A John F. Gage.
Q Is he living?   A No sir, he is dead.
Q When did he die?   A Eighteen or nineteen years ago.
Q Since the 1880 roll was made?   A Yes sir.
Q Have you married since that time?   A No sir.
Q Lived in the Cherokee Nation ever since?   A Yes sir.
Q Made your home there?   A Yes sir.

The undersigned, being duly sworn, states that as stenographer to the Commission to the Five Civilized Tribes he correctly recorded the testimony and proceedings in this case, and the foregoing is a true and correct transcript of his stenographic notes thereof.

E.G. Rothenberger

Subscribed and sworn to before me this 16th day of December, 1902.

BC Jones
Notary Public.

◇◇◇◇◇

T.W.L.   Cherokee 9629.

DEPARTMENT OF THE INTERIOR,
COMMISSIONER TO THE FIVE CIVILIZED TRIBES.

In the matter of the application for the enrollment of Sarah F. Gage as a citizen by intermarriage of the Cherokee Nation.

D E C I S I O N .

THE RECORDS OF THIS OFFICE SHOW: That at Claremore, Indian Territory, October 25, 1900, application was received by the Commission to the Five Civilized Tribes for the enrollment of Sarah F. Gage as a citizen by intermarriage of the Cherokee Nation.   Further proceedings in the matter of said application were had at Claremore, Indian Territory, November 9, 1900   The records further show that on May 27, 1902, the Commission to the Five Civilized Tribes entered its decision herein, granting said applicant the right to enrollment as a citizen by intermarriage of the Cherokee Nation.

THE EVIDENCE IN THIS CASE SHOWS: That the applicant herein, Sarah F. Gage, is a white woman and neither claims nor possesses any right to enrollment as a citizen of the Cherokee Nation other than by reason of her marriage in the state of Texas, prior to the year 1872, to one John Jackson Gage, now deceased, her admission to Cherokee citizenship by the duly constituted authorities of said nation, and her subsequent marriage to the said John Jackson Gage in the Cherokee Nation.   That the said John Jackson Gage was not, at the time of said marriage performed in Texas, a recognized citizen by blood of the Cherokee Nation, and did not become a citizen of said nation until his admission to citizenship therein by the duly constituted authorities of said Nation November 24, 1876.   Said applicant did not, therefore, marry in accordance with Cherokee law, a citizen of the Cherokee Nation prior to November 1, 1875.   Said applicant and her said husband are identified on the Cherokee authenticated tribal roll of 1880, on page 111, the former at No. 1285, as a native Cherokee, followed by the notation "dead", and the latter at No. 1286, as an adopted white.

IT IS, THEREFORE, ORDERED AND ADJUDGED: That in accordance with the decision rendered by the Commission to the Five Civilized Tribes May 27, 1902, granting the application for the enrollment of Sarah F. Gage as a citizen by intermarriage of the Cherokee Nation, be rescinded, set aside and held for naught, and that in accordance with the decision of the Supreme Court of the United States, dated November 5, 1906, in the cases of Daniel Red Bird et al., vs. the United States, Nos. 125, 126, 127, and 128, the said applicant, Sarah F. Gage is not entitled, under the provisions of Section 21 of the Act of Congress approved June 28, 1898 (30 Stats. 495), to enrollment as a citizen by intermarriage of the Cherokee Nation, and her application for enrollment as such is accordingly denied.

Tams Bixby

Commissioner.

Dated at Muskogee, Indian Territory,
this   FEB 26 1907

Copy

◇◇◇◇◇

COPY

Muskogee, Indian Territory, May 27, 1902.

W. W. Hastings, Esq.,
         Attorney for the Cherokee Nation,
         Muskogee, Indian Territory.

Sir:

There is herewith transmitted a copy of the decision of the Commission to the Five Civilized Tribes rendered May 27th, in the matter of the application of Sarah F. Gage for enrollment as a citizen by intermarriage of the Cherokee Nation.

You are hereby advised that you will be allowed fifteen days from date hereof in which to file with the Commission such protest as you desire to make against the enrollment of said person as a citizen of the Cherokee Nation. If you fail to file protest within the time allowed this applicant will be regularly listed for enrollment.

Very respectfully,

SIGNED *Tams Bixby*

Acting Chairman.

Encl. D-701.

◇◇◇◇◇

Cherokee D 701

COPY

Muskogee, Indian Territory, June 11, 1902.

Robert L. Wayburn,
         Pryor Creek, Indian Territory.

Sir:

There is herewith enclosed the decision of the Commission to the Five Civilized Tribes in the matter of your application for the enrollment of your aunt, Sarah F. Gage, as a citizen of the Cherokee Nation.

Very respectfully,

T.B. Needles.

Commissioner in Charge.

Enclosure D 701

Register

<><><><><>

Cherokee
 9629

Muskogee, Indian Territory, December 27, 1906.

Sarah F. Gage,
 Claremore, Indian Territory.

Dear Madam:

November 6, 1906, the United States Supreme Court held that white persons who intermarried with Cherokee citizens according to Cherokee law prior to November 1, 1875, are entitled to enrollment and allotments of land as citizens of the Cherokee Nation.

You are advised that to properly determine your right to enrollment as a citizen by intermarriage of the Cherokee Nation, it will be necessary for you to appear before the Commissioner for the purpose of giving testimony as to the date of your marriage and whether or not your husband, by reason of your marriage to whom you claim the right to enrollment as a citizen by intermarriage of the Cherokee Nation, was a recognized Cherokee citizen at the time of your marriage to him.

You are therefore directed to appear before the Commissioner at Muskogee, Indian Territory, at 9 o'clock A. M., on Saturday, January 8, 1907, and give testimony as above indicated.

Respectfully,

Acting Commissioner.

GHL

<><><><><>

Cherokee 9629.

ECM   Muskogee, Indian Territory, February 13, 1907.

SPECIAL.

> Sarah F. Gage,
>   Claremore, Indian Territory.

Dear Madam:

The Commissioner sent you this day a telegram as follows:

"Intermarried case incomplete.
Have witnesses appear immediately
to establish marriage. Evidence
husband's citizenship necessary".

The Act of Congress approved April 26, 1906, provides that the Secretary of the Interior shall have no jurisdiction to approve the enrollment of any person as a citizen of the Cherokee Nation after March 4, 1907.
This matter, therefore, demands your immediate attention.

Respectfully,

Commissioner.

GHL

◇◇◇◇◇

COPY

Muskogee, Indian Territory, February 26, 1907.

The Honorable,
    The Secretary of the Interior.

Sir:

There is transmitted herewith the record of proceedings had in the matter of the application for the enrollment of Sarah F. Gage as a citizen by intermarriage of the Cherokee Nation, together with the decision of the Commissioner, dated February 26, 1907, denying said application.

Respectfully,

SIGNED *Tams Bixby*

Encl. HJ-32.   Commissioner.
HJC

Through the Commissioner of
    Indian Affairs.

◇◇◇◇◇

Cherokee
    9629.   COPY

Muskogee, Indian Territory February 26, 1907.

W. W. Hastings,
        Attorney for the Cherokee Nation,
                Muskogee, Indian Territory.

Dear Sir:

        There is enclosed herewith a copy of the decision of the Commissioner to the
Five Civilized Tribes, dated February 26, 1907, denying the application for the
enrollment of Sarah F. Gage as a citizen by intermarriage of the Cherokee Nation.

        The decision, together with the record of proceedings had in the case, has this
day been transmitted to the Secretary of the Interior for his review and decision. You
will be advised of the Secretary's action as soon as this office is informed of same.

Respectfully,

SIGNED *Tams Bixby*

Encl. HJ-31.
HJC   Commissioner.

◇◇◇◇◇

FEB 26 1907

Cherokee
9629.

Muskogee, Indian Territory, February 26, 1907.

Sarah F. Gage,
    Claremore, Indian Territory.

Dear Madam:

There is enclosed herewith a copy of the decision of the Commissioner to the Five Civilized Tribes, dated February 26, 1907, denying your application for enrollment as a citizen by intermarriage of the Cherokee Nation.

The decision, together with the record of proceedings had in this case, has this day been transmitted to the Secretary of the Interior for his review and decision. You will be advised of the Secretary's action as soon as this office is informed of the same.

Respectfully,

Encl. HJ-30.
  HJC   Commissioner.

Register.

◇◇◇◇◇

D.C. 13836-1907.   SPECIAL   W.H.M.   JFJr
                    DEPARTMENT OF THE INTERIOR,
                           WASHINGTON.
I.T.D. 7840-1907.   March 4, 1907.
LRS
    DIRECT.

Commissioner to the Five Civilized Tribes,
    Muskogee, Indian Territory.

Sir:

March 2, 1907 (Land 21249), the Indian Office transmitted your report dated February 27, 1907, in the matter of the application of Sarah F. Gage for enrollment as a citizen by intermarriage of the Cherokee Nation, together with your decision of the same date, denying said application.

The Indian Office considers your decision should be reversed in view of the opinion of the Attorney-General in the John W. Gleason case.

The Department considers the position taken by the Indian Office to be correct.

Your decision of February 26, 1907, is hereby reversed, and you are instructed to enroll said Sarah F. Gage as a citizen by intermarriage of the Cherokee Nation.

The papers in the matter have been sent to the Indian Office, together with a copy hereof.

Respectfully,

(Signed)   Jesse E. Wilson,

Acting Secretary.

2 enclosures & copy hereof
to Indian Off.

WCR 3-4-07

◇◇◇◇◇

Cherokee 9629

Copy

Muskogee, Indian Territory, March 20, 1907.

W. W. Hastings,
Attorney for the Cherokee Nation,
Muskogee, Indian Territory.

Dear Sir:

You are hereby advised that the decision of the Commissioner to the Five Civilized Tribes, dated February 28, 1907, rejecting the application of Sarah F. Gage for enrollment as a citizen by intermarriage of the Cherokee Nation, was reversed by the Secretary of the Interior, March 4, 1907, and the application granted.

For your information, there is enclosed herewith a copy of Departmental decision referred to.

Respectfully,

SIGNED *Jams Bixby*

Commissioner.

Encl. H-76
JMH

◇◇◇◇◇

Cherokee 9629   COPY

Muskogee, Indian Territory, March 20, 1907.

Sarah F. Gage,
    Claremore, Indian Territory.

Dear Madam:

    You are hereby advised that the decision of the Commissioner to the Five Civilized Tribes, dated February 28, 1907, rejecting your application for enrollment as a citizen by intermarriage of the Cherokee Nation, was reversed by the Secretary of the Interior, March 4, 1907, and said application granted.

    For your information, there is enclosed herewith a copy of Departmental decision referred to.

Respectfully,

SIGNED *Tams Bixby*
Commissioner.

Encl. H-75
JMH

◇◇◇◇◇

GAW

DEPARTMENT OF THE INTERIOR
OFFICE OF INDIAN AFFAIRS,
I.T.   WASHINGTON.
References in body
of letter.   May 11, 1907.

Subject: Motions for
review in certain Chero-
kee citizenship cases.

The Honorable,
    The Secretary of the Interior.

Sir:

    There are inclosed herewith motions filed by W. W. Hastings, National Attorney for the Cherokee Nation, praying for review and rehearing of Departmental decisions authorizing the enrollment as citizens by intermarriage of the Cherokee Nation of the following persons:

42893-1907,	Jacob A. Bartles,
42895- "	Osburn J. Byrd,
42886- "	Amanda Beck,
42894- "	Sarah F. Gage,
42892- "	Phirena Harris,
42888- "	Daniel Harmon,
42891- "	Emma L. Ironsides,
42896- "	Sarah A. Jordan
42881- "	Dovie Johnson,
42882- "	Andrew H. Norwood,
42887- "	Stacy E. Perry,
42885- "	Martha Randolph, now Kernan
42893- "	John W. Smith
42884- "	John J. Smith,
42890- "	Robert H. F. Thompson,
42889- "	Hattie Wright,
42883- "	Nancy Wolfe,
42880- "	E. A. Welch.

In view of the provisions of section 2 of the act of April 26, 1906 (34 Stat. L., 137), providing that the rolls of the Five Civilized Tribes shall be fully completed on or before March 4, 1907, there appears to be no authority in law for the reconsideration of any enrollment cases at this time, and it is recommended that the office be authorized to advise Mr. Hastings that the motions for review herewith transmitted cannot be considered.

Very respectfully,

C. F. Larrabee

Acting Commissioner.

AJW-FHE.

May 13, 1907.

Approved.

Thos Ryan

First Assistant Secretary.

◇◇◇◇◇

I.T references
in body of letter.

DEPARTMENT OF THE INTERIOR,
OFFICE OF INDIAN AFFAIRS,
WASHINGTON.

GAW

May 15, 1907.

Commissioner to the Five Civilized Tribes,
Muskogee, Indian Territory.

Sir:

There is inclosed copy of Office letter of May 11, 1907, approved by the Department on May 13, 1907, recommending that motions filed by W. W. Hastings, National Attorney for the Cherokee Nation, praying for a review and rehearing of Departmental decisions authorizing the enrollment of the following persons as citizens by intermarriage of the Cherokee Nation, be denied, in view of the fact that there appears to be no authority in law at this time for the reconsideration of any enrollment case.

42893-1907	Jacob A. Bartles
42895- "	Osburn J. Byrd
42886- "	Amanda Beck
42894- "	Sarah F. Gage
42892- "	Phirena Harris
42888- "	Daniel Harmon
42891- "	Emma L. Ironsides
42896- "	Sarah A. Jordan
42881- "	Dovie Johnson
42882- "	Andrew H. Norwood
42887- "	Stacy E. Perry
42885- "	Martha Randolph, now Kernan
42893- "	John W. Smith
42884- "	John J. Smith
42890- "	Robert H. F. Thompson
42889- "	Hattie Wright
42883- "	Nancy Wolfe
42880- "	E. A. Welch

You are requested to advise the interested parties, including Mr. Hastings, of the Department's action.

Very respectfully,
C. F. Larrabee
Acting Commissioner.

AJW-FHE.

◇◇◇◇◇

Cherokee
253 et al.

Muskogee, Indian Territory, May 25, 1907.

W. W. Hastings,
　　Attorney for the Cherokee Nation,
　　　　Muskogee, Indian Territory.

Dear Sir:

You are hereby advised that on May 13, 1907, the Secretary of the Interior denied the motion filed by you for a review of its decision authorizing the enrollment of Jacob A. Bartles, et al., as citizens by intermarriage of the Cherokee Nation.

For your information, there is enclosed herewith a copy of Departmental decision referred to.

Respectfully,

Commissioner.

Encl. C-20
　LMC

◇◇◇◇◇

Cherokee
245

Muskogee, Indian Territory, May 25, 1907.

Sarah F. Gage,
　　Claremore, Indian Territory.

Dear Madam:

You are hereby advised that on May 13, 1907, the Secretary of the Interior denied a motion filed by the Attorney for the Cherokee Nation, for a review of its decision authorizing your enrollment as a citizen by intermarriage of the Cherokee Nation.

For your information, there is enclosed herewith a copy of Departmental decision referred to.

Respectfully,

Commissioner.

Encl. C-6
　LMC

Cher IW 246

◇◇◇◇◇

Department of the Interior,
Commission to the Five Civilized Tribes,
Fairland, I.T., Jul 13, 1900.

In the matter of the application of John J. Smith for enrollment as an intermarried Cherokee, and for the enrollment of his wife and children and grandchildren as Cherokees by blood; being duly sworn, and examined by Commissioner Breckenridge[sic], he testified as follows:

Q   What is your name?   A   John J. Smith.
Q   What is your age?   A   I am 65.
Q   What is your post office address?   A   Maysville, Ark.
Q   Do you live in the Indian Territory?   A   I live in the Territory, Maysville is right across the line.
Q   In what district of the Cherokee Nation?   A   Deleware[sic] district.
Q   How long have you lived there?   A   41 years: four years of that time I was in the war.
Q   This has been your residence continually during that period, since the war?
A   Yes, sir.
Q   Do you apply as a Cherokee by blood?   A   No, sir.
Q   By intermarriage?   A   Yes, sir.
Q   Is your wife living?   A   Yes, sir.
Q   What was your wife's name before your marriage?   A   Sarah P. Fields.
Q   When were you married?   A   About October 20, 1859.
(1880 roll, Delaware district, page 323, No. 2561, Sarah E. Smith.)
Q   What is your wife's age now?   A   She is 58.
Q   Do you identify that as the enrollment of your wife?   A   Yes, sir.
Q   Have you a license and certificate of marriage?   A   No, sir, I have not.
(1896 roll, page 589, No. 1517 (517), Delaware district, John J. Smith;
same roll, Sarah P. Smith, page 539, No. 3052, Delaware district.
John J. Smith on 1880 roll, page 323, No. 2560, Delaware district.)
Q   Is your wife present?   A   No, sir, she is not present.
Q   Do you want to apply for your children as well?   A   Yes, sir. I have some children living at home who are of age.
Q   Are the unmarried and living with you?   A   3 of them are, and I have some grandchildren I want to enroll.
Q   Give me the names of your children?   A   Walter F. Smith.
(On 1880 roll, page 323, No. 2564, as Walter F. Smith. On 1896 Roll as Walter F. Smith, page 539, No. 3053, Delaware district.)
Q   What is your next child?   A   Nat D. Smith, age 23.
(On 1880 roll, page 323, No. 2566, Delaware district, Nathaniel D. Smith. On 1896 roll, page 539, No. 3054, Nathaniel D. Smith. Delaware district.)

Cherokee Intermarried White 1906
Volume VIII

Q   What is your next child?   A   Homer L. Smith, he will be 21 the last day of this month.
(On 1880 roll, page 323, No. 2567, Delaware district. On 1896 roll, page 539, No. 355[sic], Delaware district.) #3055
A   That is all; I have two grandchildren.
Q   Give the name of the father and mother of those. A Jeff D. Smith is their father.
Q   Is that your son by your present wife?   A Yes, sir.
Q   Are their father and mother dead?   A   Their father is dead, and the mother is living.
Q   Do they claim through their father?   A Yes, sir.
Q   When did Jeff D. Smith die?   A In 1887.
(On 1880 roll, page 323, No. 2582, Jeff D. Smith, Delaware District.)
Q   Now give the names of the children of Jeff D. Smith. A William L. Smith, age 14.
(On 1896 roll, Willie L. Smith page 539, No. 3056, Delaware district age 10.)
Q   Now the next child?   A Pearl H. Smith, age 13.
(On 1896 roll, page 539, No. 3057, Delaware district.)
Q   Is that all?   A Yes, sir, that is all I want to enroll.
Q   Is the mother of these children still living?   A Yes, sir.
Q   What is her name?   A Her name now is Missouri Wells.
Q   What was her name in 1896?   A I don't know, she was not on any of the rolls; she married since the death of my son.
Q   Your son died in 1887?   A Yes, sir.
Q   Do they live with you?   A They will be most of the time; they stay at my place and go to school.
Q   In regard to your son and wife, did they live with you and in your neighborhood?
A   They lived on my place a while, and then on their own place.
Q   You had personal knowledge of their marriage in due form?   A They married and came to my place, I couldn't swear to the marriage.
Q   They lived always within your knowledge?   A Yes, sir.
Q   How long were they married?   A They married in 1884 or 1885.

Mr. Smith, your name and the name of your wife appearing duly enrolled on the roll of 1880, and your son[sic] Walter F., Nathaniel D., and Homer L. being likewise recorded on the roll of 1880, all of you will be enrolled at this time, you being enrolled as an intermarried Cherokee and the others as Cherokees by blood.

Your grandchildren, William L. Smith and Pearl H. Smith, being recognized on the roll of 1896, and their father being recognized on the roll of 1880, and the representatives of the Cherokee Nation making no objection to the evidence of marriage, the question of residence being established, will be enrolled as Cherokees by blood.

---------0---------

Bruce C. Jones, being duly sworn, says that as stenographer to the Commission to the Five Civilized Tribes he reported the testimony of the above named witness, and that the foregoing is a full, true and correct translation of his stenographic notes.

Cherokee Intermarried White 1906
Volume VIII

Bruce C. Jones

Sworn to and subscribed before me this the 16th day of July, 1900.

Clifton R Breckinridge
Commissioner.

◇◇◇◇◇

R.

DEPARTMENT OF THE INTERIOR.
Commission to the Five Civilized Tribes.
Muskogee, Indian Territory, October 1st, 1902.

———————

In the matter of the application of John J. Smith for the enrollment of himself as a citizen by intermarriage of the Cherokee Nation and for the enrollment of his wife, Sarah P. Smith; his children, Walter L., Nathaniel D. and Homer L. Smith, and his grand children, William L. and Pearl H. Smith, as citizens by blood of the Cherokee Nation.

———————

Supplemental to #195.

———————

W. W. HASTINGS, being duly sworn, testified as follows:
Examination by the Commission.

Q. What is your name?　A. W. W. Hastings.

Q. What is your age?　A. 35.

Q. What is your post office?　A. Tahlequah.

Q. Are you acquainted with John J. Smith, whose post office is Maysville, Arkansas, and who is an applicant for enrollment as an intermarried citizen? A. Yes, sir.

Q. Are you acquainted with his wife?　A. Yes, sir.

Q. What is her name?　A. Her name is Sarah. I don't remember her middle name. She was a Fields.

Q. Is his wife Sarah P. a citizen by blood of the Cherokee Nation?　A. Yes, sir.

Q. When was John J. Smith married to his wife Sarah?

A. It was further back than '8o[sic]; further than I can remember.

Q. Have they been living together as husband and wife continuously from 188o until the present time?　A. Yes, sir.

Q. Were they living together as husband and wife on September 1st, 19o2[sic]?

A. Yes, sir.

Q. And they have never been separated during that time?

A. Never, during that time.

Q. Has John J. Smith and his wife Sarah P. resided in the Cherokee Nation all the time since 188o?　A. All the time; continuously.

Q. Do you know his son Walter F. Smith?　A. Yes, sir.

Q. Has he lived in the Cherokee Nation all his life?   A. Yes, sir.
Q. Do you know his sons Nathaniel D. and Homer L.?   A. Yes, sir.
Q. Have they always lived in the Cherokee Nation all their lives?
A. Yes, sir. I think one of them is married now.
Q. Do you know the father of William L. and Pearl H. Smith?
A. Jeff D., yes; he was killed.
Q. Did Jeff D. live all his life in the Cherokee Nation?
A. Yes, sir.
Q. There[sic] two children were born and lived-----
A. Ever since their berth[sic] in the Cherokee Nation.

++

Jesse O. Carr, being first duly sworn, states that as stenographer to the Commission to the Five Civilized Tribes he reported the above entitled case and that the foregoing is a true and complete transcript of his stenographic notes thereof.

Jesse O. Carr

Copy

Subscribed and sworn to before me this 24th day of October, 1902.

BC Jones
Notary Public.

◇◇◇◇◇

Cherokee Card 195

DEPARTMENT OF THE INTERIOR,

COMMISSION TO THE FIVE CIVILIZED TRIBES,

Muskogee, I. T., September 4, 1902.

In the matter of the application of John J. Smith et. al. for enrollment as Cherokee citizens.

SUPPLEMENTAL STATEMENT.
o-o-o-o

An examination of the Cherokee authenticated tribal roll of 1880 for Delaware District shows that John J. Smith is identified thereon, at page 232, No. 2560.

(Signed) C R Breckinridge
Commissioner.

◇◇◇◇◇

Cherokee No._____

DEPARTMENT OF THE INTERIOR,
COMMISSIONER TO THE FIVE CIVILIZED TRIBES.
Muskogee, I. T., January 2, 1907.

In the matter of the application for the enrollment of John J. Smith as a citizen by intermarriage of the Cherokee Nation.

John J. Smith, being first duly sworn by Frances R. Lane, a Notary Public for the Western District, Indian Territory, testified as follows:

By the Commissioner:
Q What is your name? A John J. Smith.
Q How old are you? A Seventy-one years.
Q What is your postoffice address? A Maysville, Ark.
Q Do you claim to be an intermarried citizen of the Cherokee Nation? A Yes sir.
Q Through whom do you claim? A Sarah P. Fields, a Cherokee Indian by blood and resided in Delaware District.
Q When were you married to Sarah P. Fields? A The 15th of October, 1859.
Q Where were you married to her? A Maysville. It is a town right on the Cherokee line; we was married in the Territory.
Q Were you married under a license? A No, I was not.
Q Who married you? A A Methodist preacher that preached there at that time.
Q What was his name? A Hass.
Q What was his full name, do you know? A No, I forgot it.
Q Did he give you a certificate? A He gave me one at the time but I went through the war and lost all my papers.
Q Is there anyone here present here today that knows of your marriage in 1859?
A No one that I know of here, but probably I could get witnesses that could testify to the fact. There is no one here in town that I know of.
Q Were you ever married before you were married to Sarah P. Fields? A No sir.
Q Was she ever married before her marriage to you? A No sir.
Q Have you lived together continuously as husband and wife in the Cherokee Nation since your marriage to her in 1859? A Yes, I was in the war with the Cherokees, but I came back when the Cherokees came home.
Q Your wife is a citizen of the Cherokee nation[sic]? A Yes sir.
Q Did you ever marry her again under the Cherokee law when they passed a law requiring people to take out a license? A No sir.

The applicant is identified on the 1880 roll, Cherokee, opposite No. 2560. His wife is identified on said roll opposite No. 2561; also upon the final roll of Cherokees by blood of the Cherokee Nation opposite No. 636.

Q Have you appeared before the Commissioner before today?

A Yes, I have appeared before the Commission two or three times.

Q Did you furnish them evidence of your marriage in 1859?

A They didn't ask it of me. They asked me whether I was married, and when I was married and where I was married. I told them that I was maried[sic] at Maysville. My mother-in-law lived in the Territory; she lived right on the line, and she was running a hotel there when I married my wife.

Witness excused.

Frances R. Lane, upon oath, states that as stenographer to the Commission to the Five Civilized Tribes, she reported the testimony in the above entitled cause and that the foregoing is an accurate transcript of her stenographic notes thereof.

Frances R Lane

Subscribed and sworn to before me this January 2, 1907.

Edward Merrick
Notary Public.

◇◇◇◇◇

E C M   Cherokee 195.

DEPARTMENT OF THE INTERIOR,

COMMISSIONER TO THE FIVE CIVILIZED TRIBES.

In the matter of the application for the enrollment of JOHN J. SMITH as a citizen by intermarriage of the Cherokee Nation.

D E C I S I O N

THE RECORDS OF THIS OFFICE SHOW: That on July 13, 1900, application was received by the Commission to the Five Civilized Tribes for the enrollment of John J. Smith as a citizen by intermarriage of the Cherokee Nation. Further proceedings in the matter of said application were had at Muskogee, Indian Territory, October 1, 1902, Tahlequah, Indian Territory, September 1, 1903 and at Muskogee, Indian Territory, January 2, 1907.

THE EVIDENCE IN THIS CASE SHOWS: That the applicant herein, John J. Smith, is a white man and neither claims nor possesses any right to enrollment as a citizen of the Cherokee Nation other than such right as he may have acquired by virtue of his marriage in October, 1859, to one Sarah P. Smith, nee Fields, who was at the time of said marriage a recognized citizen by blood of the Cherokee Nation, who is identified on the Cherokee authenticated tribal roll of 1880, Delaware District No. 2561 as a native Cherokee, and whose name is included on the approved partial roll of citizens by blood of the Cherokee Nation opposite No. 636; that from the time of said marriage the said John J. Smith and Sarah P. Smith resided together as husband and wife and continuously lived in the Cherokee Nation up to and including September 1, 1902. It is further shown that said marriage was not in accordance with Cherokee law, the said John J. Smith having failed to secure a license as required by an Act of the Cherokee Council passed October 15, 1855. Said applicant is identified on the Cherokee authenticated tribal roll of 1880 and the Cherokee census roll of 1896 as an intermarried citizen of the Cherokee Nation.

IT IS, THEREFORE, ORDERED AND ADJUDGED: That in accordance with the decision of the Supreme Court of the United States, dated November 5, 1906, in the cases of Daniel Red Bird et al. vs. the United States, Nos. 125, 126, 127, and 128, the said applicant, John J. Smith is not entitled, under the provisions of Section Twenty-one of the Act of Congress approved June 28, 1898 (30 Stats. 495), to enrollment as a citizen by intermarriage of the Cherokee Nation, and his application for enrollment as such is accordingly denied.

Tams Bixby

Commissioner.

Dated at Muskogee, Indian Territory,
this   FEB 14 1907

◇◇◇◇◇

Cherokee
195.

Muskogee, Indian Territory, December 21, 1906.

John J. Smith,
        Owasso, Indian Territory.

Dear Sir:

November 6, 1906, the United States Supreme Court held that white persons who intermarried with Cherokee citizens according to Cherokee law prior to November 1, 1875, are entitled to enrollment and allotments of land as citizens of the Cherokee Nation.

You are advised that to properly determine your right to enrollment as a citizen by intermarriage of the Cherokee Nation, it will be necessary for you to appear before the Commissioner for the purpose of giving testimony as to the date of your marriage and whether or not your wife, by reason of your marriage to whom you claim the right to enrollment as a citizen of the Cherokee Nation, was a recognized citizen of the Cherokee Nation at the time of your marriage to her, and whether or not you were married to her in accordance with Cherokee laws.

You are therefore directed to appear before the Commissioner at Muskogee, Indian Territory, at 9 o'clock A. M., on Thursday, January 3, 1907, and give testimony as above indicated.

Respectfully,

H.J.C.   Acting Commissioner.

◇◇◇◇◇

Muskogee, Indian Territory, February 14, 1907.

The Honorable,
        The Secretary of the Interior.

Sir:

There is transmitted herewith the record of proceedings had in the matter of the application for the enrollment of John J. Smith as a citizen by intermarriage of the Cherokee Nation, together with the decision of the Commissioner, dated February 26, 1907, denying said application.

Respectfully,

Encl. H-50   Commissioner.
   JMH

Through the Commissioner
of Indian Affairs.

◇◇◇◇◇

Cherokee 195

Muskogee, Indian Territory, February 14, 1907.

John J. Smith,
        Owasso, Indian Territory.

Dear Sir:

There is enclosed herewith a copy of the decision of the Commissioner to the Five Civilized Tribes, dated February 14, 1907, rejecting the application for your enrollment as a citizen by intermarriage of the Cherokee Nation.

The decision, together with the record of proceedings had in the case, has this day been transmitted to the Secretary of the Interior for his review and decision. You will be advised of the Secretary's action as soon as this office is informed of same.

Respectfully,

Commissioner.

Register.

◇◇◇◇◇◇

Cherokee 195

Muskogee, Indian Territory, February 14, 1907.

W. W. Hastings,
        Attorney for the Cherokee Nation,
                Muskogee, Indian Territory.

Dear Sir:

There is enclosed herewith a copy of the decision of the Commissioner to the Five Civilized Tribes, dated February 14, 1907, rejecting the application for the enrollment of John J. Smith as a citizen by intermarriage of the Cherokee Nation.

The decision, together with the record of proceedings had in the case, has this day been transmitted to the Secretary of the Interior for his review and decision. You will be advised of the Secretary's action as soon as this office is informed of same.

Respectfully,

Encl. H-49   Commissioner.
JMH
◇◇◇◇◇◇

Cherokee
195

Muskogee, Indian Territory, March 11, 1907

Sarah P. Smith,
        Maysville, Arkansas.

Dear Madam:

This office is in receipt, by reference of the Secretary of the Interior, of your letter of January 25, 1907, addressed to the President, relative to the right of your husband, John J. Smith, to enrollment as a citizen by intermarriage of the Cherokee Nation.

In reply you are advised that the decision of the Commissioner to the Five Civilized Tribes rejecting the application for the enrollment of John J. Smith as a citizen by intermarriage of the Cherokee Nation, was, on February 14, 1907, forwarded to the Secretary of the Interior for review. The applicant will be advised of the action of the Secretary when this office is informed of the same.

Respectfully,

L M B   Commissioner.

◇◇◇◇◇

DEPARTMENT OF THE INTERIOR
OFFICE OF INDIAN AFFAIRS,
WASHINGTON.   GAW

I.T.   May 11, 1907.
Reference in body
of letter.

Subject: Motions for
review in certain Chero-
kee citizenship cases.

The Honorable,
    The Secretary of the Interior.

Sir:

There are inclosed herewith motions filed by W. W. Hastings, National Attorney for the Cherokee Nation, praying for review and rehearing of Departmental decisions authorizing the enrollment as citizens by intermarriage of the Cherokee Nation of the following persons:

42893-1907,	Jacob A. Bartles,
42895- "	Osburn J. Byrd,
42886- "	Amanda Beck,
42894- "	Sarah F. Gage,
42892- "	Phirena Harris,
42888- "	Daniel Harmon,
42891- "	Emma L. Ironsides,
42896- "	Sarah A. Jordan,
42881- "	Dovie Johnson,
42882- "	Andrew H. Norwood,
42887- "	Stacy E. Perry,
42885- "	Martha Randolph, now Kernan

Cherokee Intermarried White 1906
Volume VIII

42893-	"	John W. Smith
42884-	"	John J. Smith,
42890-	"	Robert H. F. Thompson,
42889-	"	Hattie Wright,
42883-	"	Nancy Wolfe,
42880-	"	E. A. Welch.

In view of the provisions of section 2 of the act of April 26, 1906 (34 Stat. L., 137), providing that the rolls of the Five Civilized Tribes shall be fully completed on or before March 4, 1907, there appears to be no authority in law for the reconsideration of any enrollment cases at this time, and it is recommended that the office be authorized to advise Mr. Hastings that the motions for review herewith transmitted cannot be considered.

Very respectfully,

C. F. Larrabee

Acting Commissioner.

AJW-FHE.

May 13, 1907.

Approved.

Thos Ryan

First Assistant Secretary.

◇◇◇◇◇

I. T. references
in body of letter.

GAW

DEPARTMENT OF THE INTERIOR,
OFFICE OF INDIAN AFFAIRS,
WASHINGTON.

May 15, 1907.

Commissioner to the Five Civilized Tribes,
Muskogee, Indian Territory.

Sir:

There is inclosed copy of Office letter of May 11, 1907, approved by the Department on May 13, 1907, recommending that motions filed by W. W. Hastings,

National Attorney for the Cherokee Nation, praying for a review and rehearing of Departmental decisions authorizing the enrollment of the following persons as citizens by intermarriage of the Cherokee Nation, be denied, in view of the fact that there appears to be no authority in law at this time for the reconsideration of any enrollment case.

42893-1907	Jacob A. Bartles
42895- "	Osburn J. Byrd
42886- "	Amanda Beck
42894- "	Sarah F. Gage
42892- "	Phirena Harris
42888- "	Daniel Harmon
42891- "	Emma L. Ironsides
42896- "	Sarah A. Jordan
42881- "	Dovie Johnson
42882- "	Andrew H. Norwood
42887- "	Stacy E. Perry
42885- "	Martha Randolph, now Kernan
42893- "	John W. Smith
42884- "	John J. Smith
42890- "	Robert H. F. Thompson
42889- "	Hattie Wright
42883- "	Nancy Wolfe
42880- "	E. A. Welch

You are requested to advise the interested parties, including Mr. Hastings, of the Department's action.

Very respectfully,

C. F. Larrabee

Acting Commissioner.

AJW-FHE.

◇◇◇◇◇

Cherokee
246

Muskogee, Indian Territory, May 25, 1907.

John J. Smith,
        Maysville, Arkansas.

Dear Sir:

You are hereby advised that on May 13, 1907, the Secretary of the Interior denied a motion filed by the Attorney for the Cherokee Nation, for a review of its decision authorizing your enrollment as a citizen by intermarriage of the Cherokee Nation.

For your information, there is enclosed herewith a copy of Departmental decision referred to.

Respectfully,

Commissioner.

Encl. C-15
   LMC

◇◇◇◇◇

Cherokee
253. et al

Muskogee, Indian Territory, May 25, 1907.

W. W. Hastings,
        Attorney for the Cherokee Nation,
                Muskogee, Indian Territory.

Dear Sir:

You are hereby advised that on May 13, 1907, the Secretary of the Interior denied the motion filed by you for a review of its decision authorizing the enrollment of Jacob A. Bartles, et al., as citizens by intermarriage of the Cherokee Nation.

For your information, there is enclosed herewith a copy of Departmental decision referred to.

Respectfully,

Commissioner.

Encl. C-20
   LMC

D.C. 28529-1907.

	DEPARTMENT OF THE INTERIOR,	
I. T.	OFFICE OF INDIAN AFFAIRS.	GAW
47958-1907	WASHINGTON.	

June 5, 1907.

The Commissioner

    To the Five Civilized Tribes,

        Muskogee, Ind. Ter.

Sir:

    The Office is in receipt for a communication from the Department dated May 17, 1907, transmitting a letter from John J. Smith, of Maysville, Arkansas, dated May 7, objecting to a motion for review of Departmental decition[sic] in the matter of his application to be enrolled as a citizen by intermarriage of the Cherokee Nation. The department says that the motion referred to has not been received.

    THE RECORDS OF THIS OFFICE SHOW: That at , Indian Territory, , application was received by the Commission to the Five Civilized Tribes for the enrollment of as a citizen by intermarriage of the Cherokee Nation. office do not show that is has been filed here, and you are requested to advise Mr. Smith of the facts in the case.

            Very respectfully,

               C. F. Larrabee,

                    Acting Commissioner.

GAW-GH.

Cher IW 247

◇◇◇◇◇

Cherokee Intermarried White 1906
Volume VIII

DEPARTMENT OF THE INTERIOR.

COMMISSION TO THE FIVE CIVILIZED TRIBES.

Vinita, I.T. October 2nd, 1900.

IN THE MATTER OF THE APPLICATION OF COLIN C. IRONSIDE THE
ENROLLMENT OF HIMSELF, HIS WIFE AND CHILD, AS CHEROKEE CITIZENS.

The said Colin[sic] C. Ironside, being sworn and examined by Commissioner T. B.
Needles, testified as follows:

Q   What is your name?   A Colin C. Ironside.

Q   What is your age?   A Sixty-three.

Q   What is your post office?   A Bluejacket.

Q   Are you a recognized citizen of the Cherokee Nation?   A Yes, sir; I am a
Shawnee.

Q   What district do you live in?   A I live in Delaware District now.

Q   Who do you desire to enroll?   A Myself, my wife and my child.

Q   What is the name of your wife?   A Emma Louisa.

Q   When did you marry her?   A In 1874.

Q   The name of your child?   A Henry T. He will be twenty next December.

Q   The name of your next child?   A That is all.

1880 Roll, page 121, No. 151 (1511), C. C. Ironside, Cooweescoowee District.

1880 Roll, page 121, No. 1512, Louisa Ironside, Cooweescoowee District.

1896 Roll, page 345, No. 240, Colin C. Ironside, Cooweescoowee District.

1896 Roll, page 310, No. 538, Louisa Ironsides[sic], Cooweescoowee District.

1896 Roll, page 345, No. 241, (Walter) T. Ironside, Cooweescoowee District.

(Henry)

Q   How long have you lived in the Cherokee Nation?   A Since the spring of
1870.

Q   Continuously?   A Yes, sir.

Q   You never lived out of it?   A Well, temporarily I have been out of it.

Q   For how long?

A   Well, some six months.

Q   How long since you lived here permanently and continuously?

A   Oh, it is eleven years. I was out then on account of the health of my wife. I was
compelled to take her.

Q   What State were you in?   A Dakota.

Q   How long did you live in Dakota?   A Well, we were there off and on--I was
back here in the mean time--off and on, I suppose we were there not quite two years.

Q   Did you ever establish your citizenship in Dakota?   A No, sir.

Q   Did you ever vote there?   A No, sir. This has been my home. All my effects
and my house and my furniture all has been here.

THE COMMISSIONER: The name of Colin C. Ironside and his wife Emma L. appear upon the authenticated roll of 1880. His name is identified as C. C., and his wife as Louisa.

The name of his child Walter T. appears upon the census roll of 1896. The said Colin C. Ironside and his son Walter T., will be duly listed for enrollment as Cherokee citizens of Shawnee blood, and his wife Emma L., as a Cherokee citizen by intermarriage.

-----0-----

The undersigned, being sworn, states that as stenographer to the Commission to the Five Civilized Tribes he correctly recorded the testimony and other proceedings in this application for enrollment, and that the foregoing is a correct and complete transcript of his stenographic notes thereof.

Wm S Meeshean

Subscribed and sworn to before me this 19th day of October A. D. 1900.

C R Breckinridge
Commissioner.

◇◇◇◇◇

Cherokee 3927.

DEPARTMENT OF THE INTERIOR,
COMMISSION TO THE FIVE CIVILIZED TRIBES.
Muskogee, I. T., October 16, 1902.

In the matter of the application of Collin C. Ironside for the enrollment of himself and his minor child, Harry T. Ironside, as citizens by Shawnee blood, and for the enrollment of his wife, Emma L. Ironside, as a citizen by intermarriage, of the Cherokee Nation.

SUPPLEMENTAL PROCEEDINGS.

EMMA L. IRONSIDE, being sworn, testified as follows:

By the Commission,

Q What is your name?   A Emma L. Ironside.
Q How old are you?   A Fifty-two.
Q Are you a white woman?   A Yes, sir.
Q Don't claim any Indian Blood?   A No, sir.
Q What is the name of your husband?   A Collin C. Ironside.
Q He is an adopted Shawnee, Oklahoma is he?   A Yes, sir.
Q Was he your husband in 1880?   A Yes, sir.
Q Your name appears on the roll of 1880 with your husband, does it?   A Yes, sir.

Q Have you and your husband been living together in the Cherokee Nation ever since 1880?   A Yes, sir.

Q Never been separated?   A No, sir.

Q Have you made your home in the Cherokee Nation all this time?

A Our home has been in the Cherokee Nation, but we have been away several times.

Q Visiting?   A My husband has been in business away, but we have never moved our household goods away.

Q How long has your husband been out of the Cherokee Nation looking after his business?   A We have been living here continuously, have not been out since '90.

Q Since '90?   A Between '85 and '90 he was out.

Q Have you any children?   A Harry T.

Q Only one?   A Yes, sir.

Q Is he living?   A Yes, sir.

Retta Chick, being first duly sworn, states that, as stenographer to the Commission to the Five Civilized Tribes, she recorded the testimony and proceedings in the matter of the foregoing application, and that the above is a true and complete transcript of her stenographic notes thereof.

Retta Chick

Subscribed and sworn to before me this 11th day of November, 1902.

BC Jones
Notary Public.

◇◇◇◇◇

L. G. D.   Cherokee 3927.

DEPARTMENT OF THE INTERIOR,
COMMISSIONER TO THE FIVE CIVILIZED TRIBES.
Muskogee, Indian Territory, January 18, 1907.

In the matter of the application for the enrollment of Emma L. Ironside as a citizen by intermarriage of the Cherokee Nation.

Applicant appears in person.

APPEARANCES:

Cherokee Nation represented by
W. W. Hastings, Attorney.

Emma L. Ironside being first duly sworn by John E. Tidwell, Notary Public, testified as follows:

ON BEHALF OF COMMISSIONER.

Q What is your name?   A Emma L. Ironside.

Cherokee Intermarried White 1906
Volume VIII

Q   What is your age?   A   56.

Q   What is your post office address?

A   Miami, Indian Territory.

Q   You claim to be a citizen by intermarriage of the Cherokee Nation?

A   Yes sir.

Q   Through whom do you claim your intermarriage rights?

A   My husband, Collin C. Ironside.

Q   When did you marry Collin C. Ironside?

A   29th of April, 1874.

Q   Where was you married to Collin C. Ironside?

A   About 10 miles from Vinita, in the Cherokee Nation.

Q   Were you ever married before you married Collin C. Ironside?

A   No sir.

Q   Was he ever married before he married you?

A   No sir.

Q   Are you and Collin C. Ironside living together at this time?

A   Yes sir.

Q   Have you lived together continuously as husband and wife since 1874 in the Cherokee Nation?

A   Yes sir; only we were away a short time.

Q   Where were you?   A   In Dakota; we never moved away

Q   You were absent on a visit?

A   Yes sir; the Indian Territory has been our home.

Q   Was Collin C. Ironside a recognized citizen by blood of the Cherokee Nation, at the time you married him?

A   Yes sir.

Q   Have you any documentary evidence of your marriage?

A   Yes sir.

   Applicant offers in evidence a certificate of marriage signed by Jas. Ketcham to the effect that she was married to C. C. Ironside on the 29th day of April, 1874.

Q   Who was James Ketcham?

A   He was a Minister of the Gospel. I think he belonged to the Delawares.

BY MR. HASTINGS.

Q   You claim your only right to enrollment through your marriage to Collin C. Ironside?

A   Yes sir.

Q   To no one else?   A   No sir.

Q   Collin C. Ironside is a Shawnee citizen of the Cherokee Nation?

A   Yes sir.

Q   He claims in the Cherokee Nation by virtue of his being a Shawnee and through the Shawnee agreement?

A   Yes sir.

Q   He doesn't claim by virtue of Cherokee blood?
A   No sir.

The undersigned being first duly sworn states that as stenographer to the Commission to the Five Civilized Tribes, she recorded the testimony taken in this case and that the foregoing is a full, true and correct transcript of her stenographic notes thereof.

Myrtle Hill

Subscribed and sworn to before me this the 22nd day of January, 1907.

John E. Tidwell
Notary Public.

◇◇◇◇◇

L. G. D.   Cherokee 3927.

(COPY)

Cherokee Nation,
Delaware Disct.
April 29th, 1874.

This is to certify that I have this 29th day of April joined together in the holy bond of Matrimony according to the rights of the M. Episcopal Church C. C. Ironside and Louisa Kibbie.

(Signed)   Jas. Ketcham.

Witness:
   G. Blakeney.
   Mrs. Hester I. West.

The undersigned being first duly sworn states that as stenographer to the Commission to the Five Civilized Tribes, she made the above and foregoing copy and that same is a true copy of the original marriage certificate on file in this office.

Myrtle Hill

Subscribed and sworn to before me this the 22nd day of January, 1907.

John E. Tidwell
Notary Public.

◇◇◇◇◇

C.E.W.   Cherokee 3927.

DEPARTMENT OF THE INTERIOR,
COMMISSIONER TO THE FIVE CIVILIZED TRIBES.

In the matter of the application for the enrollment of Emma L. Ironside as a citizen by intermarriage of the Cherokee Nation.

D E C I S I O N .

THE RECORDS OF THIS OFFICE SHOW: That at Vinita, Indian Territory, October 2, 1900, application was received by the Commission to the Five Civilized Tribes for the enrollment of Emma L. Ironside as a citizen by intermarriage of the Cherokee Nation. Further proceedings in the matter of said application were had at Muskogee, Indian Territory, October 16, 1902, and January 18, 1907.

THE EVIDENCE IN THIS CASE SHOWS: That the applicant herein, Emma L. Ironside, identified on the Cherokee authenticated tribal roll of 1880 as an adopted white, neither claims nor possesses any right to enrollment as a citizen of the Cherokee Nation other than such right as she may have acquired by virtue of her marriage to one Collin C. Ironside, who is identified on the Shawnee register at No. 432, and upon the approved partial roll of citizens of the Cherokee Nation opposite No. 9463, as a citizen of the Cherokee Nation of Shawnee blood, was a member of the Shawnee tribe of Indians, and acquired his right to enrollment as a citizen of the Cherokee Nation by virtue of his compliance with the provisions of the agreement entered into by the Cherokees and Shawnee tribe[sic] of Indians June 7, 1869, and approved by the President June 9, 1869.

In view of the foregoing, it is considered that the applicant Emma L. Ironside, acquired no right to enrollment as a citizen by intermarriage of the Cherokee Nation by reason of her said marriage to Collin C. Ironside, who is not a citizen of the Cherokee Nation of Cherokee blood.

IT IS, THEREFORE, ORDERED AND ADJUDGED: That in accordance with the decision of the Supreme Court of the United States, dated November 5, 1906, in the cases of Daniel Red Bird et al., vs. the United States, Nos. 125, 126, 127, and 128, the said applicant, Emma L. Ironside is not entitled, under the provisions of Section 21 of the Act of Congress approved June 28, 1898 (30 Stats., 495), to enrollment as a citizen by intermarriage of the Cherokee Nation, and her application for enrollment as such is accordingly denied.

Tams Bixby
Commissioner.

Dated at Muskogee, Indian Territory,
this   FEB 2 1907

Cherokee Intermarried White 1906
Volume VIII

◇◇◇◇◇

REFER IN REPLY TO THE FOLLOWING:

Cherokee

3927

DEPARTMENT OF THE INTERIOR,
COMMISSIONER TO THE FIVE CIVILIZED TRIBES.

Muskogee, Indian Territory, December 26, 1906.

Emma L. Ironside,
Bluejacket, Indian Territory.

Dear Madam:

November 26[sic], 1906, the United States Supreme Court held that white persons who intermarried with Cherokee citizens according to Cherokee law prior to November 1, 1875, are entitled to enrollment and allotments of land as citizens of the Cherokee Nation.

You are advised that to properly determine your right to enrollment as a citizen by intermarriage of the Cherokee Nation, it will be necessary for you to appear before the Commissioner for the purpose of giving testimony as to the date of your marriage and whether or not your husband, by reason of your marriage to whom you claim the right to enrollment as a citizen by intermarriage of the Cherokee Nation, was a recognized Cherokee citizen at the time of your marriage to him.

You are, therefore, directed to appear before the Commissioner at Muskogee, Indian Territory, at 9 o'clock A. M., on Friday, January 4, 1907, and give testimony as above indicated.

Respectfully,

Wm O. Beall

JMH   Acting Commissioner.

◇◇◇◇◇

Cherokee
3927

Muskogee, Indian Territory, January 21, 1907

Emma L. Ironside,
Miami, Indian Territory.

Dear Madam:

Replying to your letter of January 7, with reference to your rights to enrollment as a citizen by intermarriage of the Cherokee Nation, you are advised that the United

States Supreme Court by its decision of November 5, 1906, held that white persons who intermarried according to Cherokee law with Cherokee citizens, prior to November 1, 1875, are entitled to enrollment as citizens by intermarriage of the Cherokee Nation.

If you claim to be entitled to enrollment under the Court's decision, you will be permitted to appear before the Commissioner at Muskogee, Indian Territory, at any time in the near future and submit such testimony as you desire relative to your marriage to your Cherokee husband by reason of your marriage to whom you claim the right to enrollment as a citizen by intermarriage of the Cherokee Nation, and as to the date of your marriage.

The Act of Congress approved April 26, 1906, provides that the Secretary of the Interior shall have no jurisdiction to approve the enrollment of any person as a citizen of the Cherokee Nation after March 4, 1907, and the matter should, therefore, receive your immediate attention.

Respectfully,

Commissioner.

RPI

◇◇◇◇◇

Cherokee 3927

Muskogee, Indian Territory, February 1, 1907.

W. W. Hastings,
     Attorney for the Cherokee Nation,
          Muskogee, Indian Territory.

Dear Sir:

There is enclosed herewith a copy of the decision of the Commissioner to the Five Civilized Tribes, dated February 1, 1907, rejecting the application for the enrollment of Emma L. Ironside as a citizen by intermarriage of the Cherokee Nation.

The decision, together with the record of proceedings had in the case, has this day been transmitted to the Secretary of the Interior for his review and decision. You will be advised of the Secretary's action as soon as this office is informed of same.

Respectfully,

Enc I-77   Commissioner.

RPI

◇◇◇◇◇

Muskogee, Indian Territory, February 1, 1907.

The Honorable,
    The Secretary of the Interior.

Sir:

There is transmitted herewith the record of proceedings had in the matter of the application for the enrollment of Emma L. Ironside as a citizen by intermarriage of the Cherokee Nation, together with the decision of the Commissioner, dated February 1, 1907, denying said application.

Respectfully,

Enc I-75   Commissioner.
RPI
Through the Commissioner
    of Indian Affairs.

◇◇◇◇◇

Cherokee
3927

Muskogee, Indian Territory, February 2, 1907.

Emma L. Ironside,
    Miami, Indian Territory.

Dear Madam:

There is enclosed herewith a copy of the decision of the Commissioner to the Five Civilized Tribes, dated February 2, 1907, rejecting the application for your enrollment as a citizen by intermarriage of the Cherokee Nation.

The decision, together with the record of proceedings had in the case, has this day been transmitted to the Secretary of the Interior for his review and decision. You will be advised of the Secretary's action as soon as this office is informed of same.

Respectfully,

Enc I-78   Commissioner.

RPI
Register.

◇◇◇◇◇

309

COPY.

Refer in reply to the following:

DEPARTMENT OF THE INTERIOR,

OFFICE OF INDIAN AFFAIRS,

Land

12683-1907   WASHINGTON.

February 25, 1907.

The Honorable,
    The Secretary of the Interior.

Sir:

There is enclosed a report from the Commissioner to the Five Civilized Tribes, dated February 1, 1907, transmitting the record relative to the application for enrollment of Emma L. Ironsides[sic] as a citizen by intermarriage of the Cherokee Nation.

On February 1, 1907, the Commissioner held that the applicant was not entitled to enrollment.

The evidence shows that the applicant, who is identified on the Cherokee authenticated tribal roll of 1880 as an adopted white, neither claims nor possesses any right to enrollment as a citizen of the Cherokee Nation except by reason of her marriage to one Collin C. Ironsides[sic], who is identified upon the Shawnee register and upon the approved partial roll of citizens of the Cherokee Nation as a citizen of the Cherokee Nation of Shawnee blood, and who acquired his right to enrollment by his compliance with the provisions of the agreement entered into by the Cherokee and Shawnee tribe of Indians June 7, 1869, and ratified by the President June 9, 1869.

In view of the evidence, it is considered that the applicant, Emma L. Ironsides, acquired no right to enrollment as a citizen by intermarriage of the Cherokee Nation by reason of her marriage to Collin C. Ironsides, who is not a citizen of the Cherokee Nation of Cherokee blood.

Under the decision of the Supreme Court of the United States dated November 5, 1906, the case of Daniel Red Bird, et al. vs. the United States, the applicant is not entitled to enrollment.

It is therefore recommended that the decision of the Commissioner adverse to the applicant be approved.

Very respectfully,

C. F. Larrabee,

JPB-GH   Acting Commissioner.

◇◇◇◇◇◇

COPY

DEPARTMENT OF THE INTERIOR
WASHINGTON.

D. C. 12415
I.T.D. 5042,5044,5054,5070,5126-07.
　　　5162,5338,5340,5352,5372- "   Y.P.
　　　5408,5430,5432,5434,　 - "   FHE.

LRS
<u>DIRECT</u>.   February 28, 1907.

Commissioner to the Five Civilized Tribes,
　　　Muskogee, Indian Territory.
Sir:

Your decisions in the following Cherokee citizenship cases adverse to the applicants are hereby affirmed, viz:

Title of case.	Date of your letter of transmittal
Emma L. Ironside, (Intermarried)	February 1, 1907
Nancy Raper, (Intermarried)	February 2, 1907
John Swain, (Intermarried)	February 2, 1907
Eve Ellen Anderson (Freedman)	January 12, 1907
William M. Donaldson	December 3, 1906
Fannie W. Trott, (Intermarried)	January 8, 1907
Louisa J. Sloan, (Intermarried)	February 6, 1907
Dollie Therssa[sic] Callaway, et al,	January 25, 1907
Martha Harris, (Intermarried)	February 6, 1907
Sandy Smith, (Freedman)	November 23, 1906
Edward Chaney,	January 25, 1907
Carl E. Fishback,	January 18, 1907
Sarah E. McDonald, (Intermarried)	January 30, 1907
Mary A. Price (Intermarried)	January 30, 1907.

Copies of Indian Office letters submitting your reports and recommending that the decisions be approved, are inclosed. A copy hereof and all the papers in the above-mentioned cases have been sent to the Indian Office.

AfMc   Respectfully,
3-1-07

                                        (Signed)   Jesse E. Wilson
                                                    Assistant Secretary

14 enc. and 28 for Ind. Of.

◇◇◇◇◇

                                                        Copy

                        DEPARTMENT OF THE INTERIOR,

LAND
21116-1907   OFFICE OF INDIAN AFFAIRS,

——

                            WASHINGTON.

                                        March 2, 1907.

The Honorable,
        The Secretary of the Interior.

Sir:

Referring to Departmental letter of February 28, 1907 (I.T.D. 6042-1907), rejecting, among others, the application of Emma L. Ironside, et al., for enrollment as citizens by intermarriage of the Cherokee Nation, there is returned herewith the record in that case for reconsideration.

It will be noted that the applicant is identified on the Cherokee authenticated tribal roll of 1880 and that she married a duly enrolled citizen of the Cherokee Nation on April 29, 1874.

Although her husband appears to have been a Shawnee by blood, the applicant, by reason of her marriage as above, and her name appearing on the 1880 roll, seems to be entitled to enrollment, under the decision of the Attorney General of February 26, 1907, in the case of John W. Gleason.

It is therefore recommended that the Department rescind its decision of February 28, 1907, so far as it related to this applicant, and grant her application for enrollment as a citizen by intermarriage of the Cherokee Nation.

Very respectfully,

C. F. Larrabee,

AJW-EH   Acting Commissioner.

◇◇◇◇◇

D.C. 13835-1907.   SPECIAL   W.H.M.

DEPARTMENT OF THE INTERIOR,

WASHINGTON.

I.T.D. 7820-1907.   March 4, 1907.

LRS
   DIRECT.

Commissioner to the Five Civilized Tribes,
   Muskogee, Indian Territory.

Sir:

On March 2, 1907 (Land 21116), the Indian Office returned the record in the matter of the application of Emma L. Ironside for enrollment as a citizen by intermarriage of the Cherokee Nation, and recommended that, in view of the decision of the Attorney-General dated February 26, 1907, in the case of John W. Gleason, the Department rescind its action of February 28, 1907, and reverse your decision adverse to said applicant.

The Department considers the decision of the Indian Office correct.

Your decision of February 1, 1907, adverse to the applicant Emma L. Ironside, is hereby reversed, and you are directed to enroll said applicant as a citizen by intermarriage.

The papers have been sent to the Indian Office, together with a copy hereof.

Respectfully,

(Signed)   Jesse E. Wilson,
1 enclosure, and   Acting Secretary.
2 enclosures and copy hereof
   to Indian Office.

WCF 3-4-07

◇◇◇◇◇

Cherokee 3927   COPY

Muskogee, Indian Territory, March 9, 1907.

Emma L. Ironside,
        Miami, Indian Territory.

Dear Madam:

You are hereby advised that the decision of the Commissioner to the Five Civilized Tribes, dated February 1, 1907, rejecting your application for enrollment as a citizen by intermarriage of the Cherokee Nation, was reversed by the Secretary of the Interior, March 4, 1907, and said application granted. for enrollment as a citizen by intermarriage of the Cherokee Nation, was affirmed by the Secretary of the Interior, February 28, 1907.

For your information, there is enclosed herewith a copy of Departmental decision referred to.

Respectfully,

SIGNED *Tams Bixby*
Commissioner.

Encl. H-12
    JMH

◇◇◇◇◇

Cherokee 3927   COPY

Muskogee, Indian Territory, March 9, 1907.

W. W. Hastings,
        Attorney for the Cherokee Nation,
                Muskogee, Indian Territory.

Dear Sir:

You are hereby advised that the decision of the Commissioner to the Five Civilized Tribes, dated February 1, 1907, rejecting the application for the enrollment of Emma L. Ironside as a citizen by intermarriage of the Cherokee Nation, was affirmed by the Secretary of the Interior, February 28, 1907.

For your information there is enclosed herewith a copy of Departmental decision referred to.

Respectfully,

SIGNED *Jams Bixby*
Commissioner.

Encl. H-19
JMH

◇◇◇◇◇

Cherokee 3927

COPY

Muskogee, Indian Territory, March 121, 1907.

Emma L. Ironside,
    Miami, Indian Territory.

Dear Madam:

You are hereby advised that the application for your enrollment as a citizen by intermarriage of the Cherokee Nation, was granted by the secretary of, March 4, 1907.

For your information there is enclosed herewith a copy of Departmental decision referred to.

Respectfully,

SIGNED *Jams Bixby*
Commissioner.

Encl. I-603

R.P.I.

◇◇◇◇◇

Cherokee 3927   COPY

Muskogee, Indian Territory, March 21, 1907.

W. W. Hastings,
    Attorney for the Cherokee Nation,
        Muskogee, Indian Territory.

Dear Sir:

You are hereby advised that the application for the enrollment of Emma L. Ironside as a citizen by intermarriage of the Cherokee Nation, was granted by the Secretary of the Interior, March 4, 1907.

For your information, there is enclosed herewith a copy of Departmental letter referred to.

Respectfully,

SIGNED <i>Tams Bixby</i>
Commissioner.

Encl. I-602

RPI

◇◇◇◇◇

GAW

DEPARTMENT OF THE INTERIOR
OFFICE OF INDIAN AFFAIRS,
WASHINGTON.

I.T.   May 11, 1907.
Reference in body
of letter.

Subject: Motions for
review in certain Chero-
kee citizenship cases.

The Honorable,
    The Secretary of the Interior.

Sir:

There are inclosed herewith motions filed by W. W. Hastings, National Attorney for the Cherokee Nation, praying for review and rehearing of Departmental decisions authorizing the enrollment as citizens by intermarriage of the Cherokee Nation of the following persons:

42893-1907,	Jacob A. Bartles,
42895- "	Osburn J. Byrd,
42886- "	Amanda Beck,
42894- "	Sarah F. Gage,
42892- "	Phirena Harris,
42888- "	Daniel Harmon,
42891- "	Emma L. Ironsides,
42896- "	Sarah A. Jordan
42881- "	Dovie Johnson,
42882- "	Andrew H. Norwood,

42887-	"	Stacy E. Perry,
42885-	"	Martha Randolph, now Kernan
42893-	"	John W. Smith
42884-	"	John J. Smith,
42890-	"	Robert H. F. Thompson,
42889-	"	Hattie Wright,
42883-	"	Nancy Wolfe,
42880-	"	E. A. Welch.

In view of the provisions of section 2 of the act of April 26, 1906 (34 Stat. L., 137), providing that the rolls of the Five Civilized Tribes shall be fully completed on or before March 4, 1907, there appears to be no authority in law for the reconsideration of any enrollment cases at this time, and it is recommended that the office be authorized to advise Mr. Hastings that the motions for review herewith transmitted cannot be considered.

Very respectfully,

C. F. Larrabee

Acting Commissioner.

AJW-FHE.

May 13, 1907.

Approved.

Thos Ryan

First Assistant Secretary.

◇◇◇◇◇

GAW

DEPARTMENT OF THE INTERIOR,
I. T. references   OFFICE OF INDIAN AFFAIRS,
in body of letter.   WASHINGTON.

May 15, 1907.

Commissioner to the Five Civilized Tribes,
        Muskogee, Indian Territory.
Sir:

There is inclosed copy of Office letter of May 11, 1907, approved by the Department on May 13, 1907, recommending that motions filed by W. W. Hastings, National Attorney for the Cherokee Nation, praying for a review and rehearing of Departmental decisions authorizing the enrollment of the following persons as citizens by intermarriage of the Cherokee Nation, be denied, in view of the fact that there appears to be no authority in law at this time for the reconsideration of any enrollment case.

42893-1907	Jacob A. Bartles
42895- "	Osburn J. Byrd
42886- "	Amanda Beck
42894- "	Sarah F. Gage
42892- "	Phirena Harris
42888- "	Daniel Harmon
42891- "	Emma L. Ironsides
42896- "	Sarah A. Jordan
42881- "	Dovie Johnson
42882- "	Andrew H. Norwood
42887- "	Stacy E. Perry
42885- "	Martha Randolph, now Kernan
42893- "	John W. Smith
42884- "	John J. Smith
42890- "	Robert H. F. Thompson
42889- "	Hattie Wright
42883- "	Nancy Wolfe
42880- "	E. A. Welch

You are requested to advise the interested parties, including Mr. Hastings, of the Department's action.

Very respectfully,
C. F. Larrabee
Acting Commissioner.

AJW-FHE.

318

◇◇◇◇◇

Cherokee
247

Muskogee, Indian Territory, May 25, 1907.

Emma J. Ironsides[sic],
Miami, Indian Territory.

Dear Madam:

You are hereby advised that on May 13, 1907, the Secretary of the Interior denied a motion filed by the Attorney for the Cherokee Nation, for a review of its decision authorizing your enrollment as a citizen by intermarriage of the Cherokee Nation.

For your information, there is enclosed herewith a copy of Departmental decision referred to.

Respectfully,

Commissioner.

Encl. C-8
LMC

◇◇◇◇◇

Cherokee
253 et al.

Muskogee, Indian Territory, May 25, 1907.

W. W. Hastings,
Attorney for the Cherokee Nation,
Muskogee, Indian Territory.

Dear Sir:

You are hereby advised that on May 13, 1907, the Secretary of the Interior denied the motion filed by you for a review of its decision authorizing the enrollment of Jacob A. Bartles, et al., as citizens by intermarriage of the Cherokee Nation.

For your information, there is enclosed herewith a copy of Departmental decision referred to.

Respectfully,

Commissioner.

Encl. C-20
LMC

◇◇◇◇◇

G F 13170
Cher. Allot.
I. W. 247

Muskogee, Indian Territory, October 24, 1907.

Emma L. Ironside,
    Miami, Indian Territory.

Dear Madam:

This office is in receipt of your letter of October 19, 1907, asking that certificates describing your allotment be forwarded to you.

In reply you are advised that it appears from the records of this office that your proper name is Emma L. Ironside and that your name has been placed upon the approved roll of citizens by intermarriage of the Cherokee Nation as Emma J. Ironsides[sic]. The matter of the delivery of your certificates has been held as the matter of the advisability of making any corrections on the approved roll of Cherokee citizens has been under the consideration of this office and the Department.

If you are willing that your name shall remain upon the approved roll of Cherokee citizens as Emma J. Ironsides and will so advise this office, your allotment certificates, which of course will have to be issued in the name of Emma J. Ironsides should your name remain that way upon the roll, will be forwarded to you should no objection not now apparent appear.

Respectfully,

JOR-(GHL)   Commissioner.

◇◇◇◇◇

Cherokee Intermarried White 1906
Volume VIII

Muskogee, Indian Territory, November 2, 1907.

Subject:
Recommends change
in name of Emma L.
Ironside upon
Cherokee Roll.

The Honorable,
The Secretary of the Interior.

Sir:

On February 2, 1907, the Commissioner to the Five Civilized Tribes rendered his decision rejecting the application of Emma L. Ironside for enrollment as a citizen by intermarriage of the Cherokee Nation. This decision was approved by the Department, among others, on February 28, 1907 (I.T.D. 5042-1907), and on March 4, 1907 (I.T.D. 7820-1907), the Department rescinded its decision and ordered said Emma L. Ironside enrolled as a citizen by intermarriage of the Cherokee Nation. The name of this applicant we placed on a schedule of citizens by intermarriage, which was prepared by an employee of this office in Washington, and approved by the Department, March 4, 1907, as Emma J[sic]. Ironsides, opposite Roll No. 247.

In a letter of this office addressed to Mrs. Ironside under date of October 24, 1907, she was advised of the discrepancy in her name as it appears on the Roll and in her reply of October 26, 1907, she protested against her name remaining upon the Roll as Emma J. Ironsides, and requested that the mistake be corrected.

On September 23, 1907 (Subject: Exclusions from Tribal Rolls), the Department in a letter addressed to Messrs. Ralls Brothers, of Atoka, Indian Territory, expressed its opinion as

> "having authority to correct errors of the rolls in their nature clerical or of procedure, notwithstanding the close of the rolls against further administrative or quasi judicial action by limitation of its powers for those purposes to March 4, 1907."

I, therefore, respectfully recommend that the name of this person be changed upon the copies of the approved roll of Cherokee citizens retained by the Department and in the Office of the Commission of Indian Affairs, from Emma J. Ironsides to Emma L. Ironside, and that this office be authorized to make such change on the copies of said Roll in its possession.

Respectfully,

JOR (AV)   Commissioner.

www.ingramcontent.com/pod-product-compliance
Lightning Source LLC
Chambersburg PA
CBHW020244030426
42336CB00010B/606